Inscriptional Evidence of Pre-Islamic Classical Arabic

Selected Readings in the Nabataean, Musnad, and Akkadian Inscriptions

With a Revealing New Reading in the Epic of Gilgamesh

Saad D. Abulhab

Blautopf Publishing
New York ~ Ulm
blautopfpublishing.com

Blautopf Publishing
New York ~ Ulm
blautopfpublishing.com

Colophon
English text set in *Arabetics Latte*, designed by the author.
Arabic text set in *Jalil, Sabine, Yasmine, and Arabetics Latte* fonts, designed by author.

Cover Design by Author
A zoomed-in image of part of the *'Ayn 'Abdat* Nabataean inscription found in the Negev Desert and dated to around First Century CE, which included two verses of Classical Arabic poetry

Publisher's Cataloging-in-Publication Data

Abulhab, Saad D.
Inscriptional Evidence of Pre-Islamic Classical Arabic: Selected Readings in the Nabataean, Musnad, and Akkadian Inscriptions / Saad D. Abulhab.
p. cm.
1. Arabic Language – History. 2. Inscriptions, Nabataean 3. Inscriptions – Arabia, Southern. 4. Cuneiform Inscriptions, Akkadian. 5. Gilgamesh. I. Title.
PJ6123.A285 2013
492.711–dc22
Library of Congress Control Number: 2013901220
CIP

ISBN: 978-0-9849843-3-6 (hardcover)
ISBN: 978-0-9849843-4-3 (paperback)
ISBN: 978-0-9849843-5-0 (electronic)

First Edition

Printed by CreateSpace©, an amazon.com© company

20 18 16 14 13 8 7 6 5 4 3 2 1

DEDICATION

In memory of my father, uncle, and aunt, who raised me in a nurturing and responsible environment.

CONTENTS

Preface 1

Introduction to the History of the Arabs and Classical Arabic 5

Part 1 29

Nabataean Inscriptional Sample: The *al-Namārah* Inscription

1 Introduction to Part One 30

2 Historical and Geographical Overview 34

3 On the Usage of the Word *Nafs* by the Nabataeans and Arabs 40

4 Detailed Reading of the *Umm al-Jimāl* Nabataean Inscription 67

5 Arabic Grammar Prelude 80

6 Detailed Reading of *al-Namārah* Nabataean Inscription 86

7 Summary of Part One 111

Part 2 115

Yemen Inscriptional Sample: The *Sa'adTa'lib* Inscription

1 Introduction of Part One 116

2 Reading Musnad Inscriptions from Yemen 119

3 Detailed Reading of the *Sa'adTa'lib* Musnad Inscription 121

4 Summary of Part Two 135

Part 3 137

Akkadian Inscriptional Sample: The Epic of Gilgamesh

1 Introduction of Part Three 138

2 About the Akkadian Arabic Language and Gilgamesh 142

3 A Comparative Detailed Reading in the Babylonian Tablets 155

4 A Comparative Detailed Reading in the Assyrian Tablets 193

5 Summary of Part Three 225

Selected Bibliography 229

Preface

Some of the results of my research in this book—like my new readings of the *al-Namārah* and *Umm al-Jimāl* Nabataean Inscriptions—were first presentd in my book "*DeArabizing Arabia: Tracing Western Scholarship on the History of the Arabs and Arabic Language and Script*", which was published in late 2011. However, while translating that book to Arabic, I felt it was necessary to expand my research to further support my conclusions regarding the history of pre-Islamic Classical Arabic, or Standard Arabic, and to present all my inscriptional reasearch as an independent book in both Arabic and English languages.

In this book, I will continue with my re-tracing and re-reading of the modern Nabataean inscriptional evidence introduced by Western scholars from the 19th century until today. This evidence is, according to many, the key evidence behind the new modern-day radical theories about the history of the Arabs and Arabic language and script. In this book, I will also read an important Akkadian inscriptional sample from the Epic of Gilgamesh. It is important to note here that the intended audience of this book is not limited to the professional scholars but to anyone interested in this field of knowledge, particularly among the Arabs and Muslims, who should be most concerned with studying their own history based on the important material evidence of modern findings.

As a matter of fact, I am not a professional Arabic linguist or an archeologist. I am an Electrical Engineer in my academic training, a professional Arabic type designer in my hobby, and a librarian specialized in Arabic, science, business, and library technology, in my profession. However, I should bring to light here that the person who had finally succeeded in deciphering the Cuneiform symbols inscribed on key tablets of the Epic of Gilgamesh was not a specialist but a young English accountant working in a bank in Great Britain. That was in the early third decade of the twentieth century, sixty years after their discovery in a library of an Assyrian palace buried under a mound in the Iraqi providence of Mosul, and after their subsequent shipment to the British Library Museum.

To help the reader, I divided this book into three parts depending on the nature of the inscriptions being studied. Each part has its own introduction, chapters, and summary. I have also provided, in the beginning of the book, a detailed table containing the historical varied shapes of the Nabataean and Musnad scripts, to aid readers who are not familiar with these historical scripts.

Finally, I would like to sincerley thank all those who helped me with the research and writing of this book, particularly my wife Sabine for her continued and unlimited support and understanding; Iraqi poets *Saadī Yūsuf*, *ʿAbd al-Razzaq ʿAbd al-Wāḥid*, and *Ṣalah ʿAwwād* for reviewing my readings of key historical Arabic poem verses; my brother Osama for providing me with high resolution pictures of the *al-Namārah* inscription; Denis Carter for sharing the *SaʿadTaʾlib* Musnad inscription stone; The City University of New York Research Foundation (CUNY-RF) for their generous grants; Vladimir Wertsman for his inspiring friendship over 25 years; *Rāʾid Naʿīm* for providing online *al-Baḥith al-ʿArabi* database; University of Pennsylvania for providing the online Pennsylvania Sumerian Dictionary (ePSD); Chicago University for providing freely the Chicago Assyrian Dictionary (CAD); Project Gutenberg Literary Archive Foundation and the University of London School of Oriental and African Studies for providing the Romanized texts of the Epic of Gilgamesh.

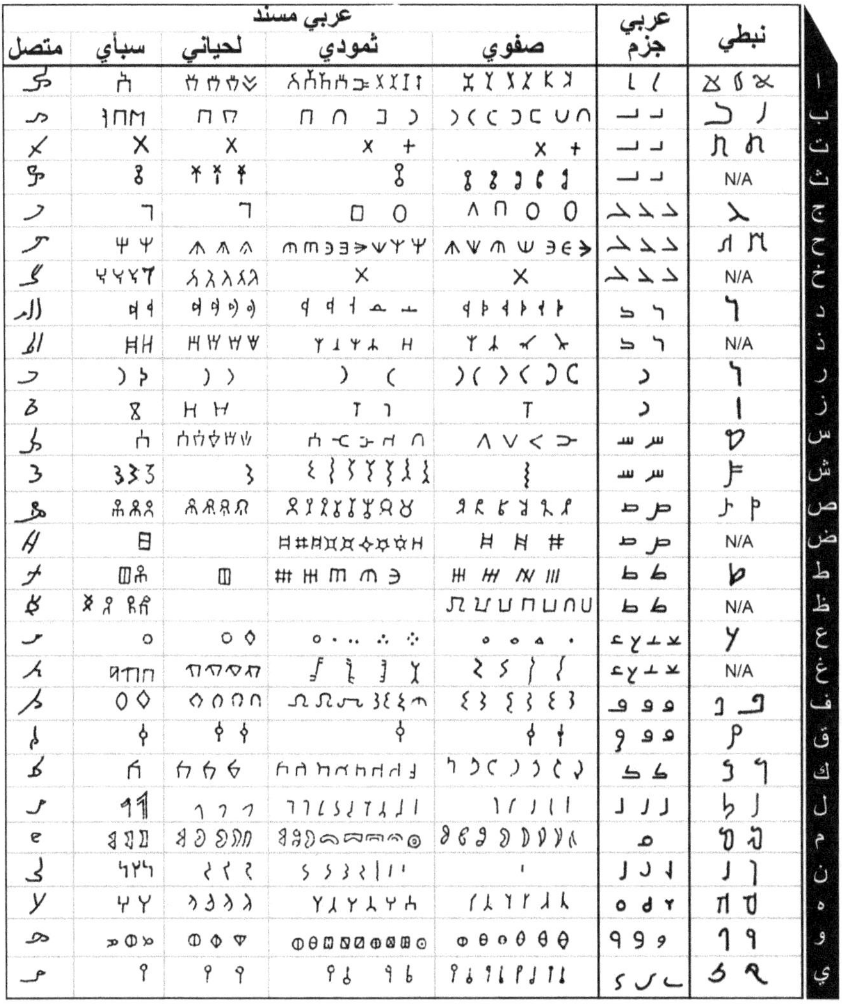

عربي مسند
متصل
سبأي
لحياني
ثمودي
صفوي
عربي جزم
نبطي
ا ب ت ث ج ح خ د ذ ر ز س ش ص ض ط ظ ع غ ف ق ك ل م ن ه و ي
N/A

A table with Nabataean and Musnad scripts letter shapes and their corresponding modern Arabic script letters, which was compiled by the author in his previous studies

Introduction to the History of the Arabs and Classical Arabic

Most modern Western theories of the nineteenth and twentieth centuries assume that Arabic language was a younger language compared to Hebrew or Aramaic. As for classical Arabic, many Arabists and Oriantalists claim it was created by the Abbasids linguists based on the language of the Quran or the tongue of the Arabs of *Hijāz*. Most Orientalists believe the dialects of the Yemenis, Thamudis, Nabataeans, and other Arab groups are independent non-Arabic languages, and that modern post Islamic Arabic writing, and other writings of the region like Phoenician, are not related to the old Musnad Arabic writing. And much more.

For example, M. S. A. Macdonald, the respected Orientalist and expert in old Arabic languages, treated the above dialects as independent non-Arabic languages, which are related to each other through their classification as "Semitic" languages. As such, the relation of Nabataean to Thamudi would be similar to the relation of Hebrew and Akkadian. As for the Southern Arabian languages, MacDonald believes "neither the Ancient nor the Modern South Arabian languages are in any sense 'Arabic'." Then he adds "Old Arabic was a minority language in the Arabian Peninsula and only became the Arabic language for the majority after Islam". [28] Generally, Western theories distinguish between the so-called "Classical Arabic" and "Standard Arabic", also known as *al-ʿArabiyyah al-fuṣḥā* among Arabs. According to them, Classical Arabic is the language of the Quran and the words of Prophet Muhammad, or *Ḥadith*, and Standard Arabic is the language used in modern day Arabic writing since the Abbasids. I think this distinction is not only arbitrary but also not logical since it assumes, firstly, the two languages were static and not evolving over time, and secondly, their vocabulary and grammatical rules were significantly different and independent. It is not clear why wouldn't Western scholars classify the two as "Old Standard Arabic" and "Modern Standard Arabic" as it is the case for English or German, for example.

Ironically, many of the supporters of the above views of MacDonald and other Arabits would rush to quote the following paragraph from the Introduction of *Ibn Khaldūn* to prove their thesis:

".. the *Muḍar* tongue and *Ḥimīr* tongue were in a similar situation before the changes that occurred to many of the words of *Ḥimīr* tongue among the people of *Muḍar*. This is evident through available historical quotes, in contradiction with those who assume through ignorance that the two were one language and attempt to measure the *Ḥimīr* language based on the measurements of the *Muḍar* language and its grammar rules, as in the claims of some that the word *al-qīl* in *Ḥimīr* tongue is derived from *al-qawl*, and many other similar examples, which are not correct. The language of *Ḥimīr* is another language that differs from the language of *Muḍar* in many of its conditions, words' roots, and vowels, as the language of the Arabs in our time differs from the language of *Muḍar*". [15]

However, and as it is clear from *Ibn Khaldūn*'s paragraph, the Arabs seem to use the word "language" as a synonym to the word "tongue", not in the meaning of independent language, and certainly not in the meaning of "non-Arabic" language. What *Ibn Khaldūn* meant to say is that the Arabs of *Ḥimīr* and the Arabs of *Muḍar*, and the Arabs of his times spoke Arabic in a different manner over the centuries, but he did not even hint that any of their languages were not substantially Arabic. In his introduction, he wrote regarding the the *Muḍar* tongue that "if we took care of this Arabic tongue", which clearly indicates he classified it as one of several Arabic tongues. His observations are obvious since languages are constantly evolving.

Regrettably, *Ibn Khaldūn* was not successful in choosing the right words to explain the evolution of the Arabic tongue from the *Ḥimīr* ages until his times. Following his accurate and correct explanation that the *Muḍar* and *Ḥimīr* tongues contained similar words and roots by saying "the *Muḍar* tongue and *Ḥimīr* tongue were in a similar situation before the changes that occurred to many of the words of *Ḥimīr* tongue among the people of *Muḍar*", he then objected to the "claims of some that the word *al-qīl* in the *Ḥimīr* tongue is derived from *al-qawl*, and many other similar examples". It is possible that *Ibn Khaldūn* wanted to say that some of the *Muḍar* words have no roots in the *Ḥimīr* language and vice versa, which is an obvious fact since the two evolved independently.

In his classification of what he called "*Muḍar* tongue", *Ibn Khaldūn* seemed puzzled and unsure. At one point he says with absolute confidence that the "Quran was delivered and the *Ḥadīth* was transmitted in its language". Then he says hesitantly that the *Muḍar* language "was not created by this generation but it was inherited, and from that it seems to be the language of early *Muḍar* people, and maybe the language of Prophet Muhammad, itself". In other words, he mixed up between the *Muḍar* tongue and Standard Arabic, which was possibly the closest to the *Muḍar* tongue, not more than that. In the past, the term "Arabic tongue" meant Standard Arabic tongue, which is the tongue the Arabs compared their diverse tongues with, including the tongues of *Makkah* and *Hijāz*. We read in the Quran (28: 34) أَفْصَحُ مِنِّي لِسَانًا in the meaning of "with a clearer tongue than mine" or a closer tongue to the standard one. In another Quranic verse (46: 12) we read وَهَٰذَا كِتَابٌ مُّصَدِّقٌ لِّسَانًا عَرَبِيًّا in the same meaning. The Quran also used لِسَانٌ عَرَبِيٌّ مُبِينٌ in other verses, in the meaning of standard or clear tongue.

It is an undisputed fact that Arabic, like most other languages, contains many locally evolving dialects, presently and in the past. Standard or Classical Arabic, which is the language of the Arabs for important and formal communications and poetry, is the common root of their tongues. It was considered their linguistic model, before and after Islam. In other words, it is the collective language which recorded over the ages the words of their prevalent and diverse historical groups. It is not an independent language that was spoken by any certain group or used in a certain geographic location, but rather the language of the elite learned community. In the Quran (13: 37) وَكَذَلِكَ أَنزَلْنَاهُ حُكْمًا عَرَبِيًّا. This clearly means Standard Arabic was a measurement language that was used for reference purposes. Accordingly, the Nabataean, Yemeni, Aramaic, Akkadian and other tongues of the Arabian Peninsula are substantially linked with the Arabic language and particularly the Classical Arabic language. This is clear since Classical Arabic linguistic reference tools are the key tools to study and explain these languages, as we will demonstrate through the inscriptional evidence presented in this book.

At the heart of the Western classification system of the languages of the Arabian Peninsula lays their classification of its people. Modern Western theories deprive the overwhelming historical majority in the Peninsula from their undisputed Arab roots and characteristics in favor of a new classification system where each group of people is presumed to belong to an assumed mother "Semitic" people. While scholars of the Islamic Arab civilization called most people of the Northern Arabian Peninsula, the Nabataeans, the Orientalist theories speak of a pre-Islamic overwhelming Aramaic majority in that area. The Nabataeans, according to these theories, were a minority group with some Arab background and unknown precise origin, living among a majority of Aramaic people. Because the classification by the scholars of the Islamic Arab civilization indicated otherwise, I will start by restating it to clarify the ambiguity and contradiction above. Particularly, I will start with what *Ibn Manẓūr* wrote in *Lisān al-ʿArab*, when he defined the word *Nabaṭ*, or Nabataean:

> "... *al-Nabīṭ* and *al-Nabaṭ* like *al-Ḥabīsh* and *al-Ḥabash* in comparison: a generation that settled in Iraq. They are al-*Anbāṭ* and one who belongs to them is *Nabaṭī*. In *al-Ṣaḥḥāḥ*: they were settling in *al-Baṭā'iḥ* among Iraqis. *Ibn al-Iʿrābī* said: *Nubāṭī*, not *Nabaṭī*. In *al-Ṣaḥḥāḥ*: *Nabaṭī* and *Nūbāṭī* and *Nubāṭ* similar to *Yamanī*, *Yumāni* and *Yumān*; and *Istanbaṭa* (was Nabatized). *Ayyūb bin al-Qaryah* said: the people of *ʿUmān* are Arabs who were Nabatized, and the people of *Baḥrayn* were *Nabīṭ* who were Arabized. It is said: *Tanabbaṭa* in the meaning that one became part of the *Nabaṭ*, and they were called *Nabaṭ* because they elicit or produce what belong in the ground. *ʿUmar bin al-Khattāb* said: *Tamaʿdadū wa-lā Tastanbiṭū* which means imitate *Maʿad* (of Yemen) not the *Nabaṭ*. In another saying: *lā Tanbiṭu al-Madā'in*, meaning do not imitate the *Nabaṭ* in their style of residence and owning real estate properties. *Ibn al-ʿAbbās* said: we the people of *Quraysh* are part of the *Nabaṭ* of *Kūtha Rabba* (historical city of Ur), which was said to be the birthplace of Abraham and the *Nabaṭ* were its inhabitants. *ʿAmru bin Maʿad Yakrub* said that *ʿUmar* asked him through *Saʿd bin Abī Waqqās* and said: *Iʿrābī fī Ḥabwatihī, Nabaṭī fi jabwatihī*. He wanted to say he was skillful in his construction and taxing practices like the *Nabaṭ*, because they were the prominent people of Iraq. *Ibn Awfá* said: *Kunnā naslifu Anbāṭ al-Shām* (we were before the Nabataeans of Syria), and in other sources: *Kunna Anbāṭan min Anbāṭ al-Shām* (we were Nabataeans from Syria)" [17]

Ibn a-Nadīm (929-996 CE) wrote in the introduction of his book *al-Fihrast* that the old language of Babylon (i.e. the Akkadian) was the language of the Nabataeans and that *al-Kildaniyyūn* (the Chaldeans) and *al-Siryāniyyūn* (the Assyrians) spoke dialects that were derived from it. He also wrote, quoting one of the Nabataean magicians who was living during his time, that the Nabataeans were people "with black complexion", and that one of the contemporary Nabataean personalities, *Ibn al-Waḥshiya al-Kildānī*, had translated many Nabataean texts to the Arabic of his time. [30]

The above quotations from *Ibn Manẓūr* and *Ibn al-Nadīm* are fairly clear. They indicate that the consensus among scholars of the Islamic Arab civilization was that the name Nabataean was used to describe generations of migrants from the Arabian Peninsula –not specific tribes– who had settled in Iraq and greater Syria, which included what we classify today as the Nabataeans, Aramaeans, and Akkadians. Accordingly, they believed that these early Nabataeans were Arabs in their roots who had migrated earlier from Southern Arabia, possibly historical Bahrain which extended then from Oman in the south to Basrah in the North, or possibly from Oman itself, and that their tongues had changed later on. They further believed that the Nabataeans of Iraq were older than those of Syria. Clearly, the Nabataeans according to their definition were open in their tribal backgrounds and varying in their composition. Based on their linguistic definition, the word Nabat was similar to the word Arab, not a specific name like *Nazār* or *Maʿad.* The above can possibly explain the overwhelming Arabian background of the Nabataeans of north-western Peninsula, since they could be the latest Arabs to become Nabataeans, and the first group to established a strong large state using explicitly the name *Nabaṭ* to distinguish themselves from other Arabs.

Even though most Western Orientalists dismissed the classification by past Islamic Arab civilization scholars and assumed it was sort of confusion, I see it a very solid and analytical classification. It is well-known, names change and vary depending on who uses them and at which historical period. Despite the usage of the name *'Ajam* by the Arabs to describe non Arab people, we are not aware of any group of people who call themselves *'Ajam*. Since there is no historical evidence to prove that there was a group of people calling themselves "Aramaeans" as in the case of the Nabataeans and because the Aramaic people (even according to the Orientalists) were semi Bedouin people who settled later like the Nabataeans, I dont see why identifying them as Nabataeans by the Islamic Arab Historians was a wrong identification. As for the lack of Nabataean inscriptions from Iraq, similar to those discovered in Syria and northern Hejaz, that does not mean necessarily their theories were wrong. We have not discovered yet any pre-Islamic inscriptions with modern Arabic writings, even though this writing style was heavily practiced and had even evolved there during that historical period. Likely, the many Aramaic inscriptions found in Iraq are themselves the inscriptions of what the scholars of the Islamic Arab civilization era called "the Nabataeans of Iraq". This may explain the reason why *al-Namārah* inscription used Aramaic shapes for the letters *Rā'*, *Kāf*, and *Dāl* rather than the usual Nabataean shapes found in Syria. As for using relatively varied languages in the Aramaic and Nabataean inscriptions, this proves the Nabataeans were of diversified roots rather than specific and definite ones.

The Arabs before Islam used the word *arām* to describe high signposts or markings, or high landmarks, which were usually built from stones to mark tombs. In the Quran (89: 7) أَلَمْ تَرَ كَيْفَ فَعَلَ رَبُّكَ بِعَادٍ إِرَمَ ذَاتِ الْعِمَادِ الَّتِي لَمْ يُخْلَقْ مِثْلُهَا فِي الْبِلَادِ. Because the Quranic verses of the *'Uthmān*'s edition were without soft vowel diacritics, extra *Alifs*, or dots, scholars of the Islamic Arab civilization differed on the meaning of the above verse. However, they all agreed that the name of the people was *ʿĀd*. Most assumed the three letters word *ʾrm* was referring to a city. It is possible this word was pronounced *ʾIrama* إِرَمَ as many read it today, but some pronounced it *Arām* أَرَام and thought it was the name of the historical city of Damascus, according to *Lisān al-ʿArab*. The usage of this word in the Quran can explain the usage of the same word in the inscription of the Assyrian king *Tukultī-abil-Ishāra* the First to announce his victory over the army of *Arām* in Syria, which was written in the Akkadian language about one thousand years CE. It may indicate that many in the surrounding area identified the people of this location as *Arām* after the name of their main city, but the Arabs to the south called them *ʿĀd*. Again, names of an identical group of people or city can vary depending on who uses it and when.

The day-to-day usage of the late Cuneiform script, which became significantly phonetic based at that stage, declined and became fully restricted to literature writings around 600 BCE until its complete disappearance in the mid third century CE. The Cuneiform writing was the predominant writing of the people of Iraq, Persia, and Syria. In this decline period, the Aramaic script gradually emerged as the vernacular script of Iraq and Syria, side-by-side the scripts of the occupying foreign powers. In fact, the decline of the Cuneiform writing was synchronous in the whole area. The oldest discovered inscription with Aramaic script belongs to the period between the eighth and sixth century CE. The oldest Nabataean inscriptions discovered belong to the third century. The Aramaic and Nabataean writing styles and languages are almost identical, despite their relative diversities. The similarities of the time period of their discovered inscriptions, the shapes of their letters, and their vocabulary, undoubtedly support the theories of Islamic Arab scholars in classifying the two as one group, namely the Nabataeans. Naturally, this does not mean the Nabataeans spoke one dialect, or that every Nabataean inscription was an inscription written by the Nabataean people. This script was also used by non-Nabataean Arab tribes and its spread was one of the main factors contributing to the gradual decline of the Arabic Musnad script.

Misnaming and denying the substantial Arab roots of the Aramaeans, Akkadians, Canaanians, and other population groups in the Fertile Crescent, and classifying them as independent and parallel ones, contradicts with the geographic and historical facts of the Arabian Peninsula. The anthropological and archeological evidence pointing to a gradual desertification of the Peninsula makes the case for repeated waves of migrations the north a very logical one. Besides, the current classification by western scholars does not seem more convincing than the one put forward by the Islamic Arab historians since it presents more questions rather than answering the original ones. If the people of the Fertile Crescent were not of Arab origin and background, what is their origin and who are the Arabs, then?

As for answering the second part of our question by the Orientalist theories, I will refere it to T. E. Lawrence, by quoting from his well-known book "The Seven Pillars of Wisdom: a Triumph" which was published in 1926 after he returned from his highly fruitfull trip to the Arabian Peninsula and Egypt. In his years there, he succeeded to become one of the closest associates of the leaders of the Great Arab Revoltion against the Ottoman Empire, if not one of its actual leaders. Lawrence studied Arabic and archeology in the prestigious Oxford University. His final thesis was about the architectural accomplishments of the Crusaders, a subject he was fascinated with, according to his autobiography. After his graduation with distinction he joined the British Royal Air Force and worked in one of the archeological expeditions in the early years of the twentieth century, like most other European archeologists positioned throughout the Ottoman Empire in preparation for World War I. According to Lawrence, "tribesmen and townsmen of Arabic-speaking Asia are of a different race", not "just men in different social and economic stages," because they have no "family resemblance" in the "working of their minds." To support and clarify his classification, he explained that the Arabs, "were a limited, narrow-minded people, whose inert intellects lay fallow in incurious resignation." "Their imaginations were vivid, but not creative." "They have no organizations of mind or body. They invented no systems of philosophy, no complex mythologies."

Despite his clearly extreme disdain of the Arabs, the key point of his view is not an isolated judgment, but the main theme of the Orientalist theories, past and current. It seems according to these theories, the Arabs cease to be Arabs once they settle down in cities and villages and evolve to different people, even if this was in the heartland of the Arabian Peninsula. Accordingly, the name Arabs is limited to the unsettled Arab tribes. At a first glance, the above Western classification does not seem to contradict with that put forward by the scholars of the Islamic Arab civilization in their distinction between the Arabs and Nabataeans. However, in actuality the two are substantially and radically different. The Orientalist's classification seems to be a pure manipulation of words and labels while that by the Islamic Arab scholars seems more analytical and connected to the actual facts of history at their times. Because Western theories cannot be scientifically convincing without answering the second part of our question above regarding the origin of the peoples of the Arabian Peninsula, they put forward their theory of the original mother Semitic people. However, this answer, which is fully based on the Jewish-Christian theology, lacks any logical or material evidence support, and therefore cannot be regarded as a scholarly or scientific answer, in my view. We do not have any scientifically-proven geographic, historic, or linguistic evidence, to prove the existence of an original Semitic group predating the rest.

Without a doubt, the success of the Orientalists in establishing the term "Semitic" as a "scientific" term to classify the languages and people of the Arabian Peninsula was the key factor behind the marginalization of the past Islamic Arab scholarly theories in our modern days. However, there is no science, whatsoever, behind this primarily theological, and even political term, which continues to play an important role in polarizing the people of the region and feeding their rivalries. Ironically, while Western theories dismiss past Islamic classification as a biased theological one lacking solid scholarly evidence, their core classifications are solely based on Jewish-Christian theology. While we continue finding Arabic names, poems, and texts on thousands of inscriptions throughout Arabia, we are yet to find one inscription that one can truly classify as a Semitic or proto-Semetic inscription.

The first scholar to use the term "Semitism" was the German seminarist, historian, and philologist August Ludwig von Schlözer, who coined it in the mid eighteen century, according to the Old Testament classifications of the peoples of Arabia and Egypt. He used it first to classify some languages of the Near East and North-East Africa, but today this term is used to classify both people and languages, and is regarded as a "scientific" fact by most specialists, including many Arab specialists, unfortunately. It may be useful to note here, even though the word *Sām* was not mentioned explicitly in the Quran, this name was not unknown to Islamic scholars. Some sources quoting *al-Tarmadhī* say Prophet Muhammad had said "Sam is the father of the Arabs". Regardless, this is clearly not relevant to the modern Western classification "Semites", which was conceived as an alternative to the term "Arabs" as a broader classification term. To conclude, the Islamic Arab scholars classified the majority of the people of the Fertile Crescent as Nabataeans of Arab background, who had migrated at various stages north from the Arabian Peninsula. Yemen was the original land of all people of the peninsula according to their classification.

Today, and particularly during the last two decades, the Orientalist theories about the history of the Middle East have multiplied manyfolds to solidify older ones. Modern theories are building new and more elaborate theoretical structures by referencing earlier assumptions as undisputed historical "facts" that were proven by modern material evidence. The mass media and even some specialized Academic journals in the West are crowded with new theories claiming that the language of the Quran was translated with many mistakes from the Syriac, that Islam actually came two centuries after the currently agreed upon date by Muslims, that its geographical inception was not in Mecca or Hejaz, that Muhammad himself is not a real person but rather a legendary Persian personality, and that Islamic battles had never actually taken place. As for the verbally transmitted pre-Islamic Arabic poetry, many Orientalists claim it was fabricated by the Abbasid authors and historians after Islam, and would rush to quote from the doctoral thesis of well-known Egyptian historian *Ṭāha Ḥusayn* in the Sorbonne to support their arguments. Some would even go as far as assuming all references of the Islamic Arab civilization, particularly the Quran, are unreliable and cannot therefore be used for any truly scientific and scholarly research in the field of Arabic and Islamic history. And much more.

Naturally, not all Orientalists are of the same opinion. In fact, Western Scholars deserve most credit for discovering and reading crucial inscriptional evidence, which did not only enrich our detailed knowledge of past scripts and languages in the greater Arabian

Peninsula, but also verified, in my opinion, the validity of the theories and conclusions of the past Islamic Arab civilization. American scholar James A. Bellamy of the University of Michigan is just one out of many such scholars. Among his long list of accomplishments, was his re-reading of two of the most important pre-Islamic Standard Arabic Nabataean inscriptions, namely the *al-Namārah* and *ʿAyn ʿAbdāt* inscriptions. The first inscription, which contained the clearest and most comprehensive Standard Arabic text found so far, will be the subject of my detailed study later. Dated between 88 CE to 125 CE, the second inscription included the oldest fully Classical Arabic text recorded before Islam, in addition to being the only material evidence we have for the existence of Classical Arabic poem in that period. Together, the two inscriptions represent undisputed pre-Islamic evidence that Classical or Standard Arabic, and Classical Arabic poetry were deeply rooted in the Arabian Peninsula and were practiced many centuries before Islam. Since the *ʿAyn ʿAbdāt* inscription included Aramaic language text side by side Standard Arabic, it also proves my observations earlier, based on the theories of the scholars of the Islamic Arab civilization, about the roots and nature of the languages of the Arabian Peninsula and their relations to Classical and Standard Arabic. Because of its utmost importance, I will provide a detailed reading of the *ʿAyn ʿAbdāt* inscription in this introduction.

ʿAyn ʿAbdāt Inscription (88-125 CE)

This inscription was first introduced to the scholarly community in 1986, by Professor Avraham Negev of the Hebrew University of Jerusalem. According to an article by Negev, it was discovered in 1979 by E. Orion, just outside the historical Nabataean city of *ʿAbdāt*, in the Negev desert. [31] The city of *ʿAbdāt* was established around 300 BCE, and was the second most important Nabataean city after Petra from the first century BCE until the beginning of the seventh century CE, when it was destroyed completely by a violent earthquake. It is believed that the Nabataean King Obados the First (96-85 BCE) is buried in this city.

The *ʿAyn ʿAbdāt* inscription was first pictured and traced by Ada Yardeni in 1982. (5) It included six lines of text, all written in the Nabataean script. The first three and the sixth lines were written in the Aramaic language, according to Negev, but the fourth and fifth lines were clearly written in Classical Arabic language. The initial paragraph in the three Aramaic lines spoke of a person named *Jurmil-lāhī bir Taymallāhī* calling for prayers and offering a statue to his god *ʿAbdāt*, possibly King Obados the First (96-85 BCE). Unfortunately the second line was severely damaged and cannot be read. The sixth and last line restated the name *Jurmillāhī*, and indicated that he was the writer of the inscription, the author of the poem, or possibly both.

A picture of the *ʿAyn ʿAbdāt* Inscription stone by *Ada Yardanī.* [31]

The entire inscription was initially read by J. Naveh and S. Shaked. [31] In 1990, Professor Bellamy of the University of Michigan provided a new reading of the two Arabic lines, based entirely on Yardeni's tracing of the stone. [8] Despite their reading differences of the two Arabic lines, Naveh and Bellamy agreed on the main theme of the inscription, which they explained primarily through their readings of the Arabic poem.

According to Yardeni's tracing, which was fully adopted by Bellamy except for reading the word ارد as ادد, the whole inscription can literally be translated from the Nabataean as follows: [31]

ذكير بطب قرا قدس عبدت الها وذكير
من [...................]
جرم الهي بر تيم الهي صلم لقبل عبدت الها
فيفعلو لا فدا ولا اثرا فكن هنا يبغنا الموتو لا
ابغه فكن هنا ارد جرحو لا يردنا
جرم الهي كتب يده

In their readings, Naveh and Shaked translated the text of the two Arabic lines in modern literary Arabic and organized it as follows:

فيفعل لا فدى ولا اثرا. فكان ان يبغنا الموت لا ابغه. فكان ان اراد جرح لا يردنا [31]

Naveh and Shaked then explained the above as follows:

> And he acts neither for benefit nor for favour. And if death claims us let me not be claimed. And if affliction seeks, let it not seek us. [31]

As mentioned above, Bellamy changed the word ارد to ادد in his new reading of the two Arabic lines, citing a Bedouin conjuration from al-*Zamakhsharī* أعزم عليك ايها الجرح ان لا تزيد ولا تديد. [8] He then assumed this word was أْدادَ, a noun of a verb in the meaning of "become infected, suppurate", which was combined with the following noun word to form the expression أدادَ جرحٌ. However, the soft diacritics of this combined expression do not match correctly according to the Arabic grammar rule regarding المضاف والمضاف اليه. Furthermore, according to *Lisān al-ʿArab*, the word أدد also means "an amazing or incredible matter" which is a more appropriate meaning. [17] Based on his reading, Bellamy re-wrote the two lines in the form of three classical Arabic poem hemistiches, as follows: [8]

فيفعلُ لا فِداً ولا اثرا
فكان هُنا يَبْغِنا الموتُ لا أبْغاهُ
فكان هُنا أدادَ جُرحٌ لا يرْدِنا

Then, he explained the three verses together as follows:

> For (Obodas -the god-) works without reward or favour, and he, when death tried to claim us, did not let it claim (us), for when a wound (of ours) festered, he did not let us perish. [8]

Both Bellamy and Naveh thought the writer was speaking about an actual wound. Naveh thought he was praying to the god to protect him from death or fatal injury. Bellamy thought he was thanking the god for his recovery from one. Thinking that this inscription was speaking about an actual wound is the common believe in the scholarly circles today. For example, based on Bellamy's updated reading, Hoyland gave only a slightly different translation, as follows:

> For he [Obodas -the god-] acts [expecting] no reward nor predilection. Though death has often sought us out, he afforded it no occasion; though I have often encountered wounding, he has not let it be my destruction. [14]

Because of the usual complex language and metaphors employed in Classical Arabic poetry, I believe a better reading of the two-line poem based on Yardeni's original tracing and Bellamy's reading of it should be:

فيفعلُ لا فِدا ولا أثرا   فكان هنُا يَبْغِنا
الموتُ لا أبْغَهُ فكان هنُا   أدَدُ جرُحٌ لا يرُدْنِا

However, after curefully tracing the inscription in Yardeni's picture, I arrived to a new Arabic transliteration from the Nabataean, which differs with her tracing and Naveh and Shaked's reading in four locations that will be pointed out in bold, below. Particularly, it updates Yardeni's tracing in four words at the beginning of the first and fifth lines. It is very clear in Yardeni's picture, and even in her own tracing, the letter *Hā'* of the word ابغه in the beginning of the sixth line was a medial shape *Hā'*. Furthermore, the letter *Fā'* of the following word فكن was actually the letter *Wāw* and it was visibly attached to that letter *Hā'*. As for the letter *Kāf* in the word فكن, it seems to me a clear letter *Mīm*.

After examining another zoomed-in image showing the first few words of the 3rd and 4th lines, I am convinced the letter sequence of the second line (4th line) was ابغه من هنا ادد. Please examine that zoomed-in image and the tracing image below it, which are provided in the next page. Clearly the letter *Hā'* was in its initial shape and it was connected to the following letter *Wāw*, which was followed in turn by a classical Nabataean letter *Mīm* in its initial form. The sand specks below the lower left-pointing tail of the letter *Wāw* are not part of that letter.

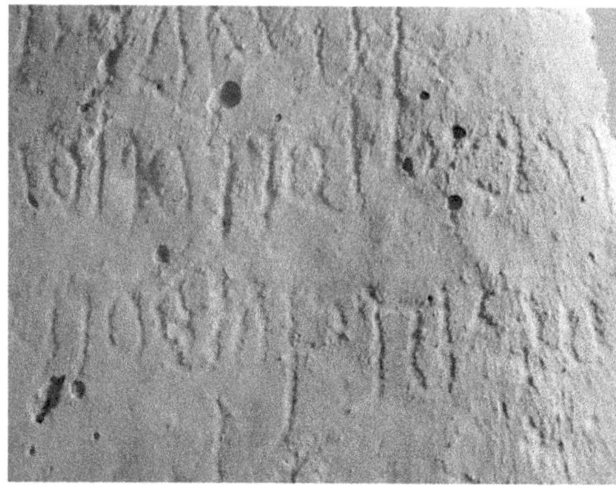

A zoomed-in picture of the *ʿAyn ʿAbdāt* inscription stone area containing the first few words of the 3rd and 4th lines which included Arabic poetry.

The following image incorporates my new tracing corrections and updates Yardeni's original tracing image:

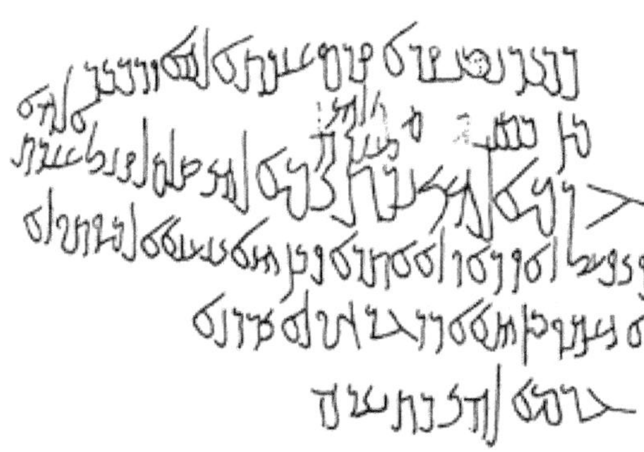

And here is my new updated literal translation of the inscription:

ذكير لمنقرا قدس عبدت الها وذكير

[]من [......................]

جرم الهي بر تيم الهي صلم لقبل عبدت الها

فيفعلو لا فدا ولا اثرا فكن هنا يبغنا الموتو لا

ابغهو من هنا ادد جرحو لا يردنا

جرم الهي كتب يده

As for the word اددا, I believe there are two other possibilities to read it. First, it could be أذذ or أذّ and both are related to the Arabic word أذى as in يؤذي, in the meaning of suffering and pain, according to *Lisān al-ʿArab.* [17] Second, it could actually be the two words إذ ذا, also based on *Lisān al-ʿArab*, which explained that the demonstrative pronoun ذا was initially the letter *Dhāl* alone, used with soft *fatḥah* diacritic sound when pointing to masculine object and with soft *kasrah* diacritic sound when pointing to a feminine object. [17]

After re-arranging the words in the Arabic poem text of the fourth and fifth lines, and after adding soft vowel diacritics, dots, and missing letters *Alif*, I concluded four possible Classical Arabic poem readings, as follows:

فيفعلُ لا فِدا ولا أثرا   فكان هُنا يَبْغِنا
الموتُ لا أبْغَهُ من هُنا   أدَدُ جرُحٌ لا يُرْدِنا

Or:

فَيَفعلَُ لا فِدا ولا أثَرا   فكانَ هُنا يَبْغِنا
الموتُ لا أبْغَهُ من هُنا   أذَذُ جرحٌ لا يُرْدِنا

Or:

فَيَفعلَُ لا فِدا ولا أثَرا   فكانَ هُنا يَبْغِنا
الموتُ لا أبْغَهُ من هُنا   أذٌّ جرحٌ لا يُرْدِنا

Or:

فَيَفعلَُ لا فِدا ولا أثَرا   فكانَ هُنا يَبْغِنا
الموتُ لا أبْغَهُ من هُنا   إذ ذا جرحٌ لا يُرْدِنا

After discussing my first three readings with the prominent Iraqi poet *Saadī Yūsuf*, he suggested the forth one and corrected the soft diacritics in few words. He further indicated that these verses could be in *al-Basīṭ* البسيط not *al-Ṭawīl* الطويل, as Bellamy thought. Another promenant Iraqi poet, *ʿAbd al-Razzāq ʿAbd al-Wāḥid*, thought the two verses were not rymed according to any Classical Arabic poetry standard. The talented Iraqi poet, *Ṣalāḥ ʿAwwād* believes the fourth reading is the most likely one. He thinks while the verses do have some indications for *al-Ṭawīl* الطويل they were actually in *al-Rajz* الرجز, and particularly in *Majzūʾ al-Rajz* مجزوء الرجز (portioned *Rajz*) which is quite common in Classical Arabic poetry. My English translations of the two poem verses, based on the three distinct meanings of the word ادد of my new four readings above, and even based on my new revised version of Bellamy's reading of Yardeni's tracing, are as follow:

> It (death) will act regardless of offering or predilection, for it is in here (life) to seek us.
> Death, which I do not seek from here (life), is an amazing act: a wound that does not kill us.

Or:

> It (death) will act regardless of offering or predilection, for it is in here (life) to seek us.
> Death, which I do not seek from here (life), is a suffering: a wound that does not kill us.

Or:

> It (death) will act regardless of offering or predilection, for it is in here (life) to seek us.
> Death, I do not seek from here (life), because it is only a wound that does not kill us.

To conclude my study of the *ʿAyn ʿAbdāt* inscription I think it is important to point out here three observations, in relation to our earlier discussion in this introduction:

First: Reading the Aramaic text in this inscription one can see clearly that the Aramaic language could not been an independent language parallel to Arabic in its roots or an older language, as most Orientalist theories claim, but a dialect of Nabataean Arabic, just as it was classified by the scholars of the Islamic Arab civilization. Evidently, any Arabic reader would find no dire difficulty understanding what the Aramaic line of this inscription wanted to say. All the following words clearly seem to have Arabic roots:

ذكير (كثير الذكر) لمنقرأ (لمن قرأ)، قدس (قداس)، إلها (إلهه)، لقبل (لقبول)، صلم (صنم)، بر (بن)، كتب يده (كتابة يده) ..

Second: The writer used Aramaic to call for prayers to the god, but he used Standard Arabic when writing his Classical poem about death. This support our observation earlier that Standard Arabic was not the tongue of Quraysh or *Muḍar*– since the city of *ʿAbdāt* was far north in the Nagev desert–, the tongue of another specific group, or the tongue of a specific geographical location. Standard Arabic was the poetic and formal communication language used by most people of the Arabian Peninsula, north and south. In a way, it is the collective record of the roots of their tongues.

Third: After reading the solid and eloquent two lines of the Classical Arabic poem in this inscription, which were written at least four centuries before the birth of Prophet Mohammad, one cannot even speculate that Classical Arabic or pre-Islamic Classical Arabic poems came after Islam, or were invented by the Abbasid linguists and historians, as many Orientalists claim today.

Because any original and scholarly research should be based first on material evidence, then secondly on documented historical references, and thirdly on a sound scientific analysis of the information provided by such evidence and references, I will restudy in this book, with an open mind and a neutral approach, the key material evidence presented by Western scholars to support their mainstream theories and conclusions regarding the nature and history of Classical Arabic, and Arabic language in general, before Islam. Specifically, I chose for my study three inscriptional samples: Nabataean, Musnad, and Akkadian. The Nabataean and Akkadian samples are from northern Arabia, where a majority spoke Arabic with various dialects in a vast area extending from northern Syria to Anbar and Babylon of Iraq in the east and including northern Hejaz. The third sample is from Yemen in southern Arabia which is known for its unique dialect and whose people constituted an important source of repeated migrations to northern Arabia.

For Nabataean, I decided first to only read the *al-Namārah* inscription as a sample Nabataean inscription, but I then decided to add several additioal inscriptions to explain and support my reading of that inscription. Particularly, I reread six other Nabataean inscriptions using the word *nafs* in the meaning of tomb, according to Western scholars' interpretation, including the Nabataean *Umm al-Jimāl* inscription. These six inscriptions were the only inscriptions using this word in that possible meaning, among more than three hundreds Musnad, Nabataean, Hebrew, Aramaic, and Palmerian inscriptions I read to conduct my study. Because *al-Namārah* inscription is complex in its language and script, its reading occupied most of the pages of this book.

Without a doubt, the discovery of the *al-Namārah* stone occupied for more than a century the front stage among modern Western Nabataean discoveries. It was used heavily to support their theories about Arabic, language and script, and it is seen by many today as an undisputed evidence to the accuracy of their research and theories in comparison to that of the scholars of the Islamic Arab civilizations. The key importance of *al-Namārah* inscription according to the Orientalist theories was in its usage of connected letters resembling cursive Arabic, which proved their assumptions regarding the origins of the modern Arabic script. This subject, which I discussed in an article regarding the history of the Arabic script, is a complex one, and is beyond the scope of this book. However, while studying *al-Namārah*, I was intrigued by the many differences in the readings of its Arabic language text. This was my major initial reason to conduct a comprehensive linguistic and historical research, which took me about a year to read the inscription.

As for the Musnad inscriptions of southern Arabia, I chose a new, never read before, inscription from Yemen. Even though it was the first Musnad inscription I read from scratch, and it was longer than *al-Namārah* inscription, Its reading did not take me very long. All what I needed was *Lisān al-ʿArab* by *Ibn Manẓūr*!

Finally, for an Akkadian inscriptional sample, I chose to read part of the Mesopotamian Epic of Gilgamesh, the oldest discovered literary work in the world. Specifically, I did a comparative reading of the two dreams of Gilgamesh as told by two different tablet editions of the epic, 1000 years apart. The first from the Babylonian edition dated to about 2000-2100 BCE. The second is from the Assyrian edition dated to around 1000 BCE. In my readings, I utilized five historical Arabic etymological references and demonstrated that the Akkadian language was substantially Arabic, and that the Epic of Gilgamesh used Classical Arabic. This is not a personal speculation. I would like to invite the readers to decide on their own whether or not the following sample lines, transliterated from the epic as is, are old Classical Arabic or not:

جِحْشِجِّحْمَش إنّ ذا أروك انطّلَ شأْناتكَ
ذوو ذأن أُشتنَذَبْكَ كا ذا

ذوو ذأن أُشَذَبَ كا ذو
اليكَ كُومَ ذأن تَفو مشذبُ إبر
أُمّاه إنَ كا إنليل مَلَك لإمقُعتَمَ
إبرِ ملِكو أنَكو لأُرسي
لأُرسِيمَ إبرِ ملِكو أنَكو

Several respectable Western scholars have read and re-read key pre-Islamic inscriptions, including *al-Namārah, Gilgamesh Epic,* and *ʿAyn ʿAbdāt.* However, a number of their readings were weak in their language, contradicting in their meaning, and superficial in their analysis. Most orientalists read these inscriptions by referencing Aramaic, Hebrew, and even Greek, first. Many explained their non-harmonious Arabic readings by invoking their theoretical assumptions that the languages of the Akkadians, Nabataeans and Yemenis were not substantially Arabic languages and therefore cannot be measured and analyzed according to the Standard Arabic language grammar rules and tools, which were introduced centuries later. However, my objective reading of many of these inscriptions prove otherwise. Here is the fact: the linguists of the Abbasid era did not invent Standard Arabic grammar but extracted it, with an incredible skilfull and scholarly elequeance, from the references of their time, like the text of the Quran, pre-Islamic poetry, and other available historical sources. Some of the Nabataean pre-Islamic inscriptions discovered today, like *al-Namārah* and *ʿAyn ʿAbdāt,* can deservingly be among these reference sources.

PART 1

Nabataean Inscriptional Sample: The *al-Namarāh* Inscription

1

Introduction to Part One

The inscription of *al-Namārah* is by far the most important, controversial, and challenging pre-Islamic Arabic inscription— it is the earliest discovered, but youngest dated inscription of only four Nabataean inscriptions, considered by Western scholars today as fully Arabic. According to some, it is the oldest Arabic document on record with relatively good classic Arabic language. Dated 328 AD and written in clear cursive forms, it was hailed by many scholars as definite evidence that the modern Arabic script had evolved from the late Nabataean script. Many prominent Muslim scholars (who lived only a few centuries after the script's assumed birth around the 3rd century) believed it was derived from the Arabic *Musnad* script. [22] *al-Namārah* inscription is also extensively cited by historians as an important reference to the historical events of the early decades of the prominent pre-Islamic Arab Lakhmid kingdom (*al-Lakhmiyyūn*) of *Hīrah*, modern day Iraq. Despite more than a century since its discovery in 1901, the reading of *al-Namārah* inscription is still questionable, even at present time.

Dussaud, the French archeologist who discovered *al-Namārah* stone near Damascus and transferred it to Paris for further examination, had possibly misread the most important part of the inscription—the first line. Based on his reading, it is generally believed today that al-Namārah was the gravestone of king *Umru'ū al-Qays al-Bid'*, the second king of the kingdom of *al-Ḥīrah* and the most significant pre-Islamic Arab leader. Dussaud's reading was partially influenced by an unfortunate ambiguity in today's Arabic language grammar textbooks. To make matters worse, other scholars who read *al-Namārah* in the past century uncritically strived to uphold Dussaud's reading fundamentals thus reinforcing its equally uncritical acceptance. To prove, at any cost, that *al-Namārah* was *Umru'ū al-Qay*'s tombstone, some were even willing to present readings that manifestly contradicted the rules of Arabic grammar, geographical facts, and recorded history.

In order to re-read *al-Namārah* inscription, I found it necessary to re-read the *Umm al-Jimāl* Arabic Nabataean inscription as well, since the two inscriptions had contained identical words and shared similar historical facts and timeframes. To read the two inscriptions, I had to also read the *Raqqūsh* and numerous other Nabataean, Palmyran, and Arabic Musnad inscriptions to study the linguistic usage of similar words and phrases.

Regarding *al-Namārah* inscription, I will demonstrate, using the tools of the Arabic language and through in-depth analytical reading, that it is not the tombstone of King *Umru'ū al-Qays bin 'Amrū*, or even about him. Written, most likely, several years after his death, the inscription recorded the important accomplishments of a previously unknown personality, *'Akdī*, who was possibly one of *Umru'ū al-Qays bin 'Amrū* army generals, an Arab tribal leader who collaborated with the Romans, or maybe a top ranking Arab soldier in the Byzantine Roman army. According to my reading, the opening sentence was only a swearing (vow) to the soul of King *Umru' al-Qays bin 'Amrū*, similar to the customary opening sentence used by Arabs and Muslims since the 7th century, *Bism Allāh al-Raḥmān al-Raḥīm* بسم الله الرحمن الرحيم. The main topic of the inscription was the apparent defeat of the prominent *Midhḥij* tribe of southern Arabia, in the hands of *'Akdī's* fighters and the possible subsequent control of part of Yemen by the Byzantine Roman Empire. The final sentence concluded the inscription by informing the reader about *'Akdī's* death, maybe in the battlefield, and stating that his parents should be happy and proud of him. This narration is consistent with how soldiers are typically mourned.

As it is always true with reading historical inscriptions, no one reading can be definitely the correct one. Going over major previous readings of *al-Namārah*, particularly of the key disputable words in the text, I can not rule out completely other reading that concluded this inscription was actually about King *Umru'ū al-Qays.* The reading by Bellamy was by far the most observing of Classical Arabic sentence structures and worth full attention. I will therefore present an alternative reading taking into account his major conclusions, particularly regarding the word *'Akdī.*

I am hopeful that my new readings of *al-Namārah* and *Umm al-Jimāl* inscriptions would prompt scholars in this field to re-examine the current readings in a fundamentally different way. I hope that future history textbooks and the Louvre museum will not state as certain that *al-Namārah* inscription stone was the gravestone or epitaph of King *Umru'ū al-Qays bin 'Amrū.* I also hope that future publications would correct the obvious current reading errors of the *Umm al-Jimāl* Nabataean inscription. As a linguistic benefit, I am optimistic that future Arabic language grammar textbooks would cease from repeating a common grammatical error regarding simple feminine demonstrative pronouns by re-examining a poem line from *Alfiyyat Ibn Mālik.* Certainly, my new readings could add even more critical, historical, and linguistic importance to *al-Namārah* inscription itself, since the language used in this inscription was clearly and essentially Classical Arabic. This can incontrovertibly prove that the grammar and language of the Quran are deeply rooted and developed in Arabia, long before Islam. That is, they are not Islamic or Abbasid inventions as many Western scholars claim.

Because a successful reading of any involved inscription, like *al-Namārah*, requires a comprehensive and organized vision, I divided my reading into convenient sections corresponding to the main topics conceived as preliminary tools to read the full inscription. I have also provided detailed sketches and images to guide the reader into a full visual understanding of the topic of this particular study. Throughout this chapter, I will transliterate (following Library of Congress rules), translate, and write in Arabic various words and phrases to benefit the expert as well as the non-expert readers.

2

Historical and Geographical Overview

It is problematic to read the inscriptions of *Umm al-Jimāl* and *al-Namārah* without studying first the historical events taking place during the second and third centuries CE — particularly during the early decades of the third century CE and during the reign of King *Umru'ū al-Qays bin 'Amrū* of the city of *al-Hīrah*. The name of this king was mentioned in the first line of *al-Namārah* inscription. Arab and Muslim historians knew *Umru'ū al-Qays bin 'Amrū*, as *Umru'ū al-Qays al-Bid'*, meaning the first. (The desert town of *al-Ḥīrah* is located less than 30 miles south of Babylon, the famed Mesopotamian city that had fallen to the Persians over eight centuries earlier.)

The first question that comes to mind regarding *al-Namārah* inscription is the following: Why was this inscription written in the Nabataean Language and script, which was limited according to the Western scholars to southern Syria and northern Hejaz, while King *Umru'ū al-Qays bin 'Amrū* was from *al-Ḥīrah* of Iraq? I have answered this question in the instroduction of this book where I pointed out that the Nabataean language was the pre-Islamic language of Babylon and nearby *al-Ḥīrah* city according to past Islamic Arab scholars.

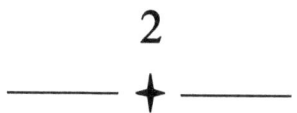

Luckily, the *al-Namārah* inscription had provided a precise date that can easily be checked against the more accurate dates provided by the remains left by the three main power players in the Arabian Peninsula during that time: the Persians, the Roman Byzantines, and the Yemenite Arabs. Several other Arab kingdoms existed too, but they were either very weak or tightly under the control of either the Persians or the Romans who fought for the conquest of new territories in the peninsula. After the fall of the northern Arab Nabataean kingdom of Petra at the hands of the Romans (105 CE), the kingdom of Yemen became the only Arab power challenging their rule in the south. Because of repeated Roman attacks, and in order to defend their territory, the Yemeni kings had occasionally forged close ties with the Persians. [6][40]

According to several Muslim scholars, *ʿAmrū bin ʿUday*, the father of King *Umru'ū al-Qays bin ʿAmrū*, was the first king of the ethnically Yemenite Lakhmid kingdom (later, called *al-Manādhirah* Kingdom by the Arabs) to designate *al-Ḥīrah* as the capital city. The *Ḥīrah* Kingdom became the most powerful member of a tribal alliance known as the *Tannūkh* Kingdom, which was established around the 1st century CE by *Mālik bin Māhir* of Yemen. The *Tannūkh* Kingdom controlled a vast area extending from *ʿŪmān* in the south to *al-Ḥīrah* and the Syrian Desert near Damascus in the north, occupying the entire west coast of the Persian Gulf, historically known as the Gulf of *Baṣrah.* Islamic Arab era scholars linked the Lakhmid and *Tannūkh* kingdom to the powerful *Maʿad* tribe of Yemen. The three kings who ruled *Tannūkh* before king *ʿAmrū bin ʿUday* visited *Ḥīrah* extensively and regularly, but probably had their capital in Bahrain or even Yemen. Most of *Ḥīrah's* original population had eventually moved north to the *Anbār* area before it was made the capital city by King *ʿAmrū bin ʿUday.* [18][26]

King *ʿAmrū bin ʿUday's* father was probably a northern Arab. His mother was the sister of *Judhaymah al-Abrash* who was the first king and the founder of the *Tannūkh* Kingdom dynasty. He maintained close relations with the Persians and ruled before and after the time of King *Ardashīr bin Bābik* (224-241 CE), the first king of the third and last Sassanid dynasty, and the son of the Zaradust priest, *Bābik*, who had earlier toppled the last king of the second Sassanid dynasty. [19]

It seems that *Judhaymah al-Abrash*, a Yemenite Arab, had decided to offer his sister to a northern Arab from the *Ḥīrah* area to establish closer blood relation with the northern tribes. The practice of marrying sisters and daughters to link with other tribes is quite common among Arab tribes. As we shall see later, both of the words *Tannūkh* and *Judhaymah* will appear briefly in the important Arabic Nabataean inscription, *Umm al-Jimāl,* found south of Damascus and believed to be dated 250 CE. According to sources, King *ʿAmrū bin ʿUday* took advantage of the temporary weakening of the Sassanid Persian Empire after the death of King *Ardashīr bin Bābik* and decided to invade the Persian-controlled Arab areas of Bilād al-ʿIrāq (Mesopotamia) with the help of the Romans and the Arab tribes north and west of *Ḥīrah*. [26][40] His action had therefore reversed the traditional alliance of the previous, purely Yemenite, kings of *Tannūkh* with the Persians.

After the death of King *ʿAmrū bin ʿUday* in the year 288 CE, his son, *Umruʾū al-Qays bin ʿAmrū* took over and decided to expand on his father's attacks even further to include all Persian-controlled areas in Arabia. He was the first Arab leader who seriously attempted to unify all parts of the Arabian Peninsula in a single kingdom challenging both the Romans and Persians, and was therefore considered the most revered man in Arabia before Islam. Taking advantage of further conflicts within the Sassanid Persian royal family, he had even crossed the Persian (Arabic) Gulf to raid the heartland of Persia. Pre-Islamic Arabic poetry spoke of several virulent raids by the Arab tribes against the Persians in Bilād al-ʿIrāq. It is known that poems are the most important record-keeping evidence of the Arab tribes who traditionally relied on memory, not writing, to document their events. King *Umru'ū al-Qays* succeeded in bringing most of the Arabian Peninsula under his control except for the powerful Yemen and the Roman-controlled Arab kingdom in Syria, known as *al-Ghasāsinah* Kingdom. History recorded that, because the Romans supported the campaigns of Umru'ū al-Qays, the Persians were forced to accept a deal with the Romans (298 CE) whereby they ceded many of their previously captured territories in Mesopotamia.

A decade later, a new powerful king took over Sassanid Persia. He was *Shabur II* (309-379 CE) known to the Arabs under the nickname *Dhū al-Aktāf* ذو الأكتاف (the owner of the shoulders). It was believed that he had pierced his Arab prisoners' shoulders to tie them together after captivity. *Shabur II* regained control over most of the areas lost to the Romans and their Arab allies. It was said that he had captured *Ḥīrah*, the seat of King *Umru'ū al-Qays*, after a bloody battle in the year 225 CE, three years before the date mentioned in *al-Namārah* inscription. [18][19] However, it is not known whether King *Umru'ū al-Qays* had survived that battle. Only after the discovery of *al-Namārah* and subsequent Dussaud's reading had experts claimed that King *Umru'ū al-Qays* had escaped to Damascus and died in the city of Bosra on December 7th, 223 Bosra (equivalent to 228 CE), which is the date mentioned in the inscription.

I have to mention, however, that there is no other evidence supporting the above claim except the supposed evidence of *al-Namārah* inscription. Nonetheless, based on my reading of the first line of the inscription as a vow to his soul, I am prone to think that he died earlier, possibly in the battle of *Ḥīrah*, 325 CE. After the death of king *Umru'ū al-Qays*, the Romans and Persians fought extensively all over Arabia until the year 363 CE when they finally signed a treaty acknowledging Persian supremacy over Iraq. [19]

Consequent to the fierce Arab attacks on the Sassanid forces stationed in Mesopotamia (330 -370 CE), descendants of king *Umru'ū al-Qays* were allowed to go back to *al-Ḥīrah* and rule under the protection of the Persians. Finally, the Muslim Arabs defeated the Persians in the battle of al-*Qādisiyyah* (638 CE) which effectively put an end to the Sassanid Empire. [18][40]

In the early decades of the 4th century CE, Yemen, the seat of the oldest known Arab kingdoms in the peninsula, was a prime target for both the Romans and the Persians. The Yemenites were generally referred to by the rest of the Arabs as *al-Ḥimīriyyīn*, and depending on whom and when, Yemen was additionally known as *Midhḥij* or *Ma'ad*. The tribes of *Midhḥij* and *Ma'ad* are the largest and most powerful tribes in Yemen. Being the most powerful among the Arab kingdoms of that time, Yemen had maintained its status as an independent kingdom.

As mentioned earlier, King *Umru'ū al-Qays* was never able to control Yemen. In fact, during his time around the year 300 CE, a Yemenite king named *Shammar Yuharʻish*, was able to unify Yemen including *Haḍramawt* to create a powerful kingdom. [6] If logic matters, It would be impossible that a defeated king *Umru'ū al-Qays*, who had just lost his capital city of *al-Ḥīrah* in a bloody battle around the year 225 CE, would accomplish the highest military victory of his times— the conquest of Yemen— at the same time of *al-Namārah* (328 CE.)

Reportedly, king *Shammar Yuharʻish* had maintained close relations with the Persians by sending a diplomatic mission to the Sasanian court at Ctesiphon, *al-Madā'in*, Iraq. [6] *Khawārizmī*, a prominent Muslim scholar who lived during the early Islamic centuries called him *Shimr Yarʻish* or *Abū Karab Bin Ifrīqis*, which could mean he was of African origins as per the use of the word *Ifrīqis*. No diacritic vowel was placed on the first word *shimr* شمر. This could indicate that his name was either *Shimr* — a classic Arabic name—, or *Shammar* — a well-known name of a prominent Arab tribe in northern *Najd.* I do believe though, it is the former because *al-Namārah* inscription has one *mīm* letter in the name. *Khawārizmī* further wrote that King *Shimr* was called *Yar'ish* (trembling) because he was suffering of a nervous condition that made him tremble. According to *Khawārizmī*, King *Shimr Yar'ish* was, as claimed by some, nicknamed king *Dhū al-Qirnayn* (the one with two horns) contrary to the belief of many who thought this was a nickname for the Macedonian conqueror, Alexander the Great. Further, *Khawārizmī* listed King *Shimr Yar'ish* as the 20th king of Yemen before Islam and listed king *Umru'ū al-Qays bin 'Amrū* as the 21st king of *al-Ḥīrah* before Islam. [18] This means, the two kings had ruled approximately during the same period. In fact, the dates reported by *Khawārizmī's* coincide well with the dates provided by historians today. Most importantly, this coincidence would make it highly probable that King *Shimr Yar'ish* was indeed the king of Yemen during the times of *al-Namārah* inscription.

While it is not impossible that King *Umru'ū al-Qays bin 'Amrū* could have died in the year 328 CE, the historical evidence, including *al-Namārah* inscription, indicates otherwise. Again, I do believe that he died between the years 309 CE after *Shabur* II took power, in 325 CE, the year *al-Ḥīrah* was captured. As we shall see later, when reading *al-Namārah*, the historical analysis above could become vital to the understanding of the events, dates, and names appearing in the inscription.

3

On the Usage of the Word *nafs* by the Nabataeans and Arabs

Before proceeding to the details of reading *al-Namārah* and *Umm al-Jimāl*, it is important to start with an introduction to the meanings and usages of the second word in both inscriptions. Specifically, one needs to answer the following question: Did the Arabs, and the Nabataean Arabs particularly, really use the word *nafs* in the meaning of tomb or funerary monument? According to Western scholars this word was individually used by the Arabs and Nabataeans in the meaning of stelé. In their reading of the word, they cited old Musnad inscriptions of Yemen and eastern Arabia, in addition to the Nabataean, Hebrew, and Palmarian inscriptions, as I will explain later.

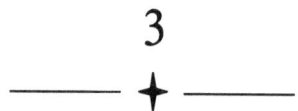

As for the Musnad inscriptions, the Arabs of Yemen and eastern Arabia used the phrase *nafs wa-qabr* in the majority of their tomb inscriptions.[41] Although studying these Musnad inscriptions in details is beyond the scope of this book, the natural and obvious meaning of this term should be "soul and tomb". Possibly, the Arabs believed historically the souls of the dead stay with them, but changed their beliefs after Islam, as it is clear from the following Quranic verse (39: 42) اللَّهُ يَتَوَفَّى الْأَنفُسَ حِينَ مَوْتِهَا. I believe the mere usage of the word *nafs* together with *qabr* indicates that it was used in the meaning of soul. According to what I learned from the Yemeni researcher *Fu'ād Yaḥyá Ḥamzah*, a lecturer in the archeology department of the *Dhumār* University, modern discoveries of ancient Yemeni tombs clearly indicated that the term *nafs wa qabr* was not the only term used on the burial stones. In the *Jawf* providence, according to *Ḥamzah*, inscriptions used *nafs wa-naṣb*, *naṣb wa-bayt*, or just *nafs*. Also, in some Sabaean tombs they used *qayf* rather than *nafs*, *maskan* rather than *bayt*, or *nasb* instead of *naṣb*, and possibly others.

The diverse linguistic usages above indicate, in my view, these words were utilized freely according to their meanings. Therefore, if the word *nafs* was used in the meaning of *qabr*, they would not have used the word *qabr* additionally. Arabic language references confirmed the appropriate usages of all the above words, but they did not hint of the usage of *nafs* in the meaning of *qabr*. For example, *Lisān al-ʿArab* clarified that *bayt* was used in the meaning of *qabr*, and that *maskan* (from *sukun* or stillness) was another word for *bayt*. As for *nasb* it clarified that it was used in the meaning of statue or just a stone to mark a location. [17] If the word *nafs* was a synonym to the word *nasb* or funerary monument, they would not have used it together with *nasb*. It is not logical to assume that the word nafs was used alone and commonly for centuries in the meaning of qabr but had somehow disappeared from all Arabic linguistic references. It is also noteworthy to mention, that Musnad inscriptions from Yemen or elsewhere did not use demonstrative pronouns, as with the Nabataean inscriptions, which can complicate our analysis or the usages of the above words.

To enrich this study, I would like to bring attention to couple more reading possibilities of the phrase *nafs wa-qabr*. First, based on my reading of the *Umm al-Jimāl* (I will discuss in a later chapter) it is possible that this phrased was pronounced *nafsu* qabr in the meaning of "itself tomb of" or "this is the tomb of" which is the common phrase used on the tombs of the Arabs after Islam, and of other neighboring people. Second, due to the similarity of the letters *Fā'* and *ʿAyn* in the *Liḥyānī* and *Sabaī* styles of Musnad, the word *nafs* could possibly be *naʿsh*, which means coffin or death bed.

In Arabic, the three-letter word *nafs* is rather complex; consequently, I have some explaining to do. The root of the word is *nafas*, meaning "breath" from which two main types of usage were derived. The first includes "soul", "life", "person", or "being"; the second "self" as in "same", "identical", "itself", "himself", and "herself". [17] This first primary usage could even be traced to the Babylonian Epic of Gilgamesh where the god-man name *Ut.napištu.m* (the Sumerian Babylonian mythological prototype which inspired the story of Biblical Noah who survived the flood) can literally be translated as "eternal great soul-being". The word *napištu* was used in Sumerian, Akkadian, and Babylonia in the meaning of "life" "being" or "soul". Arabic used nafs, Hebrew used *napšā* and Aramaic Syriac used *napištu.* The Nabataeans used several of these words due to their geographical location and diversity. The Nabataean tomb inscriptions used *l.napš.h* extensively in the meaning of "for himself"; but the words *napšā* and *napštā* had also appeared in few other cases. [13]

Palmyrenes used to portray the dead either in relief or in statues placed on tombs.[33] They usually referred to a statue as *ṣalam* (as in Arabic *ṣanam*). But they might have had also referred to it —although rarely— as *napšā*, or *napeš* to mean "the same" or "the identical", which 1) it conforms to the second main usage of the word in Arabic just mentioned, and 2) it fits well when naming a personal statue. The Nabataeans, instead, used an architectonic form (a cone topped by inflorescence) placed on a cylindrical or square base that they might have, arguably, referred to as *napšā*, or *napeš*, too. These memorial stones can be carved or engraved into rock faces with an identifying inscription that occasionally accompany them and is normally located in the base. [33] [39] In the graveyards of Umm al-Jimal south of Damascus, one can notice that most inscriptions included the name of the dead alone inscribed on individual rectangular stones placed vertically.

In his indispensable book about *Madā'in Ṣāliḥ* tombs inscriptions, Healey further opined that this "Pyramidal stele carved in the rock" could explain the "mysterious" absence of inscriptions from the numerous tombs found in the city of Petra, which he believes had banned tombs inscriptions. [12] Not surprisingly though, the *al-Namārah* and Umm al-Jimāl stones and their inscriptions do not even conform to the physical and inscriptional characteristics of a typical so-called Nabataean *napš*, which rarely included any type of text, except for an occasional name. Furthermore, the majority of the hundreds of Nabataean tombs' inscriptions found so far had consistently used the introductory phrase *dnh kapr'* or *dnh qabr'*.

Although unlikely, it is not impossible that the Nabataeans had explicitly used the word *nafash* for their architectonic-shaped personal memorial monuments, instead of their frequently used word *naṣb* (as in Arabic نصب), and for monuments they erected for their idols. It is my firm opinion, though, that scholars who read *Umm al-Jimāl*, which was discovered after *al-Namārah*, rushed to replicate Dussaud and other scholars' readings of the word *napš* to mean "memorial monument" or "funerary monument". Some even stretched its meaning to *shahidat qabr*, which can be translated to "tombstone" or "burial monument". To emphasize the usage of the word *napš*, Healey referenced *Le Nabatéen, by* the French scholar Jean Gantineau (1899-1956) who defined the word as such, offering only two Nabataean inscriptions as evidence: *al-Namārah* and *Umm al-Jimāl* which was called the *Fahrū* inscription, initially.

To be accurate, I must indicate here that the reading of the word *nafs* in the meaning of funerary monument by Gantineau and Healey was not only based on their reading of that word in *al-Namārah* and *Umm al-Jimāl*, but also on the reading by the German scholar Enno Littmann (1875-1958) of three inscriptions in his book "Semitic inscriptions of South Huran", namely the *Umm al-Jimāl, Bin Ḥūr, and Milḥ* inscriptions. These three inscriptions were the only ones among more than 107 inscriptions he read in his book, which is thought to use the word *nafs* in that manner. [20] In his study, Littmann based his reading on that of the German scholar Ulios Euting (1839-1913) and the French scholar Charles Simon Clermont-Ganneau (1846-1923), who read two Nabataean inscriptions with that word—which were three centuries older than *Umm al-Jimāl*—, and the reading of the French Scholar Eugène-Melchior de Vogüé (1848-1910) of a third older inscription. The three inscriptions are: the Strasbourg inscriptions discovered by Euting in *al-ʿUlá* north of *Ḥijāz* and dated 8-9 CE, the Madeba inscription discovered by Ganneau in the Medeba area east of the Jordan river and dated 37-38 CE, and the *Bin Ḥur* inscription discovered by de Vogüé in *Umm al-Jimāl* and dated around 150 CE.

While Healey thought in his reading of only two out of around seventy skillfully read inscriptions in his book, that the word *napšʾ* was in the meaning of "the burial monument" and the other word, *napštʾ*, as "the two burial monuments," [12] my reading of the two inscriptions led me to a different conclusion. After analyzing their texts, I concluded that the word *napšʾ* was used in its common two meanings, namely "soul" or "itself".

To illustrate the past readings of the word *nafs* —in the meaning of tomb— in the earliest discovered Nabataean inscriptions, and the disadvantages of referencing them in future studies, I will discuss the readings of the Strasbourg and Madeba inscriptions in the mid nineteenth century, which are possibly the earliest references. Then, I will discuss the readings of the *Milḥ* and *Bin Ḥūr* inscriptions in the early twentieth century. As for the readings of *al-Namārah* and *Umm al-Jimāl* inscriptions, they are the main subject of this book and I will allocate separate chapters for them. Finally, I will discuss a newly discovered inscription in *Umm al-Jimāl* —the *Shahīm* inscription— whose initial readers' haste in assuming the word *nafs* meant tomb was the key factor in preventing them from offering a lucid reading.

However, before delving into the reading details of these inscriptions, I must point out that I did not see pictures of three of the seven inscriptions above. Specifically, I was not able to obtain pictures of Strasbourg, *Milḥ*, and *Bin Ḥūr*. This prevented me from retracing them to make sure their earlier tracings were accurate, and would undoubtedly make them unreliable references, in my opinion. I say this not to question the integrity of anyone but to follow the scientific scholarly procedure. Tracing mistakes by scholars can play a decisive role in their inability to provide coherent readings. As we saw earlier, the unfortunate tracing mistakes of the *ʿAyn ʿAbdāt* inscription prevented a solid reading of its Arabic poem lines. And as we shall see later, Dussaud's tracing mistakes of *al-Namārah* were among the main factors behind our inability to obtain a sound Arabic reading of its inscription for more than a century, and Littmann's careless tracing of the *Umm al-Jimāl* inscription was the main reason to have a completely inaccurate reading of its text. Furthermore, because some of the Nabataean inscriptions did not contain complete texts, examining their actual pictures can play a crucial role in their readings. As we know, the meanings of words can change depending on their positions in sentences and paragraphs.

Strasbourg Inscription (8-9 CE)

The Strasbourg inscription was possibly the earliest Nabataean inscription used by Western scholars to define the word *nafs* as tomb, but its stone was lost according to Healey, who translated the inscription literally as follows:

دا نفشا دي ابر بر
مقيمو بر مقيمل دي بنه
له أبوهي بيرح ألول
شنت 1 لحرتت ملك نبطو

Healey translated the opening phrase in English as follows:

> This is the funeral monument of *Abār* son of *Moqimu* son of Moqimel which his father built for him ..

Translated to Arabic:

هذا النصب القبري لأبار بن مقيمو بن مقيمال الذي بناه له أبيه ...

Healey's reading is a good one if we assume that the word *nafs* meant soul, as in Yemen inscriptions, but the usage of the word بناه, or "built", afterward makes such reading unlikely as it is not possible to physically build a soul. Despite my reservation on reading an inscription without seeing its picture, or at least its tracings, I read it initially based on Healey's literal translation as follows:

هو ذا نفسُ (نفسُاو نفسه القبر او النصب) ذي (العائد الى) ابار بن مقيمو بن مقيمال الذي بناه له أبيه ...

Translated to English:

> This is the sameone (possibly same tomb or monument) that belong to *Abār* son of Muqīm son of Muqīm'l which his father built for him ...

In this reading, the first word دي is from ذي which means in this case "belonging to". The word دا in the beginning of the inscription seems to be the word ذا , the masculine demonstrative pronoun in Arabic, since the letter *dāl* and *Dhāl* have the same shape in Nabataean. The first question on this inscription should be, why did it use a masculine pronoune to point to a feminine noun, and why didn't it use the common Nabataean demonistrative pronoun *dnh*? The explanations by some Western scholars that دا was an Aramaic Hebrew feminine demonistrative pronoun with roots in Phoenician, which was used by the Nabataean, is simply not convincing. As we will see in a later chapter this word was used in the Raqqush inscription after a masculine, qabru, not a feminine word. See word #4 in Figure 6. I believe this word was not used by the Nabataean as a direct demonistrative pronoun to masculine or feminine nouns exclusively –in this or other inscriptions listed by Healey–, but rather as a neutral pronoun to define and confirm. It was probably used in the meaning of ذاته as in ذا هو and هو ذا for masculine, or in the meaning of ذاتها as in ذا هي or هي ذا for feminine. The direct demonstrative pronoun used in the Nabataen burial inscription was undisputedly *dnh* or دنه.

To put it in its correct place we must go to the classic references of the Arabic language. *Ibn Manẓūr* wrote the following in *Lisān al-ʿArab*:

> The word *dhā* ذا is a noun used to point to any object seen by the speaker or listener. It was said the noun of it is the letter *Dhāl* with *fatḥah*. It was also said: the letter *Dhāl* alone is the noun being pointed to, and it is unknown until what follows it is explained. [17]

Then he added:

> They used the soft vowel *fatḥah* with the letter *Dhāl* to distinguish a masculine from feminine as in their saying ذا أخوك, but they say ذي اختك adding soft kasrah vowel to the letter *Dhāl* for feminine; then they added *alif* with *fatḥah* for masculine, and added *Ya'* with *kasrah* for feminine. [17]

We have two conclusions from the above. First, the letter *Dhāl* alone was possibly used as a demonstrative pronoun in older inscriptions. Second, the object being pointed to can either be visible or invisible and unknown until we read the rest of the text.

After my quick initial reading of the Strasbourg inscription, I decided to examine it further, especially after seeing another inscription (will discuss it later) using ذا نفس as its first two words. The two were the only ones among the hundreds of Nabataean inscriptions I read, all of which used the word *dnh*. Eventhough I could not find a picture of the second inscription either, fortunately Littmann provided a tracing of it. Based on my new information, I am able to give a second reading for the word *nafs* in the Strasbourg inscription.

According to my new modern Arabic reading, the opening sentence was either:

ذا نّفْس (هذا، اشارة الى قبر او نصب، إلنفس، اي إلى نفس) ذي إبار (كنية) بن مقيم بن مقيمأل الذي بناه له أبيه ...

Or:

ذَ إنّفْس (هذا، اشارة الى قبر او نصب، إلنفس اي إلى نفس) ذي إبار (كنية) بن مقيم بن مقيمأل الذي بناه له أبيه ...

Translating both to English:

> This (possibly tomb or monument) to the soul of *Dhī Abār* son of *Muqīm* son of *Muqīm'l* which his father built for him ...

Accordingly, I believe the writer used the Arabic masculine demonistrative pronoun ذا but either spelled it ذا or just ذَ. In the second case, the writer omitted the letter *Alif* as it was done in the rest of the inscription. In both cases the name of the object being pointed to is not listed but assumed, namely it is either *qabr* for tomb or *naṣb* for monument, both of which are masculine.

In other words, I read the phrase of the first two words together ذانّفس. The letter *Alif* after *Dhāl* can be either part of ذا or part of the following word إنّفس in the meaning of إلنفس or إلى نفس. Not pronouncing the letter *Lām* before words like *nafs* or *rūḥ* is a common practice in the Arabic dialects of the region, until today. The rules of neglecting the sound of the preceding letter *lam* of these words in dialects are exactly the same as the rules for neglecting that of the article *al* of their Standard Arabic equivalents. As example, when reading the following verse in Quran (89: 27) يَا أَيَّتُهَا النَّفْسُ الْمُطْمَئِنَّةُ we pronounce the first two words as يَا أَيَّتُهَنَّفْسُ. In other words we do not pronounce the letter *lām* of the article al. In the phrase أَيَّتُهَا النَّفْسُ we have the letters ا أ ل ن ف س and we ommited the letters أ ل. In the phrase ذا إلنفس we have the letters ا إ ل ن ف س and we omited إ ل, or just ل. In the later case the letter إ was not omitted and was part of the second word in the inscription إنفس. It is useful to point out here that the usage of phrases like "this to memory of" or "this to soul of" on burial inscriptions, is an old Roman practice and it can be seen until today in the West, even though it is rarely found on the discovered Nabataean graves.

Finally, and according to my new reading above, the title or nickname of the dead person was *Dhī 'Ibār* ذي إبار or *Dhī 'Ibr* ذي إبر which means "the owner or handler of needles". This word is the plural of إبرة which was used by the Arabs in the old days, and even now, to name the iron needle used in sewing cloths. The possibility that his name was *Abār* as Healey indicated is very slim. Occupational adjective nouns are usually used for titles not as first names.

Madeba Inscription (37-38 CE)

There are two stones for the Madeba inscription. The first is kept in the Vatican Museum and the second in the Louvre Museum. What is even stranger than having two historical inscriptions with the same text and letters is the fact that the two inscriptions differ in the position of one word out of its eight-line text, according to Healey.

Figure (1) A picture of the Madeba inscription in the Louvre Museum. John Healey. *The Early Alphabet.* Reading the Past Series (11). University of California Press / British Museum. 1990

Healey's line by line tracing of the inscription kept in the Louvre was:

دنه مقبرتا وترتي نبشتا دي علا
منه دي عبد عبدعبدت أسرتجا
لأيتيبل أسرتجا أبوهي ولأيتيبل
رب مشريتا دي بلحيتو وعبرتا بر عبدعبدت
أسرتجا دنه ببيت شلطونهم دي شلطو
زمنين ترين شنين تلتين وشت عل شني حرتت
ملك نبطو رحم عمه وعبيدتا دي
علا عبيدت بشنت أربعين وشت له

Translated to English, Healey read the opening phrase of the inscription as follows:

> This is the tomb, and the two funeral monuments above it which ʿAbdʿobodat the governor made for Itaybel the governor, his father, and for Itaybel the camp commandant in Luhitu and for ʿAbarta, son of (this) ʿAbdʿobodat the governor, in their territory...

In my initial study of this inscription I speculated if the word ترتي was actually تلتي from ثلثي or "three", however after examining the picture of the inscription, I believe the word was actually تنتي from ثنتي from ثنين or "two", exchanging the letter *Nūn* with *Rā'*, similar to exchanging بن by بر as practiced in most Nabataean dialects. Therefore I read this inscription in modern Arabic as follows:

دنه (ادناه) مقبرتا (مقبرته او المقبرة) وثنتي نفستا (واثنتين مثلها او
والاثنتين المماثلة) الاعلى منها التي عبدّها عبدعبدات أسرتجا لأيتيبل
أسرتجا، ابيه، ولأيتيبل آمر مشريتا في لحيتو، ولعبرتا بر عبدعبدات
أسرتجا، هنا في بيت سلطانهم ...

Translated in English:

> This is the tomb (or his tomb), and the two identical ones (or two identical ones) above it which *ʿAbd ʿAbdāt* the governor made for *ʾItaybel* the governor, his father, and for *ʾItaybel* the camp commandant in *Luḥitu* and for *ʿAbarta*, son of this *ʿAbd ʿAbdāt* the governor, here in their governing house ...

Accordingly, I do not believe the word *nafshta* in this text was a noun in the meaning of tomb. As for the letter *Tāʾ*, it is related to the *Tāʾ* in the previous feminine noun word مقبرتا, not to indicate the number "two" in a speculated word نفشتان which was possibly assumed by Healey, when he read the phrase ترتي نبشتا as "the two funeral monuments". Since most Nabataean inscriptions used نبشا without the letter *Taʾ* in relation to قبرا one can speculate that this inscription had used the word نبشتا in relation to مقبرتا.

The most curious aspect in Healey's reading of Madeba was his treatment of the three structures equally. He failed to explain why would *ʿAbd ʿAbdāt* build one grave and two funeral monuments to his father, son, and camp commandant in Luhitu. Funeral monuments are usually built for the dead, but it seems possible his son and commandant were alive. On the other hand a tomb room, known in Arabic as مقبرة, is built many times for a living person in preparation to future burial. Then, what about the tomb room for *ʿAbd ʿAbdāt*, isn't it logical that he would build one for himself next to the ones he built for his father and son? To answer this question, I think the letter *Tāʾ* in the word مقبرتا was to indicate that this tomb room belongs to him as well — this letter *Tāʾ* must be pronounced unlike the letter *Tāʾ Marbuṭah*—, before pointing to the other two tomb structures above it. To support my proposed reading of *Tāʾ* as the ownership *Taʾ*, I would like to bring the attention of the reader to the usage of this *Tāʾ* in two other words in the inscription, مشريتا from مشري in the meaning of "horse camp" and عبيدتا from عبّد in the meaning of "his structures".

Healey seemed confused and not confident of his reading of the word مقبرتا. He speculated that the word *miqbarah* مقبرة, in comparison to *qabr* قبر, "could be a funeral monument indicating a less prominent structure than *qabr*". [12] He proceeded in reading the letter *Ta'* in مقبرتا as an equivalent to the letter *Tā' Marbuṭah* in the word مقبرة, and the final letter *Alif* as an indication to the article *al*. Unfortunately, his reading ignores the Arabic language definition completely, where the word مقبرة is defined as an alternative word derived from the root قبر for grave or tomb, but is a more inclusive one used in the meaning of "tombs room". The addition of the letter *Mīm* before many words is a common Arabic usage to indicate a utilization role, as in بيت and مبيت, for example. To support my reading, we notice that in the Turkumaniyah inscription the phrase مقبرا دنه used مقبرا not مقبرتا. In this inscription, Healey simply read the word مقبرا as مقبرتا too, without giving any reason why there was no letter *Ta'* there. [12]

In Medeba, Healey also seemed confused about his reading of the first word *dnh*. Without explaining why, he assumed it was the demonstrative pronoun to the feminine word مقبرتا, but he then assumed it was the demonstrative pronoun to the masculine word أسترجا. I believe *dnh* was a gender neutral demonstrative pronoun used by the Nabataeans in the meaning of ادناه or هنا. I will discuss this in the next chapter.

As a final note, Healey and other Western scholars explained the usage of the letter *Alif-Hamzah* in the end of words like نفشا in Strasbourg, and مقبرتا and أسترجا in Medeba as a parallel usage to the article *al* in Arabic. This is possible but we cannot be sure how it was pronounced: heavy *Hamzah* or high *Alif*. I believe that the use of this final *Alif* is similar or even related to the adding of the letter *waw* after names in most Nabataean inscriptions of later centuries, to emphasize, confirm, or identify. In *Lisān al-'Arab* we read that *Hamzah* has many usages "among them the illusionary *Hamzah*, according to *al-Farā'*, where some Arabs would use *Hamzah* in words usually spelled without *Hamzah* when emphasizing such words". [17] Quoting al-Jawhary, we then read that "*Hamzah* is not stable in its spelling, since it can be written as letter *Alif*, letter *Yā'*, or letter *Wāw*" and that "the letter *Alif* has two types, soft and voweled, the first is called *Alif* and the second is called *Hamzah*". [17] It is useful here to mention that the Arabs did not commonly use the article *al* when pointing to a grave. They did not use the phrase هذا القبر لفلان but the phrase هذا قبر فلان.

Bin Ḥur Inscription (~150 CE)

This inscription was discovered and was read for the first time by de Vogüé in 1875. It was estimated to belong to the year 150 CE. The stone of the inscription is 37 cm (1.2 ft) high, 72 c. (2.5 ft) wide. [20] Littmann said the stone of this inscription was part of the outer wall of a burial chamber that included also the Milḥ inscription, but he thinks it was placed originally over its door header. Despite the good and clear tracing of the stone by de Vogüé's assistant, Littmann decided to retrace it to give a better sense of its dimensions. See Figure (2).

Littmann noticed that this inscription had used connected letters and new shapes not seen before, like the shape of final letter *Yā'* in the end of the second line, which was inverted both vertically and horizontally in comparison to its usual shape in Arabic and Nabataaean. Littman believed it was an *Alif-Maqṣurah* shape. However, despite its peculiar look, this shape was commonly used by many of the Nabataean inscriptions discovered later. [38]

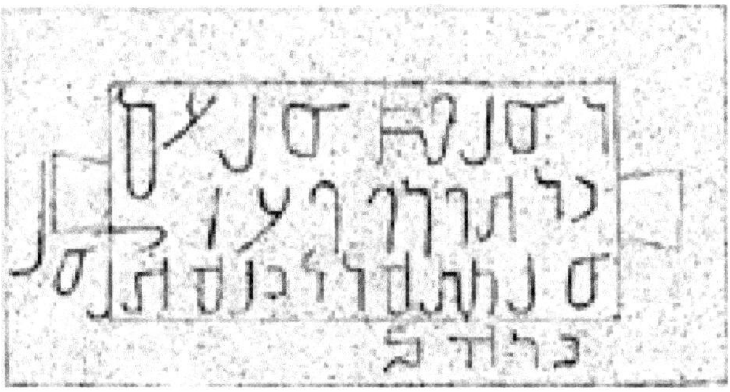

Figure (2) Littmann's tracing of the Bin Ḥur inscription based on de Vogüé's original tracing. [20]

Littmann's literal translation was identical to the one by de Vogüé 40 years earlier:

دا نفش أنعم
بر حورو وعزي
التته ذي بنه حنأل
برهم

Littmann then translated it to modern language as follows:

> This is the tomb of *An'ām*, son of *Ḥur*, and of *'Uzzai*, his wife, which was built by *Ḥann-'īl* their son.

Even though Littmann's translation seems solid and clear, it did not actually reflect the original text. For example, he does not explain why he translated the word *nafsh* with the article *al*, even though it was without letter *Alif* at the end. As we will see, he did believe that the word *nafsha* was in the meaning of *al-nafsh*, like all other Western scholars believed.

It seems that Littmann was convinced that the letter Alif after the word *nafs* was not part of it because of the large space between them —possibly due to the disappearance of the left-pointing horizontal stroke of the letter Shīn as a result of stone damage—, or maybe because he believed that name can not be other than *An'ām* أنعام. He referred his readers to another inscription in his book that listed the same name. However, when I looked into that inscription, I did not find the name, but another three-letter word *n'm* نعم. Still, the name can actually be *An'ām* since, earlier, Littman read many Musnad inscriptions which included that name. [21] However, one cannot be absolutely sure since, according to old Arabic references, the name *Ni'ām* نعام was another known name which was used for "tribe" and for two important geographic locations in the Arabian Peninsula. In such case, the *Alif-Hamzah* after the word *nafs* can be part of it, just as it was part of the same word in other Nabataean inscriptions, like Strasbourg and Madeba.

The possibility that the first word *dha* was used as a demonstrative pronoun to point to the feminine word *nafs* in the meaning of "soul" is slim since the inscription used the word *bnh* بناه, or "built", afterwords. I think the writer of the inscription was particularly careful in spacing his words and in writing them completely in the same line before moving to new lines. This may explain why he used large spaces between the letters *Dāl* and *Hamzah* in the beginning of the text, and between the letters *Hamzah* and *Nūn* of the word أنعم. This observation is the reason why I believe that the letter *Dāl* was actually *Dhāl*, and was used alone as a masculine demonstrative pronoun, as I indicated in my reading of the Strasbourg inscription earlier. In this case, it is pointing to an invisible masculine name of what the inscription was about, namely tomb قبر or monument نصب, which are both masculine.

In other words, I read the phrase of the first two words together ذاْنّفس . The letter *Alif* after *Dhal* can be either part of ذا or part of the following word إنّفس in the meaning of إلنفس or إلى نفس, as I explained in my detailed reading of the Strasbourg inscription.

Therefore, my new literal translation based on Littmann's tracing, is the following:

د انفشا نعم
بر حورو وعزي
التته ذي بنه حنأل
برهم

And my translation in modern Arabic is:

ذَ إنّفْس (هذا، اشارة الى قبر او نصب، إلنفس، اي إلى نفس) نعام بن حور
وعزى أنثته (زوجته)، الذي بناه حنئيل، ابنهم

Or:

ذا نّفْس (هذا، اشارة الى قبر او نصب، إلنفس، اي إلى نفس) نعام بن حور
وعزى أنثته (زوجته)، الذي بناه حنئيل، ابنهم

As a final note regarding both this and the Strasbourg inscription, and regardless of which reading is the correct one, I think their extremely rare usage of the word نفش as part of the phrase دا نفش in the beginning of the text, can not be generalized when reading this word in other inscriptions.

Milḥ Inscription

As stated earlier, this inscription was discovered in the early years of the last century by Littmann in *Umm al-Jimāl*, Syria. According to his description, the stone of the inscription was 30 cm (1 ft) high and 90 cm (3 ft) wide. It seems clear this stone was the right piece of a much wider stone that was estimated by Littmann to be 150 cm (5 ft) wide. [20] He also believed that this stone was used as main component of the structure of the room. Even though this stone was discovered placed on top of two columns on the right wall, Littmann believes it was originally placed in the outside as a header over the main entrance of the room. However, I do not believe it was placed as a header for the door but as a lentel carrying the ceiling with the inscription showing inside the room. After reading the inscription of this stone, I am convinced it was part of a longer inscription that was probably displayed around the high perimeters of the room, from the inside. See Figure (3).

Figure (3) Reduced tracing image of the right part of the Milḥ inscription that was offered by Littmann. [20]

Littmann's line by line literal translation from the Nabataean was:

[د]نه نفشا ذي عبد [.....]
لملحو برته ول [......]

He then translated it to:

> This is the tomb which was made (by ... son of ...) for *Milḥ*, his daughter, and for (......)

In other words, he made several assumptions to read the inscription. First, he assumed that the right edge of the stone was the original edge. Second, he assumed the existence of the letter *Dāl* from the word *dnh*. Thirdly, he assumed the existence of the letter *Lām* in the word لملحو. However, his last two assumptions are not possible because the very large letters of a high inscription cannot be inscribed exactly on the edges of a stone, since attaching neighboring stones requires building materials that can cover these edges. It is clear to me that the right space on the stone, which was about 10 cm (4 in) wide, was an intentional empty space. Even if Littmann was right in assuming the existence of two letters in this space, it is too coincidental to assume that both would be damaged equally.

Littmann read the first, very clear, letter of the inscription as the letter *Nūn*, even though the writer had exaggerated in lengthening its vertical stem down and in pointing it up afterward, as Littmann himself noticed. The shape of this letter was identical to the last letter of the second line, which Littmann read correctly as the letter *Lām*. As for the very faded shape on the extreme right edge in the beginning of the second line, which Littmann read as the letter *Lām*, I think it is actually just a scratch. Finally, I think Littmann's tracing of the letter *Shīn* was not very convincing as it appeared unusually small.

My reading of this inscription based on Littmann's tracing from the Nabataean is as follows:

[....] له نفشا ذي عبد [....]
[....] ملحو برته ول [....]

Accordingly, I believe the first letter was actually *Lām* and the word *nafs* in this inscription meant نفسه or "same as". Most importantly, I think one cannot fully read this inscription because its text was likely completing another text which was displayed on its right on a lost stone. It is also possible that this stone was broken in three, not two pieces. Besides, it is particularly hard to use this inscription as a solid reference, because I could not find any picture of it to make sure it was traced accurately. For example, the last letter *alif* in *nafsā* could have been a final *Hā'* making the beginning phrase له نفسه الذي.

Shahīm Inscription

As mentioned earlier, assuming that the word *nafs* in the beginning of a Nabataean inscription means "tomb" can result in an overall inacurate reading. To explain my point, I chose a recently discovered inscription from *Umm al-Jimāl* which was read for the first time by S. Said and M. al-Hamad in 2003, and was re-read by A. M. Butts and H. H. Hardy from the University of Chicago in 2010. [9] See Fig (4).

The four specialists read the first line identically, but differed on reading the second line. Said and al-Hamad translated the inscription literally from the Nabataean as follows:

[د]ا نبشا ذي بنه شهيمو
[بر] علت بنا له ابوهم
[.. ل]ربئل ملكا ملك نبط[و ..]

They translated it ito English as follows:

> This is the tomb which *SHYMW* son of *ʿLT* built. He built (it) for himself *ʾBWHM* ... of king Rabel, king of the Nabataeans ...

Figure (4): High resolution picture of the Shahimu inscription according to Said and al-Hamad. [9]

It seems the two readers believed the word al was only an emphasis word, and the phrase should be read "He built it for *'BWHM*, himself". Because their reading did not clearly make sense, even in their own acknowledgement, they asked the scholarly community to help re-reading this inscription. [9]

Butts and Hardy accepted the challenge, according to their article, and provided a new literal translation of the second line only, as follows:

[]ا نبشا ذي بنه شهيمو []
[]ع بره بأله ابوهم []

Despite their relative success in tracing the second complex line, their overall reading of the two lines was linguistically weak and not smooth. They translated the two lines to English as follows:

> [Th]is is the tomb which *SHYMW* ... built ... [for P]N, his son, through (the help of) the god of their father ...

Restated in a clearer manner, their translation was:

> [Th]is is the tomb that was built by *SHYMW* [.... for NAME]', his son, through (the help of) the god of their father ...

The reading of Butts and Hardy was clearly not reasonable in assuming the existence of the rest of *Shahīm*'s name and the first part of the name of his son ending with the letter *'Ayn* and preceded by the letter *Lām* —in the meaning of "for"—, in the small space between the end of the first line and the beginning of the second line. Furthermore, they read an isolated letter *'Ayn* even though it was clearly attached to the first visible word of the second line. Their use of the word ألَه for "god" was correct, linguistically, but it did not match in the overall reading of this inscription.

Despite several damaged areas in the inscription—indicated between square brackets—, which can force a reader to guess some words, we fortunately have a clear image of the stone. This image was instrumental in my ability to examine the Nabataean letters' tracings of the first two lines by the four researchers, particularly, the first two clear words of the inscription, which were نبشا دي according to them. According to Butts and Hardy, their retracing was based on this same picture that was published in the article by Said and al-Hamad. This image is exactly what I used too in my retracing of the two lines shown in the bottom of Figure (5) below.

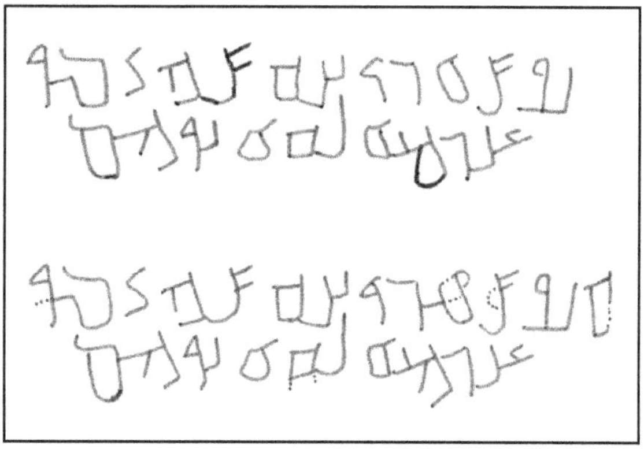

Figure (5): Above is a tracing image of the first two lines of *Shahīm* inscription according to Butts and Harding's reading, and below it is the author's new tracing, where the dotted lines could be part of actual letters or due to stone damage.

Because of the poor quality and missing letters of this inscription, one cannot provide one definite modern reading. However, I can provide a literal Arabic transliteration of the two Nabataean lines in Arabic, as follows:

[دن]ه نفش[و] قبرو بنه شهيمو
[ذي] عبد هنا له ابوهم

My translation in modern Arabic language is one of the following:

دنه (ادناه) نفسو قبرو (روح وقبر او هو قبر) بنه شهيمو (ابن شهيم) [الذي]
عبّد (شيّد) هنا له ابوهم (اي ابوهما او جدهم) ...

Or

دنه (ادناه) نفسو قبرو (روح وقبر او هو قبر) بنه شهيمو (ابن شهيم) [الذي]
عبّد (شيّد) هنأله (اسم) (اي ابوهما او جدهم) ...

Or

دنه (ادناه) نفسو قبرو (روح وقبر او هو قبر) بنه شهيمو (ابن شهيم) [الذي]
عبّدهنأ (شيّده) له ابوهم (اي ابوهما او جدهم) ...

The first possibility above can be translated to English as follows:

> Here is the soul and grave of son of *Shahīm* that was built here for him by *Han'allah*, their father ....

The English translation of the second and third possibilities is:

> Here is the soul and grave of son of *Shahīm* that was built by their father ....

Accordingly, I do not think the large prominent shape following the letter Shin in the first line was the relatively small Nabataean *Alif-Hamzah*, which can be seen in three other words in the inscription. One can clearly follow the small circle of the Nabataean letter *Qāf*, which started from the right in a counterclockwise direction then formed a straight downward line, before pointing left and proceeding upward to connect to the medial letter *Bā'* that was clearly connected to the following letter *Rā'*. As for the letter *Yā'*, which was read by the four specialists as part of the word *dhī*, I read it as Nabataean letter *Wāw*, whose top loop was a bit rectangular with its top line slightly extended to the right before connecting to the previous letter *Rā'*, intentionally, or as a result of a scribe mistake or damage. We can clearly see that the shape of this letter *Wāw*, including the downward line's slightly left-pointing tail, was similar to that of the other two letters *Wāw* in the inscription. One cannot rule out that the phrase نفسو قبرو in this inscription was altered later by the original writer or someone else. The inscription image shows an 8 or B-like shape, which I pointed out in dotted lines, and a small circle attached directly to the letter *Shīn* to possibly indicate the word should be read *nafsu.*

My three proposed readings assume the existence of the word ذي in the meaning of "which" before the word عبد. This is a very reasonable assumption since the size of the space was very appropriate. Based on this reading, the word بنه which was read by the four scholars as بناه in the meaning of "built" cannot be so, because, first, the writer used the word عبّد in the second line, and second, it is after the phrase نفسو قبرو without the word ذي before it. I think بنه means ابنَ and the final *Hā'* indicates a fathah soft vowel or *Tā' Marbūṭah.* In other words, it was part of the deceased nickname, ابنَ شهيم or "son of Shahim" where شهيم was possibly his father's name. Generally, most Nabataean inscriptions used the word بر instead of بن, but such usage was between two names, not as part of a nickname.

The first clear word of the second line was positively the word عبد because the letter *'Ayn* was completely connected to it. Even though my tracing of the letters of this line was identical to that of Butts and Hardy, I believe the final letter *Hā'* of the word بره, according to their reading, was actually an initial letter *Hā'*, which is very clearly connected to the following letter *Nūn*, which is also clearly connected to the letter *Alif-Hamzah* after it, producing the word هنا. This word could be the independent word هنا in the meaning "here" —as we have seen in the *'Ayn 'Abdat* inscription, which used it twice—, to form the phrase هنا له in the meaning "here for him". Or, it was connected to the following word له, forming the name هنأله, or هناء الله which is similar in its meaning to the name commonly found in the Musnad inscriptions سعدأله or, سعد الله. Or, it was connected to the previous word, forming the word عبدهنأ in the meaning of "built it". Possibly, the use of the final *Hamzah* was to point to the single masculine name قبرا, following the local dialect of the writer.

The usage of the last word in the second line, ابوهم or possibly ابوهما meaning "their father", indicates that the father of the deceased was dead and the builder of the tomb was the father of both, which means he was his grandfather. As we saw earlier, the Strasbourg and Madeba inscriptions used ابوهي to indicate a single dead person, and the *Bin Ḥur* inscription used برهم to indicate that the builder was the son of two dead persons. The above can explain why this inscription used the nickname ابن شهيم instead of his first name. However, it is possible that the word بنه was إبنا to indicate two sons, which would explain *Hana'illah*'s usage of the word ابوهم instead of ابوهي. If we assume the word بنه meant "built", and the word عبد was part of the dead person's name and was preceded by the letter *Lām*, we can read the two lines as follows:

دنه نفس وقبر بناه شهيم [بر اسم أو واسم] لعبد هنأله، ابوهم ...

Translated in English:

> This is the tomb built by *Shahīm* [(son of name) or (and name)] for *'Abd Han'allah*, their father ...

This, however, is unlikely because, first, the name *'Abd Han'Allah* does not make sense. Second, the space before عبد was too small to include a letter *Lām* preceded by the word بر and a father's name, or a letter *Wāw* and a brother's name, to justify using the word ابوهم instead of ابوهي.

To conclude this chapter, after reading more than three hundred Nabataean, Palmyran, Aramaic, and Hebrew inscriptions, I found only seven inscriptions using the word *nafs* alone in the opening phrase in the meaning of "tomb", according to the current readings. After re-tracing and re-reading the seven inscriptions, I found two of them had used the word *qabr* too. As for the other five inscriptions, I found that the the word *nafs* was used in the meaning of "same" or "soul". It became clear to me that there was no solid evidence to presume that the word *nafsh* or *nafs,* in an opening phrase of an Arabic or Nabataean burial inscription, was used in the meaning of "funerary monument" or "memorial monument". As a result of my study, I also concluded that any successful analysis of the Nabataean inscriptions must utilize standard Arabic references, since the Nabataen language was not a parallel language to Arabic but one of its derived tongues.

4

Detailed Rereading of the *Umm al-Jimāl* Nabataean Inscription

As mentioned earlier, according to Western scholars, among the numerous Nabataean inscriptions discovered so far, only three were written fully in the Arabic language. Dated 328 CE, *al-Namārah* was the latest inscription of the three. The two earlier inscriptions are *Umm al-Jimāl,* found in the same area, around Damascus, where *al-Namārah* was found, and *Raqqūsh*, found in *Madā'in Ṣālaḥ*, not very far south of Damascus in Northern *Ḥijāz*. Both areas were previously Nabataean territories. *Raqqūsh* indicated the date of 267 CE while *Umm al-Jimāl,* which explicitly mentioned the names *Judhaymah* and *Tannūkh,* was dated around the year 260 CE, clearly a successful estimate when checked against our geographical and historical review in the previous section. The two inscriptions are therefore older than *al-Namārah* by at least 60 or even 70 years. This would make them useful references for this study. As we shall see later, reading the three inscriptions together is valuable for the separate reading of each one of them correctly.

While *Raqqūsh* and *Umm al-Jimāl* were decidedly gravestones, *al-Namārah* could be either a gravestone or an honoring monument (I shall come back to this subject later.) Further, *Raqqūsh* included several text lines while *Umm al-Jimāl* was brief. Unlike in *al-*

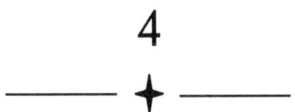

Namārah and *Umm al-Jimāl*, the language used in *Raqqūsh* was not Classical Arabic entirely.

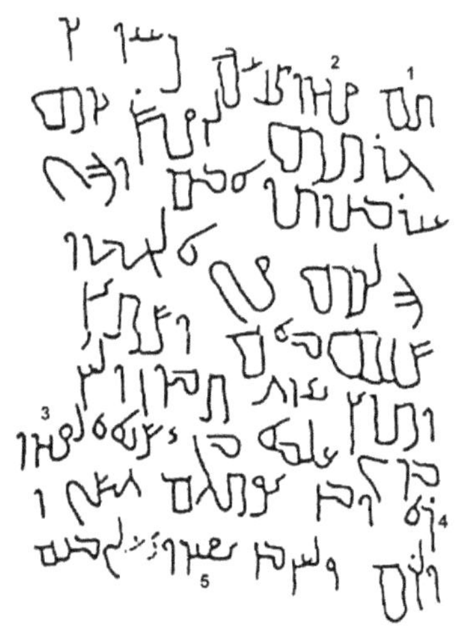

دنه قبرو صنعه كعبو بر
حذتت لرقوش برت
عبذ منرتو امه وهي
هلكت في الحجرو
سنت مئه وستين
وتنين بيرخ تموز ولعن
مري علما من يشنا القبرو
ذا ومن يفتحه خشي و
ولذه ولعن من يقبر ويعلي منه

Figure (6) Current tracing of the *Raqqūsh* Arabic Nabataean inscription (left), with author's improved modern Arabic reading. Numbers added to facilitate discussion.

Both *Umm al-Jimāl* and *Raqqūsh* clearly started with the word *dnh* دنه, but scholars read the word differently in *Raqqūsh* where the first letter *Dāl* was slightly attached to the second letter *nūn* forming another possible shape. The Arabic word *qabrū* (tomb) was mentioned three times in *Raqqūsh*, and was read as such by all scholars. The same exact word though in *Umm al-Jimāl* was read as a personal name, *Fahrū*, which clearly was an error, as I will demonstrate later. [13]

دنه نفسو قبر فرء بر سلي ربو جذيمت مملك تنوخ	دنه نفسو فهرو بر سلي ربو جذيمت ملك دنوخ

Figure (7) Top: A high resolution picture of the *Umm al-Jimāl* Nabataean inscription (right) with an enlarged picture of the left side of the stone. Bottom: current tracing and reading of the inscription (left) side-by-side author's new tracing and reading. Numbers added to facilitate discussion.

Unfortunately, I was not unable to obrain enough photographic details of either inscription. However, for the purpose of this study, I feel it is adequate to rely on the available Nabataean tracing of *Raqqūsh.* A word of caution: without retracing *Raqqūsh* personally, I would be reluctant to offer a full letter-by-letter transcription or modern Arabic reading.As for *Umm al-Jimāl,* examining couple high-resolution pictures of the stone was very sufficient to illustrate the validity of my new tracings of a few key words in the inscription. Accordingly, I provided here the above original photo and another zoomed-in photoshoped image of the eroded re-traced area of the stone, along with current tracing — a letter-by-letter Arabic transcription and corresponding modern Arabic translation. Based on this new tracing, a new detailed reading emerges that significantly differs from the current reading.

In Figure (6), the first word in *Raqqūsh* and *Umm al-Jimāl* was clearly a three letter word *dnh*, but scholars differed both on its tracing and reading in *Raqqūsh*. Some read it as *tah* ته, claiming it was an Arabic simple feminine demonstrative pronoun; this is neither correct nor possible since the following word *qabr* is a masculine noun. [32] Others read it as the Arabic letter *dhāl*, probably for the simple masculine demonstrative *dhā* ذا, which would contradict directly with the reading of word #4 in the same inscription showing *dhā* spelled as letter *dāl* with dot above followed by *alif*. [13] Yet, few traced it as *dh.n.h* for *dhnah* ذنه claiming this was a northern Arabic feminine demonstrative pronoun.

However, most scholars traced word #1 in both inscriptions as *dnh*, a word present in numerous other fully Nabataean inscriptions, and read it as an assumingly Aramaic demonstrative pronoun. I traced it in both as *dnh*, too, but I read it as *adnāh*, أدناه, a word used in Arabic to point to a nearby object or text that is located generally below the horizontal visual level. The beginning *alif* with *hamzah* above was possibly omitted because the word was possibly pronounced *dnāh* دناه, in the local Arab Nabataean dialect. *Raqqūsh* and most other inscriptions used several local dialect words, notably *bir* for *bin*, or *ʿabdh* for *ʿabd*. Otherwise, beginning *alif-hamzah* could have been omitted, just as the second *alif* between the letters *nūn* and *hāʾ* was omitted, consistent with Arabic writing throughout the

8th century CE, as evident in all available inscriptions and manuscripts. Less likely, this word could be *idnah* إدنه for the imperative: "come close to," omitting beginning *alif-hamzah* with *kasrah*.

The Arabic word *adnāh* is utilized extensively today in the meaning of "see by, or near, you", "see below" or "the following below." It can be used effectively as a gender neutral demonstrative in the meaning of *hunā* هنا as in "here" or "here in". When I searched for the use of this word in older Arabic references, I was surprised that I could not find any documented evidence of its usage in that contest. Assuming my reading is correct, this would make the two inscriptions the earliest Arabic references documenting the usage of the word in such manner. The word *danā*, a classical Arabic verb, means "became physically close or near to someone or some object." [17] Among numerous examples, the Quran (53:9) used it in ثُمَّ دَنَا فَتَدَلَّى فَكَانَ قَابَ قَوْسَيْنِ أَوْ أَدْنَى. Also, the Islamic *Ḥadīth* used *ʾadnāh min nafsih* to describe how Prophet Muhammad had a visiting Arab king sitting —physically— very close to him. [23][35]

In his valuable doctoral dissertation on the Nabataean and Aramaic inscriptions, al-Dhuyayb wrote —possibly based on Western scholars' readings— that the word *dnh* was used by the Nabataeans as "the singular demonstrative pronoun "this" for both genders". However, he read inscription #6 in the dissertation as follows: *dnh naṣbayyā dī ʾḤwā* دنه نصبيا ذي أحوا; explaining that the word *naṣbayyā* meant more than one monument and it was in the form of *jamʿ al-mudhakkar al- sālim* جمع مذكر سالم (Perfect Masculine *Plural*). In other words, he contradicted his earlier definition of the word *dnh* as a *singular* demonstrative pronoun. [38] Clearly, one can only eliminate this and other contradictions by reading this word as a gender-neutral and number-neutral demonstrative pronoun word similar to Arabic *adnāh*.

Regardless of how one would read the first word *dnh*, the most important fact is that it was explicitly used as a word pointing to both a masculine object like *qabr* and a feminine *maqbarah*, and it was consistently used as an opening word for most Nabataean gravestones.

In *Umm al-Jimāl* scholars spelled the next word after *dnh*, as *n.f.sh.ū*, and read it نفشو supposedly from a "Semitic" feminine noun *napš'* or from Arabic *nafs* as in the Quran (89:27) يَا أَيَّتُهَا النَّفْسُ الْمُطْمَئِنَّةُ. This same word can also be pronounced in Arabic as *nafas* in the sense of "inhalation or breathing" which would be a masculine noun. It is not clear, how scholars pronounced this word found in various Nabataean inscriptions as *napš* or *napiš*. Still, it would be a feminine noun in both cases. Even before analyzing the meaning and usage of *nafsh*, one can already suspect through *Umm al-Jimāl* that its current reading is questionable since the word *dnh* was used in *Raqqūsh*, and many other Nabataean inscriptions to point to *qabrū*, a masculine noun. This contradiction can only be solved by reading *dnh* as *adnāh*, a neutral Arabic demonstrative pronoun, as I argued above.

Alternatively, and as a second possibility, the word *nafsū* was not a noun, and *dnh* was pointing to a third masculine noun following it (I shall discuss this later.) And yet a third possibility, the word *nafsū* was actually *naqshū* نقشُ, for the Arabic masculine noun, *naqsh* (etching or inscription), used to indicate the act of writing or sketching on all mediums including epitaph's stones and even sand. [17][29] Unlike the Nabataean letter *Fā', which* is a left starting loop with a right side downward vertical stem, the letter *Qāf* can look like a circle attached in the middle to a downward vertical stem. This was evident in the three inscriptions.

However, reading the second word (we call it #2) of *Umm al-Jimāl* as *naqshū* can conflict with the current reading of word #3 of the inscription, which is thought to be *Fihrū* for *Fihr*فهر , a classical Arabic name. Even though it is possible to read the opening phrase as *adnāh naqshu Fihrū bin Sāllī*, after examining the photo of Figure (7) and even according to the current tracing it is clear that word #3 of *Umm al-Jimāl* is not *Fihrū*. It is *qabrū*, followed by a first name containing the letters *Fā'*, *Rā'* and *Alif/Hamzah* as in *Fara'* فَرء or *Firā'* فِراء, an old Arabic male name meaning "wild donkey" which is known for its excellent skills to escape hunters! This name was possibly modified to *Faru'* فرُء according to old Northern Arabic and Aramaic practice of using *wāw* sound at the end of names.In the Hadith, Prophet Muhammad told *Abū Sufyān:* "You are as they say, all hunting is in the belly of the wild donkey". Translated from the Arabic text: يا أبا سفيان! أنت كما قال القائل : كل الصيد في جوف الفرا . [17]

The three partially damaged letters in the name *Faru'* can clearly be traced in the subsequent space, which is suspiciously wide for an intentional space! To illustrate my point, I provided a partial image of the stone utilizing the Brush Strokes filter utility in Photoshop to emphasize stroke edges and reveal the new traced letters.

Back to the the third word *qabru* (ndicated with #3), one can easily trace a prominent long horizontal stroke connected to the letter *Rā'* on the left, just as it was the case with medial letter *Bā'* in the words for *qabru* in *Raqqūsh* (words #3, #4, and #5). There is a short downward line pointing to the left that seems to be a stone discoloration, not a stroke. Nevertheless, even if it were a stroke, the formed shape would surely not resemble a Nabataean letter *Hā'*. A second short, left-pointing, downward line just below the letter *Rā'* is not a stroke either, as it resembles an extensive crack. The only difference between the word *qabr* we see in *Umm al-Jimāl* and the one in *Raqqūsh* is that the upward line stroke forming the medial letter *Bā'* in *Umm al-Jimāl* was not vertical. Instead, it was pointing left as it was the case with the previous word *nafsū* and the following word *Fara'*— clearly a scribe hand-writting style. One can even spot another faded parallel, left-tilted line connecting to the horizontal stroke of that letter thus forming a classic Nabataean medial letter *Bā'*, slightly affected by a possible scriber style or error, stone discoloration and crack, or a subsequent alteration. Moreover, the first letter of this word is clearly *Qāf*, not *Fā'*, which can easily be compared to the many letters *Qāf* in *al-Namārah* and *Raqqūsh*.

Reading word #3 in *Umm al-Jimāl* as *qabrū* or *qabr* would allow more possibilities for the meaning and usage of the previous word. A likely alternative to my earlier reading of the word as *naqshū*, is *nafsū*, in the meaning of *nafsuhū*, or *hūwa nafsuhū*, for "itself", referring to *qabr*. This reading would fit well with reading *dnh*, either as a masculine, or as a neutral demonstrative. The beginning phrase could then be "this itself is the tomb of" similar to *hadhā hūwa qabr* هذا هو قبر, a standard usage on gravestones in Arabic, or *hadhā nafsuhū qabr* هذا نفسُهُ قبر. To summarize, we have two initial readings of the opening phrase of the *Umm al-Jimāl* inscription: *dnh naqshū qabr Faru' bir Sāllī* هذا نقشُ قبر فرُء بن سالّي (this is the inscription of Faru' bir Sāllī), or *dnh nafshū qabr Faru' bir Sāllī* هذا نفسه (هو) قبر فرُء بن سالّي (this is the tomp of *Faru' bir Sāllī*).

However, I should now bring attention to a curious fact: my reading of the opening phrase in *Umm al-Jimāl* as *nafsū qabrū* or *nafsū qabr* is intriguingly identical to the usual opening phrase in the Arabic *Musnad* script found on eastern Arabian tombs' inscriptions: *nafs.w.qabr* نفس وقبر. King *Judhaymah*, whose name appears in the *Umm al-Jimāl* inscription, was linked to the eastern Arabian area where the *Tannūkh* kingdom was supposedly situated before moving to *al-Ḥīrah*, as I indicated in my review section above.

According to my analysis of the phrase *nafs wa-qabr* in the previous chapter and following my reading of the opening phrase in this inscription as *dnh nafsu qabr* it is very likely the meaning of this phrase was روح وقبر (soul and grave). In other words, I can now offer a third possible reading of the *Umm al-Jimāl* inscription as follows: *dnh nafs wa-qabr Faru' bir Sāllī* هنا روح وقبر فرءُ بن سالّي (Here is the soul and tomb of *Faru' bir Sāllī*). Based on this reading, it would be impossible to assume that this inscription was only a "memorial monument" without an actual grave.

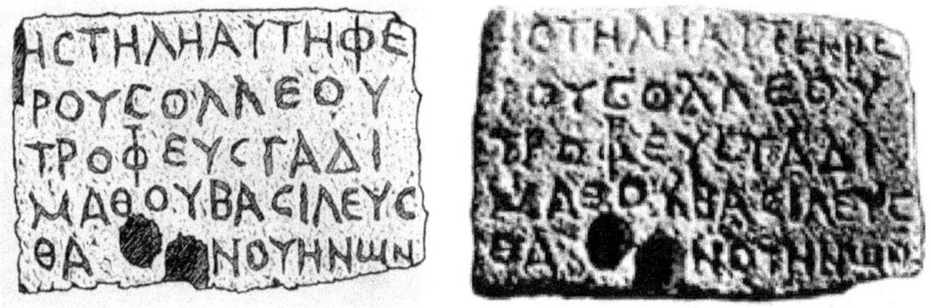

Figure (8) Littmann's tracing of the Greek *Umm al-Jimāl* inscription, which was a translation of its Nabataean text (left). A picture of the inscription squeeze (right). [20]

Before analyzing the final line of the *Umm al-Jimāl* inscription, it is worth mentioning that although this inscription was not a bilingual inscription, it was discovered next to a separate stone with a Greek inscription, which appears to be an exact translation of the Nabataean text. See Figure (8). Despite my belief that the Nabataean inscription should be the main reference to use in our ongoing analysis (pronouncing Arabic names can be deceiving in the Greek translation), I will analyze the first four or five words of the Greek inscription which, by all accounts, seems to support our new reading of the Nabataean text. Although there were no spaces in the Greek inscription, as evident in Figure 3.2, the words of the opening phrase were:

Η CΤΗΛΗ ΑΥΤΗ ΦΕΡΟΥ CΟΛΛΕΟΥ ΤΡΟΦΕΥC ....

According to my reading of the Greek text above, the first line can be translated in English as "This is the stele of Feroo Salleoo ..". Clearly, the first name was ΦΕΡΟΥ (Feroo), not Fehroo — there is no indication of the guttural sound of the Arabic letter *hā'* anywhere in the word, unless the reader was invoking past Phoenician letter *he* origin of the Greek E! My belief, the inscription used the Greek sound OY (sounds like oo as in wood) at the end of the first name ΦΕΡΟΥ to substitute for either *Alif-Hamzah* or *Dhammah-Hamzah.* You may recall, according to my reading of the Nabataean inscription, the word was either *Fara'* or *Faru'.* The sound OY was repeated at the end of the last name COΛΛΕΟΥ (Salleoo) too — in spite of the existence of the letter *Yā'* at the end of that word in the Nabataean text. The repeated use of the sound OY further indicates that the first name was not necessarily ending with a *wāw* as experts (evidently depending mainly on the Greek text) mistakenly assumed. I will discuss again this Aramaic and Northern Arabic usage of the sound *wāw* after names, later. In addition, using the word CTHΛH (Stele) would not necessarily mean that this word was an exact translation of *nafs,* because translating a text is not linear; that is, it is not a word-for-word process. At best, this type of usage could mean that some Nabataean Arabs used *nafsu qabr* combined to mean stele.

More observations on the *Umm al-Jimāl* inscription reading include the following:

1. Most specialist read the word *Rabbu* in the meaning of "care taker" or "gardian". This reading is possible. However this word was used in other Nabataean inscriptions (Madeba for example) in the meaning of camp commaner. Among the many meanings offered in Lisān al-Arab, we have *al-qayyim* and *al-mudabbir,* meaning "the one in charge". Since the following word in Greek

was TPOΦEYC, I think this word meant in this inscription the "top military leader".

2. Word #4 was read by Littmann as *malk* for Arabic king. However, after careful tracing of the Nabataean text, I can clearly see a second letter *mim*; therefore, the correct reading should be *mmlk*, for classic Arabic *mumallik* مُمَلّك, which literally means, "the one who crowned or gave kingship to"; meaning in current context: "the founder of the dynasty of". Moreover, reading word #4 in this way would accurately fit the meaning conveyed by word #5 *Tannūkh,* king *Judhaymah's* tribe, which, as you will see below, was inaccurately read as *Dannūkh.*
3. Word #5 (*Tannūkh*): The first letter of this word is clearly a Nabataean letter *tā'*, not a *dāl.* As stated earlier in our history review section, King *Judhaymah al-Abrash*, *Umru'ū al-Qays'* uncle, was the founder of the *Tannūkh* kingdom, or, using the inscription words, he was the one who crowned them. This assertion can be substantiated by the fact that Arab history never recorded the existence of a tribe or kingdom in Arabia under the name *Dannukh.*

To summarize, a leter-by-letter transcription of *Umm al-Jimāl* is as follows: "*dnh nfsu qbr fra bir sali rabu jdhimat mmlik tannukh.*" Line-by-line, the Arabic text is:

دنه نفسو قبر فرء
بر سلي ربو جذيمت
مملك تنوخ

Translated to Modern Arabic after adding the missing letters *Alif*, removing the letters *Wāw*, and adding punctuations:

أدناه (هنا) روح وقبر فرأ بن سالّي، ربّ (امر جيش او ربما مربّي) جُذيمة،
مملك (مؤسس مملكة) تَنّوخ

Or:

أدناه (هذا) نفسو (هو نفسه) قبر فرأ بن سالّي، ربّ (امر جيش او ربما مربّي) جُذيمة، مملك (مؤسس مملكة) تَنّوخ

Translated to English:

> Here is the soul and grave of *Faru' bin Sālī*, the military comander (or custodian) of *Judhaymah*, crowner of *Tannūkh*

Or:

> Here is itself the grave of *Faru' bin Sālī*, the military comander (or custodian) of *Judhaymah*, crowner of *Tannūkh*

Before proceeding to the next section, I need to elaborate on the important usage of the letter *wāw* at the end of nouns in most nabataean inscriptions. For example, notice the words *qabrū* for *qabr*, *Ka'bū* for *Ka'b*, and *Ḥijrū*, for *Ḥijr* in *Raqqūsh*. This practice is consistent with that of most pre-Islamic northern Arabic inscriptions that are available today, whether written in Nabataean or Arabic *Jazm* scripts. As we shall see later, *al-Namārah* added *wāw* after all names too. The Arabic inscriptions of al-*Jazzāz* (410 AD), *Sakkākah* (late 4th Century), *Zabad* (512 AD), and *Ḥarrān* (568 AD) had all added *wāw* after the names. This is a known Northern Arabic usage which has roots going back to old Akkadian and possibly Sumerian, and was likely incorporated into their languages due to the influence of the neighboring groups to the north of them. [1][27] In fact, this consistent use of final *wāw* is a solid proof that most, if not all, Arab tribes which migrated north—long centuries before the *Tannūkh* kingdom era—, had routinely adapted to neighboring cultures. On the other hand, classic Arabic teaches us that the *wāw* of *'Amrū* is added to distinguish the Arabic name *'Amr* from *'Umar*. My belief is that *wāw* originally existed in the name *'Amrū*, and should be pronounced, at least when it is applied to *'Amrū bin 'Uday*, father of *Umru'ū al-Qays*, who was likely a northern Arab, not a Yemenite.

5

Arabic Grammar Prelude: Is *tī* a Simple Feminine Demonstrative Pronoun?

Before reading *al-Namārah*, it is important to thoroughly examine the first word of the inscription. The word is clear and legible and has two letters: *tī* تي. Dussaud claimed this word was an Arabic simple feminine demonstrative pronoun, meaning "this is." Throughout the 20th century, all subsequent readers of *al-Namārah* agreed with him without any debate!

For example, in his comprehensive reading of 1985, Bellamy allocated only one line to address the word where he referred his readers to consult with two old reference books for further explanation. [7] The first book was an enhanced English translation of an older Arabic grammar textbook that was initially published in 1857 in German; and the second was a British book published in 1930 and had for a subject the history of the Arabs of the western peninsula.

The author of the first book listed among his other references, *Alfiyyat Ibn Mālik*, a long Arabic poem comprising one thousand verses summarizing the grammar of the Arab language. [42] Written by the great Arabic linguist, *Ibn Mālik*, about eight centuries ago, the *Alfiyyah* is the most authoritative reference for textbooks on modern Arabic grammar. Notably absent from his references was an important Arabic language reference book, *Lisān al-ʿArab,* written during the same period of *Alfiyyah* by another great Arabic linguist, *Ibn Manẓūr.* Both of these references are manuscripts that became widely available after the emergence of Arabic typography in the 18th century.

Being a collection of poems, *Alfiyyat Ibn Mālik* is only useful when read by a professional linguist. In fact, many revered scholars, like *Ibn ʿAqīl,* wrote volumes of manuscripts to explain it. Unfortunately, these scholars had to rely on a manuscript that could have possibly included unclear words, missing verses, and scribes' mistakes. Contemporary scholars mainly rely on these older explanations of the manuscript, known as *tafsīr.* On the other hand, *Lisān al-ʿArab,* predating *Alfiyyat Ibn Mālik,* was written with explicit explanations by the original author along with generous examples from pre-Islamic poetry and the Quran.

To summarize the simple demonstrative pronouns in Arabic grammar, *Ibn Mālik* wrote a single line (verse) of a poem:

بِذا لِمُفْرَدٍ مُذكَّرٍ أَشِرْ   بِذي وذِهْ ؟؟ تا على الأنثى اقتَصِرْ

Translated into English the line says "use *dhā* to point to a masculine noun, and limit yourself to *dhī* and *dhih ?? tā* for a feminine." In the original manuscript, the unclear and disputed word between *dhih* and *tā* (marked with two question marks by the author) was either a genuine word, a corrected word, or a crossed out word. Researching several old *tafsīr* books, I discovered that scholars had read this unclear word quite differently.[10] However, most scholars of the Islamic Arab civilization era decided to omit this unclear word and simply list the only three known Arabic simple demonstrative pronouns for a feminine noun: *dhī, dhih,* and *tā.* I am listing below in Arabic a few of these verse readings.

بذا لِمفرَدٍ مُذكـرٍّ أشـرْ   بـذي وذِهْ تـا على الأنـثى اقـتَصـِرْ
بِذا لِمُفْرَدٍ مُذكـرٍّ أَشـِرْ   بِذي وذِهْ تي تا على الأنـثى اقـتَصِرْ
بذا لِمفْرَدٍ مُذكـرٍّ أشـرْ   بذي وذِهْ نسى نا على الأنثى اقتَصِرْ
بذا لِمفْرَدٍ مُذكـرٍّ أشـرْ   بذي وذِهْ تي ته على الأنـثى اقـتَصِرْ

Apparently, some persistent scholars decided to read this unfortunate scribe's error by replacing it with one or more words. Almost all of these scholars justified their readings in Islamic religious terms. Those who claimed it was *tī*, explained how this reading would be consistent with the Islamic teachings allowing four wives for one man [sic]! With the passing of time, more Islamic scholars joined in to give more personal interpretations. Some had even claimed that Arabic has nine simple demonstrative pronouns for a feminine noun. Others claimed that, unlike a man, a woman does not have a specific social status; therefore, she must be pointed to with multiple pronouns. To conclude, unfortunately, the Arabic grammar textbook listed by Bellamy, which most likely was Dussaud's main reference too, listed nine simple demonstrative pronouns including *tī*, as many Arabic grammar textbooks do today.

It is inconclusive whether the scribe's error in the manuscript of *Alifiyyat Ibn Mālik* was the reason behind these claims. Clearly, *Ibn Mālik* used the word, *Iqtaṣir*, which is an imperative verb meaning "limit yourself to." My impression is that some Muslim scholars during *Ibn Mālik's* time were busy making up feminine pronouns to support their religious claims and theories, a trend that evidently prompted *Ibn Mālik* to write his grammatical poem in that strong manner to correct them. [16] A simple online search today would lead to more of such Muslim scholars who are overly obsessed with the topic of females and Islam. Ironically —I must observe— to support their arguments, some Muslim scholars desperately tried to explain that the imperative verb *iqtaṣir* was referring to the masculine in the meaning of "do not use any of these pronouns for masculine" rather than what *Ibn Mālik* intended the meaning to be, which is, "use only these pronouns for feminine."

Regrettably, I could not examine the original manuscript of *Alfiyyat Ibn Mālik.* Fortunately though, the text line being discussed is a poem text line; meaning it can easily be checked against the well-known Arabic poetry rhyming scale Arabic typography background with an eye to distinguish and ميزان الشعر to determine the correct reading. Coming from an understand Arabic letters' shapes, and using the simple fact that *Ibn Mālik* had used *Wāw* between *dhī* and *dhih*, I concluded that the puzzling word before *tā* must be another *Wāw*, since in Arabic, one cannot add another item to an existing item without using *wa* before. It is my impression that the scribe had simply written a badly executed letter *Wāw* with very small loop and long downward stroke, which can easily be confused with final *Yā'*. Here is what I believe *Ibn Mālik* poem line said:

بِذا لِمُفْرَدٍ مُذكَّرٍ أَشِرْ   بِذي وذِهْ و تا على الأنثى اقتَصِرْ

To test if my belief holds any truth, I sent an emil enquiry to *Sa'dī Yūsuf*, one of the most prominent Arab poets, with the five versions of the *Ibn Mālik* poem verse, including mine, and asked him which one would be the correct one according to Arabic poem rhyming rules. He replied promptly, stating that the correct one was my version, using *Wāw* before *tā*. I was not surprised that this would be his answer since *Ibn Manẓūr*, who had studied the most important Arabic grammar books of his time, did not list *tī* as a simple feminine demonstrative pronoun in his dictionary textbook, *Lisān al-'Arab.* [17]

The second reference listed by Bellamy for the word *tī* was page 152 of *Ancient west Arabian*, by Chaim Rabin. [7] Rabin hinted that *tī* was used as a simple feminine demonstrative noun by quoting from *Bukhārī*, who wrote that prophet Muhammad had addressed *ʿĀʾisha*, his youngest wife, with the phrase *kaifa tīkum* كيف تيكم. Rabin must have thought that using *tī* in the compound demonstrative word *tīkum* would mean that it was also used as an independent simple feminine demonstrative pronoun. Writing his book three decades after the discovery of *al-Namārah*, he then listed the *tī* of *al-Namārah* as second reference! [34] Plainly said, this is wrong and misleading. The *tī* of *tīkum* is derived from *tā*, the classic simple feminine demonstrative pronoun. *Ibn Manẓūr* extensively discussed this topic in his introduction to the letter *Tāʾ* in *Lisān al-ʿArab*. He explained that *Tā* is the simple feminine demonstrative pronoun and that it can be used as a standalone word to point to a single feminine. He further explained: *Tayyā* is the diminutive demonstrative pronoun of *Tā* which can possibly be used for a younger female too. Clearly, when pointing to a single feminine noun as a third distant party, *Tā* can be combined to form a new compound demonstrative pronoun, as *tī*, but one cannot use this part as a standalone word. For example, the words *tīka*, and *tilka* are derived from *Tā*, not *tī*. The Arabs used *tīka* instead of *tāka*, but some had used *tālika*, instead of *tilka*, which *Ibn Manẓūr* called the ugliest usage in the language. [17].

It should be pointed out here that *Lisān al-Arab* did mention the word *tī*, twice. Once, casually, in its extensive coverage of the origins of the simple demonstrative pronoun word *hadha* in the chapter about the letter *Dhāl*. Here is what it said:

> *Abā al-Haytham* said: to use *hādhā* as feminine pronoun you use a prolonged *hādhihi*, as if pronouncing final letter *Yaʾ* at the end; some said: prolonged *hadhī*, and prolonged *tī*, and prolonged *tā*.

Because *hādhihi* and many other demonstrative pronoun words are all derived from the main four simple demonstrative pronouns. In his explanation, *Ibn manẓūr* indicated that the letter *Hā'* in the beginning of *hādhihi* was *Hā' al-Tanbīh*, which is used to bring attention. The prolonging of final sound is clearly to bring attention. Therefore, it is possible that the *tī*, which is likely derived from *tā*, was used to call attention, not as an alternative simple feminine demonstrative pronoun. This suely explain why *tī* was not even mentioned in the section for the letter *Tā'* and it was not mentioned in poetry or other historical texts.

I must point out here, *Lisān al-'Arab* did mention *tī* for a second time, explicitly and clearly, under the dedicated entry for the word*tayā* تَيَا. Unfortunately, the online version I used originally placed this entry by mistake under the letter *Jīm*, not *Tā'*. However, I confirmed it's listing in couple printed versions. The entry contained a single line of text stating the following: "*tī* and *tā*: feminine for *dhā*". While this entry can indicate *tī* was possibly used as feminine demonstrative pronoun by some Arabs, it does not explain why it would be used in *al-Namārah* alone, out of thousands of inscriptions, in that meaning.

To summarize, I did not find any evidence for a usage of this word as a simple feminine demonstrative pronoun, be that in the Quran or Arabic poetry or anywhere else, except for the usage claimed by the readers of *al-Namarāh*. Even if one were to find such an example, it would be of a wrong usage and likely a post Islamic example. The three simple feminine demonstrative pronouns in Arabic are *tā*, *dhī*, and *dhih*.

6

Detailed Reading of the *al-Namārah* Nabataean Inscription

Taking into account the numerous *Musnad* Arabic inscriptions available today, *al-Namārah* or any of the three other known Nabataean Arabic inscriptions cannot be classified as the earliest Arabic language documents on record. Although the classic Arabic language of *al-Namārah* is truly remarkable, the inscription quality is not impressive. Moreover, the quality of the stone and the efforts put to prepare it, are much higher than the quality of the inscription and the efforts put by the scribe, and most likely, this scribe was definitely not the same person who prepared the stone. Surely, *al-Namārah* stone as a whole does not look like a stone worthy of a king's tomb or monument. Despite visible damages, possibly including a complete breakup of the stone into two or more pieces, most of the words of *al-Namārah* inscription are uncomplicated to read by a person familiar with the Nabataean and Arabic scripts. Out of the several erosions that afflicted the stone, only one or two areas of erosion had somewhat affected the reading of the inscription. Although reading *al-Namārah,* a fascinating archeological and philological task, can be very challenging, it is not very complicated once the first two lines, and particularly the first two words, of the inscription are read correctly. Numerous scholars studied *al-Namārah* after Dussaud, but Professor Bellamy of the University of Michigan should get the highest credit for re-reading *al-Namārah* from scratch and presenting original corrections along with fresh new pictures, in the eighties of last century.

The first time I read *al-Namārah* was in 2008, the year I published my first article about the history of the Arabic *Jazm* script. My involvement in Arabic typography brought me earlier into the field of history of the Arabic script. In my earlier readings, I utilized available pictures and tracings, particularly those provided by Bellamy. However, I was able to obtain numerous detailed pictures later which enabled me to carefully study the highly disputed area by previous readers including myself.

I have provided in Figure (10) below, the original Nabataean tracing of *al-Namārah* by Dussaud, along with his initial Arabic reading as referenced today by most textbooks. I have also provided my new tracing of *al-Namārah* with eleven new changes —out of the eleven, three are Bellamy's and six are mine. See Figure (11). To assist the readers locating these new tracings and compare them with the old ones, I assigned a number to each affected area on Dussaud's original tracing in Figure (10). Also, I provided in Figure (11) my own letter-for-letter Arabic transcription followed by my translation into Arabic of the inscription, where I added all necessary dots, diacritic vowels, punctuations, and missing letters *alif* in accordance with my new reading, with a full Arabic explanation of my reading. See an image of *al-Namārah* stone in Figure (9)

Line 1

Demonstrating that Dussaud's reading of the first word *tī* was inaccurate, would most certainly open the way to question all current readings of the inscription. After all, if the writer of *al-Namārah* inscription had wanted to use a demonstrative pronoun for a tombstone, he would have certainly used *dnh*, the one utilized in *Umm al-Jimāl*, *Raqqush*, and all other Nabataean tombstone

Figure (9) A photo of *al-Namārah* stone hanging on a wall at the Louvre Museum, Paris. © Marie-Lan Nguyen/Wikimedia Commons.

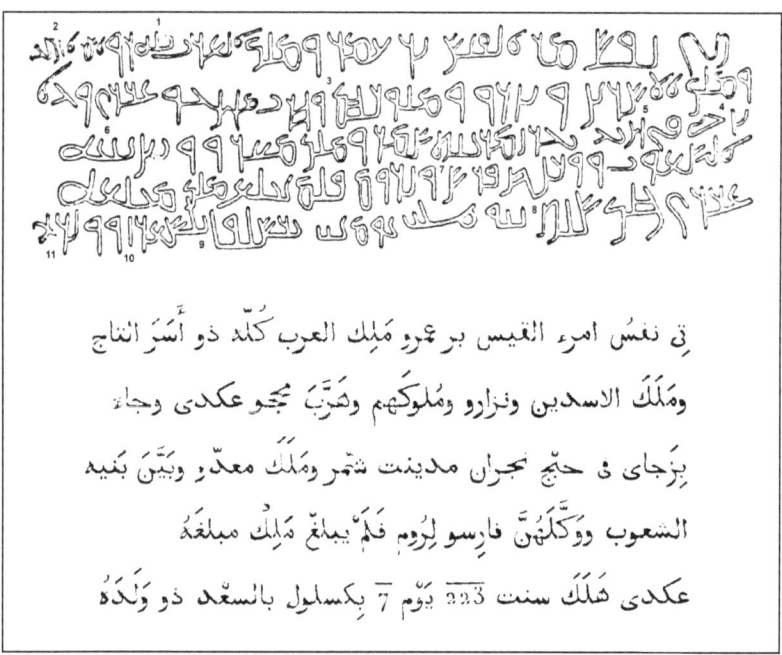

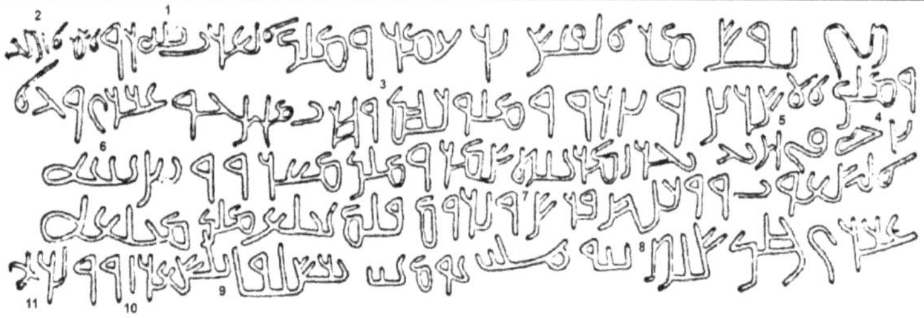

تِى نفسُ امرء القيس بر عمروٍ مَلِك العرب كُلّه ذو أَسَرَ التاج

ومَلَكَ الاسدين ونزارو ومُلوكَهم وهَرَّبَ مذحجو عكدى وجاء

بِزَجاى ى حبّج نجران مدينت شمّر ومَلَكَ معدّو وبَيَّنَ بَنيه

الشعوب ووَكَّلَهُنَّ فارسو لِرُومِ فَلَمْ يبلغ مَلِك مبلغَهُ

عكدى هَلَكَ سنت 223 يَوْم 7 بِكسلول بالسعْد ذو وَلَدَهُ

Figure (10) Dussaud tracing of *al-Namārah* inscription with his revised letter-for-letter Arabic transcription and translation. [13]

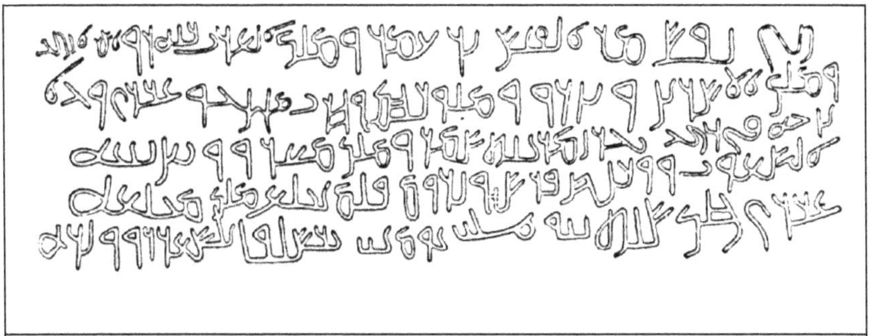

تي نفس مرء لقيس بر عمرو ملك العرب كله ذو اسد التج
وملك الاسدين ونزرو وملوكهمو هرب مذحجو عكدي وجء
يزجه في رتج نجرن مدينت شمرو ملك معدو وبين بنيه
الشعوب ووكلهن فرسنولروم فلم يبلغ ملك مبلغه
عكدي هلك سنت 223 يوم 7 بكسلول يلسعد ذو ولده

تَيا نَفسُ امرؤ القيس بن عَمْرو، مَلِكُ العَرَبِ كُلّها، ذو أسَدَ التاج،
ومَلِكُ الأسَديين ونَزارٍ ومُلوكَهُمو. هَرَّبَ مِذْحِج عكْدي، وجاءَ
يزُجُّها في رُتِجِ نَجران، مدينةُ شِمِرْ، مَلِكُ مَعَدٍ، وبَيّنَ بَنيها
الشعوب، ووكَّلَهُنَّ فُرْسانو الروم، فَلَمْ يبلغْ مَلِكُ مَبلَغَه.
عكْدي هَلكَ سَنَة 223 يَومْ 7 بكسلولْ ، يالِسَعْدِ ذو وَلَدَه.

Figure (11) New tracing by the author of the Nabataean text of *al-Namārah* inscription (top) with an equivalent letter-by-letter Arabic transcription (middle) and his modern classical Arabic translation (bottom)

inscriptions. Still, in order to fully accomplish the difficult task of challenging Dussaud's reading, we are faced by an even more difficult task — how to read this unusual word? To begin, I started in

Aramaic where *tī* is thought to be a simple demonstrative pronoun for a singular masculine noun. The name of the Syrian village *Tīshūr, Ṭarṭūs* providence, is believed to be derived from an Aramaic compound name made of *tī* (this) and *shūr* (wall), a masculine noun in both Aramaic and Arabic. [3][11]

However, the second word, *nafs,* of *al-Namārah* is a feminine noun — as I have pointed out when re-reading the *Umm al-Jimāl* inscription. The extremely rare instance where *nafs* can be treated as a masculine noun in Arabic is not applicable here. Considering that al-*Namārah* language is clearly classical Arabic, it is seriously unlikely that it would start with an Aramaic word, let alone the wrong Aramaic word.

Regardless of the nature of the word *nafs,* feminine or masculine, one needs to first reinvestigate its meaning and usage in *al-Namārah.* As I illustrated through my reading of the *Umm al-Jimāl,* Madeba, Stratsbourg, and other inscriptions in the previous chapters, this word was likely misread or even mistraced in these inscriptions. Among the long list of its usage in Arabic (compiled by major Muslim scholars who lived a few centuries after *al-Namārah*), "tombstone" or "funerary monument" were both clearly absent. Two Arabic Nabataean inscriptions, dated few decades before *al-Namārah* and found in the same geographic area, and numerous other Musnad and Nabataean inscriptions, had consistently used the word *qabr* in relation to a burial place. Why would *al-Namārah* then use *nafs* alone?

Even if the word *nafs* was actually used individually in few inscriptions to mean tombstone, this should certainly not limit it to that usage or exclude others, especially since the absolute majority of the other inscriptions had consistently used it otherwise. The fact that *Umm al-Jimāl* had used *nafsū* with final letter *Wāw,* while *al-Namārah* used *nafs* without *wāw,* is by itself a significant piece of information that needs to be examined closely. Furthermore, *al-Namārah* stone does not even resemble a typical Nabataean or non-Nabataean *nafesh.* I am of the opinion that in the context of *al-Namārah*, the word *nafs* should be read as "soul" — its common usage —, or "blood" — a less common but a very valid usage, given the events surrounding *Umru'ū al-Qays* defeat in *al-Ḥīrah.* As it will be emphasized throughout my re-reading, the overall text contents, paragraphs, sentences, and information on the events cited in the inscription — whether read with classical Arabic or having Nabataean Arabic in mind — do not match the current reading of this word as "funerary monument."

My reading of *nafs* in the meaning of "soul" would leave only a couple of possibilities for the reading of the previous word *tī.* It was either used to swear by or call upon the soul or blood of *Umru'ū al-Qays*, a very common Arab practice even today; or to bring the attention to or call upon his glory. It was customary that the Arabs, even before Islam, use introductory sentences before starting with their main topic, just as Muslims routinely do today by starting with an attention-grabbing swear sentence such as, *Bism Allāh al-Raḥmān al-Raḥīm.* Accordingly, I believe there could be four possible readings for the word *tī.*

The first and most likely reading of *tī* is *tayā* تَيا, a combined word composed of two parts, *ta* and *yā.* The first part is the swearing letter *tā'*, known as *tā' al-qasam* تاء القسم, as in *ta-Allāh* تالله. Despite its exclusive usage with name of god, *Allāh*, after Islam, swearing letter *Tā'* was commoly used before. For example, the Arabs used *ta-Ḥayātika* تحياتك when swearing by someone's life. They also used *ta-rabbi al-ka'bati* تربّ الكعبة when swearing by the god of *ka'bah* in Mecca— even before Islam. [4][17] Based on this reading, they may have used *tayā rabbi al-Ka'bati* تيا ربّ الكعبة. The second part, the letter/word *yā* is *ḥarf tanbīh* حرف تنبيه commonly used to call, or call upon, the attention of someone or something as in *yā Allāh*, or *yā fulān*, or *yā ʿIrāq*. [17] Therefore, I read the first two words of *al-Namārah* as *ta-yā nafs* تيا نفس, as in *qasaman yā nafs* قسما يا نفس, or *bikī yā nafs* بكِ يا نفس, which would mean, "swear by thee O'soul of", or "in thee, O'soul of."

The second possible reading is that *tī* could also be *tayā* تَيا, but this time the two parts are used together as *ḥarf tanbīh*. *Ibn Manẓūr* listed several examples where *Yā al-Tanbīh*, combined with additional letters before it were used as one word in the meaning of *yā*. The additional letters before *yā* were possibly used to add more emphasis, admiration, or to express feelings for revenge and sorrow. The few examples listed in his *Lisān al-ʿArab* included *āyā* آيا, *ayā* أيا, and *hayā* هيا, but not *tayā* تيا. [17] My thinking, based on *Ibn Manẓūr* examples, is that *tayā* and several other combinations of *yā* had existed in classical Arabic.

The third possibility is that *tī* itself was a swearing letter *Tāʾ* or تاء القسم with final letter *Yāʾ* added to replace a *kasrah* diacritic. In this case it would be read *tī nafs* as in *bi-nafs* بنفس or *wa-nafs* ونفس, commonly used to swear by someone's soul. Swearing *Tāʾ* is normally attached to a word with a *fatḥah* diacritic added, but it is possible that in this case *kasrah* was needed because it was followed by a feminine noun, *nafs*. This would be consistent with the typical Arabic association of *kasrah* with feminine. Since pronouncing swearing *Tāʾ* with *kasra* when attached to *nafs* is awkward, a final letter *Yāʾ* was probably used to represent *kasrah*, as practiced in prediacritic Arabic poetry writings. [17]

The forth possibility is that *tī* تي could actually be a feminine demonstrative pronoun like *hadhihī* هذه but is used here in the meaning of *ḥarf tanbīh* or for swearing. Accordingly, *tī* would be pointing with admiration (or revenge) to the soul of the king within an isolated, unrelated, opening sentence, before proceeding to the main subject of the inscription text. This usage is possible, since *tī* was mentioned casually in *Lisān al-ʿArab* in the meaning of *hadhihī* هذه, which according to that reference is a feminine demonstrative pronoun used to point at while call for attention. For example, one can say *hadhihī ummat al-ʿArab* before starting unrelated speech.

The fifth, an extremely unlikely possibility, is that *tī* could also be *tayā*, but in the meaning of *ṭawbá* طوبى or *taḥyā* تحيا (long live.) The inscription may have started with the phrase *taḥyā nafs* تحيا نفس but the letter *Ḥa'* after *Tā'* was possibly omitted by design or by mistake. This possibility is highly unlikely since I have not found any evidence linking *tī* or *tayā* with such usage. Also, *taḥyā* is usually used with a living person, not the soul of the dead.

Reading the first two words of *al-Namārah* is crucial to the reading of the rest of the inscription. In the case of the first four reading possibilities here above reported, swearing by or calling upon *Umru'ū al-Qays'* soul, the phrase should then be followed by a single major action or event announcement, not a group of events. As for the fifth possibility, the non-swearing readings above, a list of accomplishments is certainly possible. Regardless of which reading is used, the inscription has become much less likely a burial epitaph than a memorial monument. The first four swearing readings open up other possibilities for reading the rest of the inscription, since they indicate that this inscription is not necessarily about *Umru'ū al-Qays*.

The next questionable word of the first line was *klh* كله. Dussaud traced the word as *klh* accurately, but read it wrongly as *kulluh*. It should be *kulluhā* (meaning, "all of them") referring to the previous word *al-ʿArab* (the Arabs, or the Arab tribes); both are feminine nouns. However, the next challenging words of the inscription are *dhū* and the two words following it. As I explained prviously, in Arabic *dhū* is usually used in the meaning of *ṣāḥib* or *wa-lahu* ("owner of" or "he who owns"), normally for *laqab* or *kunyah* (nick name), or in the meaning of "which belongs to", "who belongs to", or "of". In both cases, it should be followed by a noun. However, in classical Arabic, *dhū* was also used in the meaning of *alladhī* (he who), followed by a verb. In *al-Namārah*, the next word was either *asad* (lion) or *asara* (took someone as prisoner). I believe it was the noun *asad*, and the previous word was either *dhū*, normally used for nicknames or other titles, or *dhū* in the meaning of "who belogs to", not *alladhī*.

It follows, I read the last three-word phrase as *dhū asadu al-tāj* in the meaning of "the one who owned *asad al-tāj*," possibly a nickname or a title referring to a figure of lion adorning the top of an actual crown. Or in the meaning of "the one who belongs to *asadu al-tāj*". This refers to the *Asad* tribe as the one with the crown or the one whose kings wore a crown, a well-known history fact.

In order to read *dhū* as *alladhī*, to fulfill Dussaud's and all current readings of the inscription, one must read the word after *dhū* as a verb. Scholars, who read the word after *dhū* as a verb, possibly *asara*, *assara*, or even *asada*, claimed that the word which followed and which can easily be traced as the noun *al-tāj* (crown,) was actually referring to the well-known historical city *Thāj* or *Thaʾj* near the modern-day city *al-Ḍahrān*.

Even so, if this were true, one would not refer to it as *al-Thāj* using *al*. In fact, Arabic poetry had never used *al* with city names like *Thāj* or *Najrān*. Additionally, in Arabic the object of the verb *asar* or *assara* must be people, not a city. One does take people, particularly soldiers, as prisoners and not a city! Tweaking the reading of *al-tāj*, some scholars claimed it was actually *al-Tājiyyīn*, possibly a tribe name, or *al-Thājiyyīn,* the people of the city of *Thāj.* However, I was not able to trace the two or three additional letters needed for *al-tāj* to become *al-Tājiyyīn* or *al-Thājiyyīn.* Since those who read the word as the verb *assara* had also read each subsequent word *mlk* as the verb *malaka,* one may ask as why *al-Namārah* would use *assar* only for *al-Taj* or *al-Tājiyyīn.* A more pertinent question would be, why not use *malaka*? It would certainly fit the meaning better.

Those who opposed reading *al-tāj* as "the crown" explained that Arab kings had never wore crowns. This is erroneous. History teaches us that some of the northern Arab kings of *Ḥīrah* and even *Najd,* home of the *Bani Asad* tribes, wore crowns. Even if this were not true, we do know that *Umru'ū al-Qays* had carried many attacks in Persia whose kings did wear crowns. Since Persia historically used a lion as a national symbol, we cannot exclude the possibility that *Umru'ū al-Qays* had managed to seize a crown with a lion effigy — this earned him the appellation: *dhū asad al-tāj* (the one with the lion of the crown), a valid Arabic phrase in terms of grammar and semantics. According to Muslim scholars, King *Umru'ū al-Qays* was known for his many appellations. Doing so, that is to have multiple nicknames, is an established Arab tradition since time immemorial, through the Abbasid times, and even today. One would be surprised, if *al-Namārah* would mention king *Umru'ū al-Qays* without following it with one of his many titles or appellations. It is unfortunate that the appellation listed in *al-Namārah* was not among those that Muslim historians accorded to him. [18][40]

Struggling to read the word following *dhū* as a verb to prove Dussaud's general classification of *al-Namārah,* some scholars hypothesized that *assar* was an equivalent to the verb *nāla* (won). They read the second word as "is"; that is, as *al-tāj* (crown), and read the three-word phrase as *alladhi nāla al-tāj* (he who won the crown).

Yet, I found no evidence that the words *assara* or *asara* was used in such manner.

Bellamy read the last four-word phrase as *wa-laqabahu dhū Asad wa-Midhḥij* (and his appellation as "the one who owned *Asad* and *Midhḥij* tribes".) I do agree with his tracing of the loop following *Asad* as a possible letter *Wāw*, but disagree with his tracing of the word that followed as *Midhḥij*. Doubly important, why would *al-Namārah* lists *Umru'ū al-Qays'* as king of *Asad* and vanquisher of *Midhḥij* in Line 2 (according to Bellamy's reading) when his appellation already included them on Line 1? However, I believe Bellamy's tracing of *alif* as possible letter *Wāw* would change *dhū asad al-tāj* ذو اسد التاج to *dhū asadūl-tāj* ذو اسدوالتاج which would conform to the way with which *al-Namārah* pronounced the name *Umru'ū al-Qays* as *Umru'ul-Qays* مرءلقيس and, as I shall discuss later, the way it pronounced *fursān al-Rūm* as *fursanūl-rūm* فرسانولروم. On the other hand, even if all Bellamy's tracing and reading of the last phrase of Line 1 were correct, this would still agree with my reading of *dhū* as the common *dhū* and not *alladhī*, and with my reading of the phrase as one of the king's titles or appellations.

Line 2

Reading the first two and the last three words of the first line was, without a doubt, the most demanding task in reading the Arabic language of *al-Namārah*. In comparison, reading the rest of the inscription is straightforward. If *dhū* was *alladhī*, one would expect a series of action (i.e. verbs) afterwards, all connected by *Wāw* (and). If it was simply the typical word *dhū* for appellations, one should then expect either additional titles connected by *Wāw*, or an announcement for an extraordinary event or a decree. Only in the second case could one start a new sentence with the letter *Wāw* (not in the meaning "and"), which would normally be followed by a non-verb, as in *wa-qad*, or *wa-akīran*. The fact that *Umru'ū al-Qays* was the king of *Asad* and *Nazār*, is neither new nor an extraordinary announcement. The Quran started many sentences with *Wāw*, but it consistently used non-verb afterwards, as in the example of Quran (53:1) *wa-al-najmi idhā hawá* والنّجم إذا هوى, where the word *al-najm* (the star) is a noun.

In my opinion, reading the word *mlk* ملك, which appears twice in the second line, as the verb *malaka* is a major mistake since the first one was preceded by the letter *Wāw*. I read both as the noun *malik* (king of), as this same word was read by all scholars in Line #1 in the phrase *malik al-'Arab*. Muslim scholars wrote that *Banī Asad* of *Najd* and *Banī Nazār* of *Ḥijāz*, are *'Arabun musta'ribah* (Arabized Arabs), not *'Arabun 'āribah* (pure Arabs.) They are the descendants of *'Adnān*, not *Qaḥṭān* (presumably a "pure" Arab.) Accordingly, *'Adnān*, a descendent of *Isma'īl*, is the father (some wrote grandfather) of *Nazār* of *Ḥijāz* and *Ma'ad of* Yemen, and great grandfather of *Muḍar*. Depending on what time period, these mixed Arab groups were customarily referred to as *Ma'ad*, *Nazār*, or *Muḍar* instead of *'Adnān*. [2][37] It is evident, therefore, that after stating that *Umru' al-Qays* was the king of all Arabs — the single largest group of people in the area — the writer of *al-Namārah* needed to state that *Umru'ū al-Qays* was *also* the king of both *Asad* and *Nazār*, two of the largest three mixed tribes in Arabia. The third group is *Ma'ad* of Yemen. Yet, it is also possible that the term "all Arabs" was referring to all nomadic Arab tribes as distinguished from tribes that had settled down in cities and specific geographic areas and established kingdoms.

Based on my readings of the word *malik* above as noun, I had suspected right from the begining, that the letter *Wāw* after the next word, *mulūkahum,* should actually be a part of that word. This would make reading Arabic smoother, especially since the next word, *hrb* هرب is a definite verb, as we shall see that later. This, of course, was not required for my reading of *al-Namārah* up to the word *mulūkahum.* As explained above, a sentence announcing an extraordinary event, like defeating the powerful *Midhḥij,* can start with *Wāw* in the meaning of *wa-akīran* (at last or finally), or *hā-qad.* However, tracing and inspecting the Nabataean text, I can unmistakably see that the *Wāw* after *mulūkahum* is actually connected to it. The downward stroke of this *Wāw* is not vertical. It is pointing to the right. The final letter *Mīm* of *mulūkahum* has a prominent lower-connecting stroke fading just before it reaches the downward stroke of *Wāw.* I read this word as *mulūkahumū* not *mulūkahum.* This final *Wāw* is referring to the people of *Asad* and *Nazār.* In Arabic grammar, it is called *wāw al-Ishba'* (saturation *Wāw*) or *wāw al-ṣilah* (relating *Wāw*) and is usually used after *mīm al-Jam'* (plural *mīm*) to emphasize its *dhammah* diacritic. The word *mulūkahumū* is the last word of the opening sentence of *al-Namārah.* It does not only conclude the opening sentence in anticipation of the main subject of the inscription, but it surely makes the reading of the first word of *al-Namārah, tī,* as a simple "this", impossible.

The Arabic root of the word after *mulūkahumū* could either be *haraba* هرب (run away) or *hadhdhaba* هذّب (disciplined), a verb in both cases. Tracing this word as *hrb* is accepted by all scholars. Since the word that comes after was *Midhḥij,* the name of the prominent Yemenite tribe, this verb must be in past tense and when read in Arabic must have a *shaddah* on the letter *Rā'* to become *harraba* هرّب (forced the object to run away) in order to refer to the subject committing the action of the verb. If *Midhḥij* is the object, as I read it, the subject can then be a name appearing before or after the verb. The only other possibility is to treat *Midhḥij,* a feminine noun, as the subject, not the object of the verb; in such case, one must say *harabat Midhḥij*, adding the feminine letter *Tā'* after *Bā'*. Since there was no *Tā'*, this word must be *harraba* (defeated them or made them run away.) *Hadhdhaba* would not make sense after reading the next line.

Given that *harraba* was the first word of the new main event announcing a sentence/paragraph that followed an unrelated opening sentence, and since it was definitely a verb followed by a name within a three-word sub-sentence, the next word *'Akdī* عَكْدي must be the subject name according to classic Arabic. It cannot be an adjective or adverb since this would leave the three-word sub-sentence incomplete. I agree with Dussaud's reading of the phrase as *harraba Midhḥij 'Akdī*, but I read it in the meaning of the phrase *harraba 'Akdī Midhḥij*, where *'Akdī* is the subject فاعل who defeated the object مفعول به *Midhḥij*. In Arabic, one can use both phrases, but should differentiate between them by using appropriate vocal accents on the object and subject. This vocal differentiation was never marked in writing until after Islam. The Quran and Arabic poetry have plenty of similar examples. In the Quran (35:28) *innamā yakhshá Allāha min 'ibādihi al-'ulamā'u* إنَّمَا يَخْشَى اللَّهَ مِنْ عِبَادِهِ الْعُلَمَاءُ, where the verb *yakhshá* is the first word followed immediately by *Allāh*, the object, and then comes the subject, *al-'ulamā'u*. [24][25]

However, assuming that *'Akdī* was a name in the phrase *harraba Midhḥij 'Akdī*, one should also consider the possibility that *Midhḥij* was a personal name and is the subject. In such case, *'Akdī*, as the object, would be the personal or tribe name of the defeated party. Although this possibility is valid from a grammar and language angle, it would not fit at all with all readings of the last line of the inscription where the victorious (either *'Akdī*, or *Umrū'ū al-Qays*) was treated as a hero, not a villain. Similarly, the assumption that

ʿAkdī was a last name, as in *haraba Midhḥij ʿAkdī,* would not work with the rest of the inscription.

Luckily, from the viewpoint of research, the word *ʿAkdī* appeared twice in the inscription. The last sentence started with the two-word phrase *ʿAkdī halak* (*ʿAkdī* died.) This phrase is, by itself, solid proof that *ʿAkdī* is a name of a person and that this inscription is about him, not *Umru'ū al-Qays.* The main event of the inscription was his triumph over *Midhḥij.* Not a very common name, *ʿAkdī* sounds like a classic Arabic name. Many of Arabic names are formed by adding final *Yā'* after a noun or after another name derived from a three-letter Arabic root, as in *Ramzī* from *Ramz, Saʿdī* from *Saʿd, Ḥusnī* from *Ḥusn,* ... etc. The name of the hero of *al-Namarāh* was *ʿAkdī* derived from the classic Arabic word *ʿakd* عكد. It is that simple! With a simple Arabic Google search for the name *ʿAkdī,* one can find many using it as a last name in an Arab desert town in Algeria, called *Umāsh* أوماش ! The fact that the name *ʿAkdī* was mentioned without the name of his father could mean that he was either an associate of *Umru'ū al-Qays,* from a slave background like the famous Arab hero *ʿAntarah* (who many think was originally a slave) or a high ranking Arab soldier of the Roman Army.

According to *Lisān al-ʿArab,* although the root word *ʿakd* can be used in a variety of meanings; however, its primary meaning is, "the lower back part of the tongue." For that reason, it was used in the meaning of *aṣl* (origin) as Libzbarski suggested. The word is probably related to *ʿiqd* عقد (tie). [7][17] Likely, the derived word *ʿakdi* does not mean "strong" or "powerful", as most Arabic publications desperately claim today following Caskel's reading, but "original" اصلي. Besides, one can not see how anyone could read the same word *ʿakdī* in two ways at the same time: as "the strong" القوي, and "with strength or strongly" قوّةً!

Bellamy thought this word was *'akkadá* عكّدى or *'akdá* عكْدى which he derived from a two-word phrase *'an kaḍá* عن قضى assuming the letter *Yā' was Yā' Maqṣūrah,* the letter *Nūn* was assimilated, the letter *Qāf* was replaced by *Kāf,* and the letter *Dhād* was replaced by *Dāl.* His assumptions are possible. As we will see in Part Three, the Akkadian language included many Arabic words with assimilated letters and sounds. Bellamy gave this word the meaning "thereafter", which is a good meaning in term of Classical Arabic. [7] Surely, his reading of the word as an adverb would make sense if one would go along with Dussaud's reading of the previous text and the inscription. But even then, his convoluted assumptions to arrive to this unknown word, *'akkaḍá,* raise more questions but give no answers. For example, why is there no reference to *'akkadá* in any historical Arabic reference? And why would the writer of the inscription use a non-crucial adverb twice, in the first place? Still, because Bellamy's reading of this word as an adverb meaning "thereafter" is a very valid possibility and would fit well in both lines, I will provide an alternative reading in the summary section using the word *'akdī* in this meaning, not as a name. However, in such case, the word *asada* أسدَ in the first line should be a verb, possibly in the meaning of "to wear", which could have been derived from the Classical Arabic root verbs *asada* أسد, *sadada* سدد, or *sadā* سدا. Historical Arabic references gave "clothing" as one of the meanings for all of three roots.

Line 3

Bellamy should be given due credit for tracing and reading two higly debated words in the beginning of Line #3. I verified his tracing and I agree with it. He traced the first word as *yzjh* يزجه and read it *yazujjuhā.* The missing final *alif* after the letter *Hā'* is consistent with the word *kulluh* for *kulluhā* in Line #1 and with another word *banīh* for *banīhā*, in the end of Line #3. The word *Yazujju* has many meanings, but in *al-Namārah* context, it means, "to engage someone in a fierce battle." Dussaud traced that word as *bzji* and read it as *bi-zjāy*, a non-existing Arabic word! The second traced word by Bellamy was *rtj* رتج, which he read as *rutuji* in the meaning of "gates of". I agree with his tracing of the word, but disagree with his Arabic reading and the meaning he gave to it. The presence of *fī* (in) rather than *'alá* (on) before the word indicates that it does not mean gates in this context. The word *fī* (in) needs a location where one can be physically "in" not "near to". One cannot say in Arabic *fī abwāb Najrān* (in the gates of *Najrān*), but *'alá abwāb Najrān* (on/at the gates of *Najrān*.) I read the word *rtj* as *rutuji*, or possibly *ritāji*, in the meaning of "narrow roads of" or "narrow road of" as given by *Lisān al-'Arab*, which indicated that the words *rutuj* or *marātij* are the plural forms of the word *ritāj* for "narrow road", as in the Quran verse وأرض ذات رتاج. [17]

Categorically therefore, only this reading is grammatically correct as it is in agreement with the historical and geographical facts of *Najrān* and Yemen, which are known for their narrow roads and mountainous valleys. The use of the word *harraba* in the second line was apparently deliberate. The crushing battle was in and around *Najrān*, where *Midhḥij* had escaped to for cover. Further, scholars read the word *Shimr* as *Shammar*, probably hinting to the well-known *Shammar* tribe of northern *Najd*. Reading the word as a tribe name rather than an individual name is clearly influenced by reading the following word *mlk* ملك as the verb *malaka*. This hasty reading is yet another example of how scholars did all they can do to prove that *al-Namārah* was listing *Umru'ū al-Qays* accomplishments.

Two facts attest to the above conclusion: 1) geographically, in the sense of distance and location, the *Shammar* tribe had nothing to do with *Najrān* or Yemen, and 2) a renowned king of Yemen who ruled in the time of *al-Namārah* carried the first name *Shimr.* [2][6][18] Moreover, I wonder why *al-Namārah,* which had added the letter *Wāw* after every single name in the inscription, would skip that practice only with the name *Shammar!* I read the word *Shmr* and the *wāw* that followed as one word, *Shimrū,* referring to King *Shimr Yarʿish* of Yemen, and therefore, I read the next word that followed as *mālik* (king of), not the verb *malaka* (owned).

The last two words of the third line are *wa-bayyana banīhā,* as in *wa mayyaza bayna banīhā* (distinguished appropriately between its people). Bellamy read the two words as *wa-nabala bi-nabahi* (treated its nobles gently). His reading would fit fine with his and my reading of the fourth line, which included two important words, *al-shuʿūb* followed by *wa-wakkalahunna.* For a victorious army, discriminating between the defeated (as in treatment of women, children, and elders differently) is contrary to the usual indiscriminate rampage. In other words, it is a sort of gentle treatment reserved for the vanquished. Tracing the first word by Bellamy as نبل *nbl,* which he read as *nabala,* is possible. Conversely, tracing the second word as *bnbh* بنبه, which he read as *bi-nabahi* is impossible since the third letter is clearly *Yā',* not *Bā'.* I read the first word as *bayyana,* as did Dussaud even though the vertical stem of the final letter *Nūn* was unusually high.

In Arabic *bayyana* in the meaning of *mayyaza* (distinguished between) or in the meaning of *wadhdhaḥa* (clarified) is the past tense for *yubayyin.* Among many diverse modes of usage, the Quran (2:118) used the following: قَدْ بيّنّا الآيَاتِ لِقَوْمٍ يُوقِنُونَ. The root word, *bayn* بين is among the few Arabic words that can be used to give an opposite meaning. Generally, it is used to express either separation or togetherness. [17] As for the second word, I believe it is *banīhā* بنيه, as in *abnā'ihā* ابنائه (its sons or people). The word *bnh* should be read as *banīhā,* since we are referring either to the *Midhḥij* tribe or *to Maʿad,* both of which are feminine nouns. Dussaud read this word *banyihi* بَنْيِهِ, as in *quwwatihi* (his steadfastness). This would fit well with the rest, but it needs to be followed by *lil-shuʿūb*, not *al-shuʿūb* as illustrated in the next word of Line 4.

Line 4

The fourth line presents no obstacles to read. In the beginning, Dussaud read it correctly, but a few decades later, he reversed position. The word *wwklhn* ووكلهن should be read *wa-wakkalahunna* (put them under the protection of), a classic Arabic word that is grammatically correct. [17] As it happened, *al-Namārah* included the required letter *Nūn* with *shaddah* diacritic at the end, which is needed to refer specifically to the plural feminine noun *al-shuʿūb*. This word is the second widely-utilized taxonomic term used in the Arab tribal and modern systems as synonym for the word "people". A tribe or *qabīlah* is divided into *shuʿūb*, plural for *shaʿb*, which in turn is divided into *buṭūn*. We read in the Quran (9:36) إِنَّ عِدَّةَ الشُّهُورِ عِندَ اللَّهِ اثْنَا عَشَرَ شَهْرًا فِي كِتَابِ اللَّهِ يَوْمَ خَلَقَ السَّمَاوَاتِ وَالْأَرْضَ مِنْهَا أَرْبَعَةٌ حُرُمٌ ذَٰلِكَ الدِّينُ الْقَيِّمُ فَلَا تَظْلِمُوا فِيهِنَّ أَنفُسَكُمْ. The word *fīhhunna* فِيهِنَّ is referring to the plural feminine word *shuhūr* (months); therefore the letter *Nūn* was added in the end. [24][25] The word *shahr* (month) is a single masculine noun, but when converted to plural form, it becomes *shuhūr*, a feminine noun. Similarly, the word *shuʿūb*, plural of the masculine noun *shaʿb*, is a plural feminine noun. This may explain, at least partially, why the word *al-ʿArab*, a single feminine noun, in the first line was referred to with *kulluhā*, not *kulluhunna* or *kullahum*, and why the feminine noun, *Midhḥij*, for a single tribe, was referred to with the words, *yazujjuhā*, not *yazujuhunna* or *yazujuhum*, and *banīhā* not *banīhunna*, or *banīhum*.

The contested word(s) of the fourth line was *frswlrwm*. The first three-letter part *frs* فرس can be *faras* فَرَسْ (horse), *fāris* فارس (horseman or equestrian), or *Fāris* بلاد فارس (Persia). Reading the word as "horse" cannot be considered. To read history correctly, it is literally impossible for the word to be read as Persia and that is because the previous word was clearly *wa-wakkalahunna*, and the following word was clearly indicating the Romans —there has never been an incidence in old Arabia where an area was put under the simultaneous protection of the Romans and the Persians. During the time of *al-Namārah*, found in a Roman-controlled territory, these two powers were engaged in heated battles. Consequently, it was highly improbable to share domination of Arabia as partners.

At this point, we are left with only one possibility as how to read *frsw*, which is *fursānū* فرسانو (horsemen) plural of *fāris*. I am inclined to believe there is a medial *nūn* between the letters *Sīn* and *Wāw*, which I will discuss in detail later. Accordingly, I read the two words as a compound: *fursānūl-rūm*, فرسانولروم, for *fursān al-Rūm*, فرسانُ الروم, similar to the reading of *Umru'ul-qays* مرُءلقيس earlier in the inscription for *Umru'ū al-Qays* أمرُؤُ القيس. The letter *Alif* of the article *al* in *al-Rūm* الروم was omitted because it was preceded by a word ending with the letter *Wāw*, namely *fursānū*. This practice has largely fallen out of use in modern Arabic writing. The name *Umrū' al-Qays*, is pronounced with heavy *dhammah* accent (as if there was a letter *Wāw*) after *Hmazah* as in *Umru'ū-l-qays* أمرُءولقيس or *Umru'u-l-qays* أمرُءُلقيس. This is why the beginning letter *Alif* of *al-Qays*, not same as *Hamzah*, was also omitted. In fact, in modern Arabic, a majority of people write the name with the letter *Wāw* beneath *Hamzah* as in *Umru'ū al-Qays* أمرُؤُ القيس. Some still write it as *Umru'u al-qays* أمرُءُ القيس. In comparison, the *Alif* of the article *al* is not omitted when the previous word ends with a soft *dhammah* diacritic, like *maliku al-Asadiyyīn* in the second line. The letter *Wāw* after theN*nūn* in *fursānū* could be the plural *Wāw* normally seen when a perfect masculine plural noun ending with *Wāw* and *Nūn*, is added to another noun to complete its meaning, as in *Banū Asad* for *banūn Asad*. This is known as *jamʿ al-mudhakkar al-sālim* جمع المذكر السالم. The word *fursān* is called *mudhāf* مضاف (qualified) or translated literary from Arabic "the added word," while the word *al-Rūm* is *mudhāf ilayh* مضاف إليه (qualifier) or literally translated from Arabic "the word which has been added to." Otherwise, this letter *Wāw* could also be *wāw al-ṣilah* or *wāw al-ishbāʿ* to emphasize the *ḍammah* diacritic on the *nūn*, as explained earlier when discussing the word *mulūkahumū* in Line #2.

Dussaud, who initially read the word *frsw* as *fārisū* فارسو (plural for *fāris*?), appeared not convinced of his reading. This explains why he decided to get rid of that reading later (when he reread *al-Namārah* in the 1950s.) A justification does exist to explain this obvious confusion: the area of the stone occupied by the letters *frsw* appears significantly damaged. However, all what the word needs to become *fursānū* is the letter *Nūn* between the letters *Sīn* and *Wāw*.

Fortunately, we do not need to dream up the letter *Nūn*. Retracing that area extensively by using several photos, I observed that the down stroke of the letter *Wāw* was pointing to the right, not perfectly vertical as traced by Dussaud. More important, the downward stroke of the previous letter *Sīn* is clearly making an upward u-turn, probably to form the small missing letter, medial *Nūn*, which was then connected to the letter *Wāw* just at the loop area. Furthermore, the space between the letters *Sīn* and *Wāw* is suspiciously wide. Nevertheless, and given that this particular surface is severely damaged, we may never know for sure if there was ever a letter *nūn* in that area of the inscription.

I believe my reading of *frsw* as *fursānū* is more convincing than Dussaud's. It is surely more convincing than Bellamy's reading of it as *fa-ra'asū* فرأسو (to appoint someone as their head or leader.) He read the two-word phrase *fa-ra'asū li-Rūmā* فرأسو لروما. I cannot see how he traced a letter *Alif- Hamzah* between the tightly spaced letters *Rā'* and *Sīn*. *Hamza,* unlike *Alif,* cannot be omitted in this case since *al-Namārah* used it consistently everywhere else. Bellamy's reading seems acceptable at first; but it would quickly crumple when combined with the previous word *wa-wakkalahunna* (placed them under the protection of.) According to Bellamy's reading, the defeated *Midhḥij,* were put under the protection of the defeater (*Ūmru' al-Qays*), and then accepted the Romans as their ultimate protectors. Why would an Arab king work so hard for the benefit of the Romans? The Arab kings were never enthusiastically subservient to either the Romans or the Persians. Their relation was primarily for mutual protection. [6] Bellamy's elaboration on the differences between *ra'īs* and *malik* is not convincing. Also, his reading of the last word as the city *Rūmā* روما is confusing. Even though the Arabs called the Byzantine Romans *al-Rūm*, these Romans were not the Romans of *Roma* (current Rome of Italy). Why *al-Namārah* would then speak of *Rūmā*?

We have no clue as to how and why some readers read the word *wwklhn* as *wa-kullahum* وكلهم in order to read the whole phrase as *wa-kullahum fursānan lil-Rūm* ووكلهم فرسانا للروم (and made all of them knights for the Romans). This highly speculative reading adds arbitrarily an additional letter *Wāw* and dreams up a final letter *Mīm*, to replace the letter *Nūn*, in *wwklhn*. Additionally, it adds a letter *Nūn* after *Sīn* (as I did) and replaces the letter *Wāw* by *Alif with tanwīn* in the word *frsw*. It also adds, arbitrarily, a second letter *Lām* before the word *lrum*. This and other peculiar readings are unfortunately the most popular ones in the Arab world today; probably because the current major Western readings of *al-Namārah* have failed to convince many! [36]

The last phrase of Line #4, *fa-lam yablugh malikun mablaghah* فلم يبلغ ملك مبلغه which was read that way by all scholars, is clear but tricky. It can mean, "Not even a king could accomplish what he has accomplished" or "no other king has accomplished what he has accomplished". There is a subtle difference between these two interpretations. The second could lead the reader to believe that it is referring to the only king mentioned in *al-Namārah*, king *Umru'ū al-Qays*. I beg to differ; that is, it refers to the first interpretation of the first phrase — that is, the one referring to the accomplishments of *ʿAkdī*. It is worth mentioning that it is common in the usages of Arabic to brag about something by stating, "not even a king has done such or had owned such." As I have explained already, according to history textbooks before Dussaud's reading of *al-Namārah*, king *Umru'ū al-Qays* was not able to control Yemen or *Midhḥij*.

To summarize, the third and fourth lines of *al-Namārah* are describing the sole event of the inscription, namely the defeat of *Midhḥij*, which was introduced in Line 2. Their specific purpose appears to be informing the reader about where the battle took place, how it was conducted, and what was its aftermath. All of the keywords appearing in the two lines, *Midhḥij*, *Najrān*, *al-shuʿūb*, *malik*, *Shimr*, and *al-Rūm* are linked to one geographical location: Yemen, and to a single timeframe: circa 328 CE.

To continue, I read the single event paragraph starting by the word *harraba* (in Line 2) until the end of the Line #4 as follows: "*ʿAkdī* defeated *Midhḥij*, then engaged them in a fierce battle in the narrow road(s) of *Najrān*, the city of *Shimr*, the king of *Maʿad*, and separated its people as it fits before placing them under the protection of the Roman cavalry, a task that not even a king had accomplished before." This reading is by no means speculative. I based it on historical and geographical facts— especially on the linguistic aspects of the inscription itself.

Line 5

The final line of *al-Namārah* started with the word *ʿAkdī*, which we have already discussed (and seen) when we read the second line. Starting with this word in the final line was not a coincidence. The letters of the final word of the previous line, *mablaghahu*, were exaggerated in size and a generous space was left blank after it. It seems, therefore, that the scriber deliberately wanted to start the conclusive sentence in a new line. Starting with the name *ʿAkdī*, he wanted to remind the reader, once more, that the inscription was about him. The second word after *ʿAkdī* was clearly *halaka* (perished) therefore, the first phrase of the sentence was *ʿAkdī halaka* (*ʿAkdī* perished) The subject name here is after the verb, exactly as it was in the older Arabic Nabataean inscription, *Raqqūsh*, which had used the phrase *hiya halakat* (she perished). [13] In good classical Arabic, the verb is usually placed *before* the subject, but this is not required for correct Arabic grammar.

After stating the year, month, and day of his death, the scriber concluded the inscription (according to Dussaud) with the phrase *bil-saʿd dhū waladahu* بالسعد ذو ولده. In Arabic language terms, this interpretation is incomprehensible. That is, we cannot understand it in Arabic. However I do agree with his tracing with exception of the first letter, which I think was the letter *Yaʾ* not *Bāʾ*, as Bellamy correctly indicated. One can easily see that the stroke for the letter *Bāʾ* was a vertical straight line throughout the inscription, unlike the stroke for the initial *Yā'*, which had always included a little dent.Nor can I understand the details of Bellamy's reading of the phrase *yā-la-sa'di dhū wālawhu* يالسعد ذو والوّه in the meaning of, "O', happiness for those who followed him". I am unable to see the second letter *Wāw* of *wālawhu* that Bellamy traced with the intention to replace the letter *dāl* of *wldh*. It is my judgment that Bellamy's reading of this word was clearly influenced by the assumption that *al-Namārah* was King *Umru'ū al-Qays*' epitaph.

I read the last phrase as *yā li-sa'di dhū waladah* يالسعد ذو ولَدَه (O', the happiness of those who gave birth to him). The first word is the letter *Yā* known as *yā' al-tanbīh* which is an exclamation letter used when calling upon for either attention or admiration. This is the same as the letter *Yā'* of *tayā*, the first word of *al-Namārah*. It is used here to draw attention to the word *sa'd* (happiness). Unlike the earlier word *dhū* in the first line, *dhū* in this phrase was followed by a verb *waladahu* (gave birth to him), and therefore it is used in the meaning of *alladhī* (those who). The closing phrase should be read in the meaning of "Oh, how happy should his parents be," a classic and familiar line used even today when bringing the bad news of a fallen young soldier, not a king, to his parents!

7

Summary of Part One

For more than a century, it was assumed that *al-Namārah* stone, which Dussaud discovered in 1901 was the tombstone of one of the most important pre-Islamic Arab kings, King *Umru'ū al-Qays bin 'Amrū*. My tracing and reading of the inscription suggests that such an assumption (based on Dussaud's initial reading) is inaccurate. In fact, by rereading *al-Namārah* and the two other known fully Arabic Nabataean inscriptions, *Raqqūsh* and *Umm al-Jimāl*, according to Western scholars, I found out that *al-Namārah* inscription was actually about a previously unknown military or tribal person named *'Akdī*, who, while working with or under the Roman Byzantine army, managed to defeat the powerful *Midhḥij* tribe of Yemen in the early 4th century. The inscription included only three parts: an opening introductory sentence swearing by the soul of king *Umru'ū al-Qays bin 'Amrū*, a long paragraph detailing the specifics of *'Akdī*'s accomplishments in a single battle, and a closing sentence announcing *'Akdī*'s death.

Below is my modern Arabic translation and explanation of the *al-Namārah* inscription:

تَيا (قَسماً يا؛ يا ؛ او تي: هذه) نَفسُ (روحُ) امرؤ القيس بن عَمْرو، ملَكُ العَربِ كلُّها، ذو أسَد التاج (كُنية)، وملَكُ الأسَديين (نَجْدْ) ونزَارٍ (بنو نَزار، الحجاز)

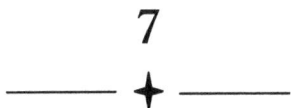

ومُلوكَهُمُ. هَرَّبَ مِذْحِجِ (قبيلة يمانية) عكْدي (اسم قائد)، وجاءَ (اي عكْدي) يزْجُّها (يُقاتلها بضراوة) في رُتِجِ (طُرُقْ ضَيِّقة) نَجران، مدينة شِمْر (شِمِر يَرعش)، ملَكُ مَعَدٍ (بنو مَعَدْ)، وبَيَّنَ (مَيَّزَ بَيْنَ) بَنيها الشعوب (فروع قبيلة مذْحِج)، ووكَّلَهُنّ (وضَعَهُنَّ تحت حماية) فُرْسانُ الروم، فلَمْ يبلغْ ملَكٌ (اي حتّى ملَكٌ) مَبلَغَهَ (ما بلَغَهُ عكدي). عكْدي هلَكَ (مات ؛ قُتلَ) سنَةَ 223 (328م)، يَومْ 7 بكسلولْ (كانون الاول)، يالِسَعْدِ (يالسعادةِ) ذو (الذي) ولَدَه (أنْجَبَهُ).

And the following is my reading of the inscription translated to English:

> In thee O' soul of *Umru'ū al-Qays bin ʿAmrū*, king of all Arabs, holder of the crown lion, and king of *al-Asadiyyin* and *Nazār* and their kings. *ʿAkdī* has defeated *Midhḥij* engaging it in a heated battle in the narrow roads of *Najrān*, city of *Shimr*, king of *Maʿad*, and befittingly differentiated between its people and placed them under the protection of the Roman cavalry — not even a king could accomplish what he had accomplished. *ʿAkdī* died on December 7th, 223 AD, O' the happiness of those who gave birth to him.

Even if one assums Bellamy's reading of the word *ʿakdī* as adverb meaning "thereafter" was correct, this inscription would still be an example of solid pre-Islamic Classical Arabic text. Here is an alternative reading of the inscription based partially on Bellamy's reading of the word *ʿakdī* as *ʿakdá*:

تي (هذه) نَفسُ (روحُ) امرؤ القيس بن عمْرو، ملَكُ العَربِ كلُّها، ذو (الذي) أسَدَ (لبس) التاج، وملَكَ الأسَديين (نَجْدْ) ونَزارٍ (بنو نَزار، الحجاز) ومُلوكَهُمُ. وهَرَّبَ مِذْحِجِ (قبيلة يمانية) عكْدى (عن قضى: بعد ذلك)، وجاءَ يزْجُّها (يُقاتلها بضراوة) في رُتِجِ (طُرُقْ ضَيِّقة) نَجران، مدينة شِمْر (شِمِر يَرعش)، وملَكَ مَعَدَ (بنو مَعَدْ)، وبَيَّنَ (مَيَّزَ بَيْنَ) بَنيها الشعوب (فروع قبيلة مذْحِج)، ووكَّلَهُنَّ (وضَعَهُنَّ تحت حماية) فُرْسانُ الروم، فلَمْ يبلغْ ملَكٌ مَبلَغَهَ. عكْدى (عن قضى: بعد ذلك) هلَكَ (مات ؛ قُتلَ) سنَةَ 223 (328م)، يَومْ 7 بكسلولْ (كانون الاول)، يالِسَعْدِ (يالسعادةِ) ذو (الذي) ولَدَه (أنْجَبَهُ).

The following is the English translation:

> In thee O' soul of *Umru'ū al-Qays bin ʿAmrū*, king of all Arabs, who wore the crown, and ruled *al-Asadiyyin* and *Nazār* and their kings, and then defeated *Midhḥij*, engaging it in a heated battle in the narrow roads of *Najrān*, city of *Shimr*, and ruled *Maʿad*, and befittingly differentiated between its people and placed them under the protection of the Roman cavalry. No king had accomplished what he had accomplished. *Then, he* died on December 7th, 223 AD, O' the happiness of those who gave birth to him.

PART 2

Yemen Inscriptional Sample: The *Sa'adTa'lib* Inscription

1

Introduction to Part Two

Choosing a Musnad inscription from Yemen (or from anywhere else in the Arabian Peninsula) to support the research and main conclusions of this book is quite easy —there are more than 90,000 Musnad inscriptions found all over Arabia — from the farthest southern territory of Yemen to the farthest northern areas of the Fertile Crescent. Musnad is the oldest known pre-Islamic Arabic script. The mere abundance and vast geographical coverage of these inscriptions is, by itself, an extremely valuable piece of information. It confirms that in those historical times, an overwhelming majority of the inhabitants of the Arabian Peninsula shared a uniform linguistic tool—the script. Emphatically, despite local dialectical variations, all Musnad inscriptions shared uniform and universal linguistic characteristics. It is most certain (or logical to hypothesize) that other minor tongues (with significantly different linguistic characteristics) that existed in the areas bordering with the core of old Arabia, had evolved with time into distinct languages. Decidedly though, they could not have been sister-languages — they were only derivative languages or even dialects.

To illustrate the common linguistic characteristics between classic Arabic and any old Arabic dialect, I decided to read a typical Musnad inscription from Yemen which is known for its distinct Arabic dialect. Reading a Musnad inscription from scratch, for the first time, I chose a never-read-before inscription to illustrate how easy can one, with proper classical Arabic background, read these inscriptions —more than eighty percent of all available Musnad inscriptions are yet to be read. Dennis Carter, a retired American finance executive who lived for 53 years in the Arabian Gulf region, brought this inscription to my attention in August 2009. In 1967, Carter's father obtained the inscription, along with a few other alabaster heads and votive figures, when he visited southern Arabia. See Figure (12). He was told that the inscription stone (and the other pieces) were all found in the *Ma'rib* region of Yemen. For the purpose of this study, I named this inscription the "*Sa'adTa'lib* Inscription," after the man who scribed it (or had it scribed). The inscription appears to belong to the period 250-300 CE, and it recorded the gold offering by *Sa'adTa'lib* to the south Arabian god *al-Miqh* (or *al-Maqah*) of the temple of *Awwm*, also known as *Maḥram Balqīs*, few miles from *Ma'rib*.

To be accurate, I did not personally inspect the *Sa'adTa'lib* stone tablet. However, with Mr. Carter's help, I was able to obtain high quality photographs. According to his description, the well-preserved stone is of a light color, possibly granite; it weighs about 13.64 Kg (30 lb), and is 30 cm (12 inches) high, 35 cm (14 inches) wide and about 5 cm (2 inches) deep. The overall quality of the inscription is good to excellent. It contained a total of eleven text lines in classic Sabaean Musnad script, all of which were written from right to left. The language of the inscription is — remarkably and clearly — Arabic. It included several solid usages of classic Arabic words, flavored by local south Arabian dialect that is no more complex than my southern Iraqi Arabic dialect, for example.

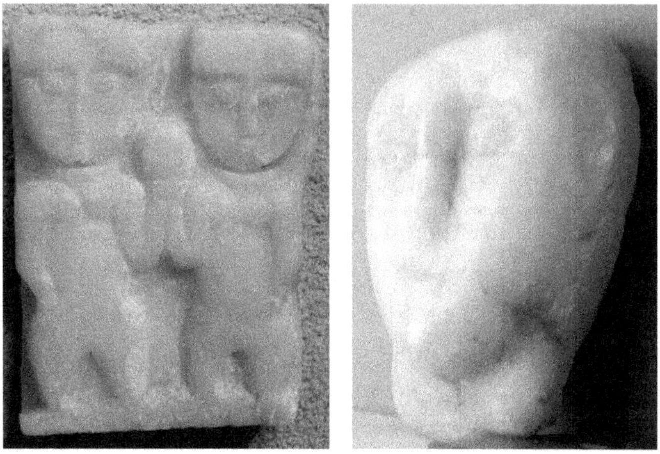

Figure (12) Alabaster head and votive figures from *Ma'rib*, Yemen. From the private family collection of Denise Carter, Santa Fe, New Mexico.

Reading my first Musnad inscription from scratch eliminated any remaining doubt that the old Yemeni language might not be Arabic. Not surprisingly, the only reference source I needed to read the inscription was the Arabic etymological dictionary: *Lisān al-ʿArab*, written by *Ibn Manẓūr* over one thousand years ago. [17]

The *SaʿadTa'lib* inscription is a valuable comprehensive inscription, in that, it coherently illustrates several usages in the old Yemen's dialect, and sheds some light on the nature of the word *Saba'* and a confusing period of Yemen's history.

2

Reading Musnad Inscriptions from Yemen

As with the language of similar old Yemenite inscriptions, reading the *Sa'adTa'lib* inscription for the first time could induce one to believe that this language might not be Arabic. However, a more diligent examination would definitely reveal otherwise. To my surprise, reading this inscription was much easier than my first reading of a Nabataean Arabic inscription. This is because both grammar and vocabulary are clear and can be explained with classical Arabic tools. For example, the inscription used the definite article *al* four times for names and nicknames, which by itself is an overwhelming evidence of its "Arabicness." All what I needed to read the text successfully was to follow several observations:

1. Written words are always spelled as pronounced in the dialect.
2. Each name mentioned in the inscription was followed immediately by either a nickname or a "wish verb," which seems to be a common old practice, as evidenced by numerous other Musnad inscriptions found in Yemen.
3. The letter *Mīm* at the end of a noun adds a factor of "greatness" or "plentiful" to it. This is referred to as *tamwīm* and has some of the effects of the classic Arabic *tanwīn,* but it is not a Yemenite replacement of it, as some believe. Using *Mīm* to indicate greatness can even be seen in names used in other civilizations of the region, notably the Mesopotamian (Babylonian)

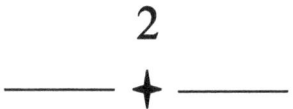

mythological figure *Ut.napištu.m* (the Sumerian Noah's archetype who survived the flood in the Epic of Gilgamesh.)

4. The letter *Nūn* at the end of a word is actually the letter *Nūn* sound of Arabic *tanwīn*, not a Yemenite equivalent of the heavily used Arabic article *al* for "the", as some scholars of Musnad believe today. Eventhough its use can lead to the same effect.
5. The letter combination *Alif* and *Lām* before a word is indeed the classic Arabic article *al* (the), which can be observed in several words in the current inscription.
6. The letter *Hā'* at the beginning of a verb indicates the letter *Alif* or *Hamzah* forming the special case past tense verb as in *'a'ṭá* (gave) from *ya'ṭī* (to give).
7. The letter *Hā'* at the end of a word could be the equivalent of classic Arabic usage of the letter *Tā' Marbūṭah.*
8. The letter *Dhāl* in the beginning of a noun or a verb could indicate *alladhī, dhī, dhā, dhū* الذي، ذي، ذا، ذو.
9. The letter *Yā'* was used to represent both heavy *Yā'* and *Alif Maqṣurah.*
10. Vertical slashes mark spaces or words' separations.

3

Detailed Reading of the *Sa'adTa'lib* Musnad Inscription

To illustrate the details of my reading, I provided an Arabic line-by-line, letter-by-letter transcription of the Musnad text of the inscription along with a translation in modern Arabic. See Figure (14). Incidentally, I found no critical need to provide an image of my tracing since the picture of the stone, Figure (13), is remarkably clear. However, to help those who would like to learn Musnad, I included in that figure an image with Musnad the letters according to my tracing, using their modern general study shapes. Missing letters or seperators, which I could not confirm physically, are added between square brackets. Note: I will only discuss selective words in my reading, since the majority of words in this inscription are self-explanatory to anyone familiar with classic Arabic.

Line 1

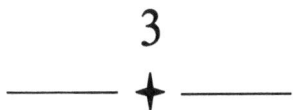

The first word *Sa'adTa'lib,* or *Sa'dTa'lib* (pronounced *Sa'duTa'lib*) is the compound name of the person who initiated this inscription and presented the gift to the god of the temple. The first part of the name *Sa'd* or *Sa'ad* is a very common Arabic name meaning "happiness," which is often combined with a second noun in the meaning of "joy of" as in *Saʿdu-al-Dīn* for "joy of the religion" or *Saʿd-Allāh* for "joy of god". The name *Saʾad Taʾlib* means "joy of *Taʾlib*", where *Taʾlib* is either a name of a tribe or one of Yemen's gods. It should be noted, the combined name *Saʾd Taʾlib* seems to be a common name at that time, since it had appeared in several other Musnad inscriptions and is also believed to be the name of the top military leader of the most famous king of Yemen, *Shimr Yarʿish*, who ruled, according to most accounts, c. 250-300 CE.

The following word *Yaqliṭ* يقلط is a verb used as a "wish or desire" verb for that person; it should not be confused with a standard nick-name, which is usually an adjective or a noun. Using verbs in such a manner is a common old southern Arab ian practice seen in most Musnad inscriptions. As tradition had it, following a name with a "wishing verb" that is in the past tense when a person is dead, and in the present tense when the person is alive, was a common Arabian practice that survived till present time. After Islam, many "wish verbs" were linked to personal names as in *raẓiyah Allāh ʿanh* رضي الله عنه (may God be pleased with or accept him), *waffaqahū Allāh* وفقه الله (may God make him successful), *yaḥfuẓuhu Allā* يحفظه الله (may God protect him), and many more. It seems that in southern Arabia, these "wish verbs" were more personalized, but some of them were reserved for a shared figure, too. A good example for re-serving a "wish verb" to an important figure is the Islamic use of the phrase *ṣallá Allāh ʿalayhi wa-sallam* صلى الله عليه وسلم (God prayed for him and saluted him,) each time the prophet Muhammad is men-tioned. The present tense verb *Yaqliṭ* used in the *SaʿadTaʾlib* inscrip-tion, means "move ahead" or "move on." This verb is still being used today in many Arabian regions, including southern Iraq.

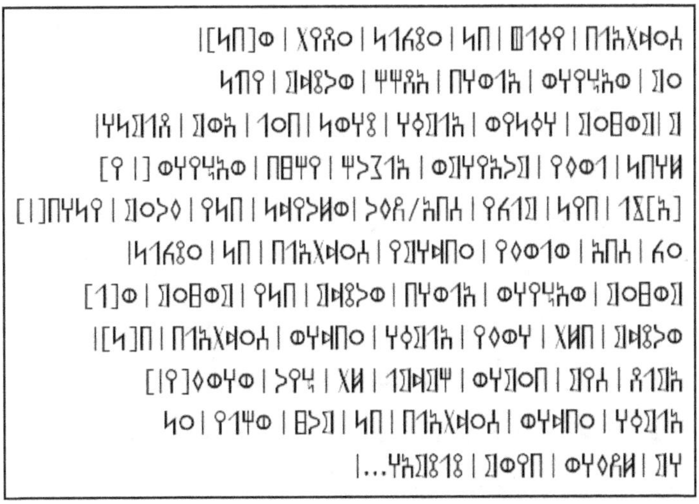

Figure (13) The *Sa'adTa'lib* Musnad inscription stone, top, and an image of its letters using a modern font, Sultan Musnad, designed by the Yamani designer *Sulṭān al-Maqṭarī*

سعدتألب | يقلط | بن | عثكلن | عصيت | و[بن|]
عم | وأخيهو | ألوهب | أصحح | ورثدم | يغن
م| موضعم | هقنيو | ألمقه | ثهون | بعل | أوم | صلمنه |
ذهبن | لوفي | مرأيهمو | ألشرح | يحضب | وأخيهو | [ي]
[أ]زل | بين | ملكي | سبأ/ظفر | وذريدن | بني | فرعم | ينهب [ا]
عك | سبأ | ولوفي | عبدهمي | سعدتألب | بن | عثكلن |
موضعم | وأخيهو | ألوهب | ورثدم | بني | موضعم | و[ل]
ورثدم | بذت | هوفي | ألمقه | عبدهو | سعدتألب | ب[ن|]
أملص | سيملأ | بعمهو | حمدمل | ذت | خير | وهوف[ي] |
ألمقه | عبدهو | سعدتألب | بن | مرض | وحلي | عن
هم | ذظفهو | بيوم | ثلثمأه |...

سَعْدْ تألب، يَقلِط، بن عثكلان، عَصَيْتَ، وبن عمو أخيهُ الوهاب، الصُحاح، ورثدم، يَغنمْ، مُوضِعً ، أقنيو المقهْ، ثُهون، بَعْلُ أوْمْ، صَلْمَنَةِ ذَهَبٍ، لوفي سيديهمُ الشرح، يَحضِب، وأخيه يأزل، بيِّنْ، ملكيّ سبأ وذي ريدِن، بنو فارعٍ، يَنْهِب، عَكْ سَبَأ، ولوفي عَبداهما سَعْدْ تألب بن عثكلان مُوضِعً واخيهُ الوهاب ورثدم، بنو مُوضِعٍ، ولوَفي ورثدم بذاتهِ. أوفى المقهْ عَبْدَهُ سَعْدْ تألب من إمْلاص، سَيعيش بفضل عمّه، حمداً له، ذات خير. وأوفى المقهْ عَبْدَهُ سَعْدْ تألب من مَرضٍ وحِلي. عَنْهُمُ الذي اضافهُ بيومِ ثلاثِمئة ..

Figure (14) The *Sa'adTa'lib* inscription with authors's line-by-line and letter-by-letter transcription from *Musnad* and translation into modern Arabic.

The word *bin* after *Yaqliṭ* means "son of" but it can also be used in the meaning of *min* من (from), clearly a matching usage since a son is "from" his father. The word *ʿthkln* عثكلن which is likely *ʿAthkalān* (a well-known name of a contemporary tribe in Yemen) is actually the first name of his father. It was followed by the word *ʿṣyt* عصيت, which is possibly *ʿaṣayta*, past tense of *yaʿṣī* (to resist). A past tense verb was used in this case, maybe because it was assigned to him after he died.

Line 2

Unfortunately, the first word بن of the phrase *bin ʿam waʾakhīhū* بن عم واخيه had to be speculated based on parts of a letter in the damaged area at the end of the first line. The natural and likely way to read this phrase is "his cousin and brother;" however I think it meant "his cousin and stepbrother;" since there was no letter *Wāw* or *Hāʾ* after the *Mīm* in the word *ʿam*, it is possible that the *Wāw* of *waʿakhīhu* is referring or related to the first word *ʿam* (uncle), thus turning the phrase into *bin ʿammū akhīhū*, which literally means "his cousin, his brother." The word *ʿam* does not fit here by itself without an attached referral article. The argument in this speculative reading is similar to my early argument on the topic of the introductory phrase *nafs wa-qabr* found in many eastern and southern Arabian tombs, which according to that reading was possibly pronounced *nafsū qabr*. Recall my reading in the *Umm al-Jimāl* and *Shahīm* Arabic Nabatatean inscriptions.

Very likely, the word *ʾlwhb* ألوهب is the name of *SaʾdTaʾlib's* cousin. It is possibly either *al-Wahb* or *al-Wahhāb* as in the common Arabic first names *Wahb* or *Wahhāb*. In such case, the addition of *al* in the beginning, is for extra recognition or acknowledgment, another common classical Arabic practice. The word *ʾṣḥḥ* أصحح is likely his nickname. This word could be starting with *Alif-Hamzah* or the Arabic article *al* but with the letter *Lām* removed since it is not pronounced, as in the case of *al-Wahb*. There are two possibilities in reading this word. In the first one, it would be a wish verb in the meaning of *aṣḥiḥ or ṣaḥḥiḥ*, as in "make correct." In the second and more likely one, the word could be *al-Ṣaḥḥāḥ* الصحاح to mean "the corrector" or "the justice maker." Another possibility for the second case is that this word stands for al-*Ṣiḥḥiḥ, al-Ṣiḥḥāḥ*, or even *al-Ṣaḥḥāḥ*, in relation to the Arabic verbs ṣiḥ or *aṣḥiḥ* from *ṣiḥḥah* صحة which means "health." Therefore, it would mean "the healer," which is possibly his profession. The next word *Wirthdam* ورثدم is *al-Wahb's* father name, as in *Wirth al-Damm*. Alternatively, it could be another name with the added letter *Mīm* for "greatness." The wish verb following his cousin and stepbrother's father name, *yaghnim* يغنم, is a present tense verb in the meaning of "wish he becomes more prosperous." Using a present tense indicates he is still alive.

Line 3

The first two words were traced as *Mwdhʿm* haqnayū موضعم هقنيو. The grandfather's name *Mwdhʿm* is possibly *Mūdhiʿ* with the final letter *Mīm* added for "greatness." The word *haqnayū* is *aqnayū* which is derived from *aqnā* أقنا for "gave forever" or "granted."

The next phrase is traced as *ʾlmqh thhwn baʿl ʾwm* المقه ثهون بعل أوم and is referring to their god. The first word *ʾlmqh* is claimed by some scholars to be derived from *īl* (supposedly the word god in Hebrew) and *maqah* (protecting.) I found no evidence supporting this reading. *Ibn Manẓūr* indicated in *Lisān al-ʿArab* that the root word مقه (no diacritics were added) has plenty of meanings, including "bright white." According to his dictionary, *al-maqh* (could also be *al-miqh*) and *al-amqah* are all adjectives in the meaning of "the shining white." It follows clearly, in this inscription, as in the numerous other Musnad inscriptions of Yemen, this word is *al-Maqh* or *al-Miqh,* using the Arabic article *al* (not Hebrew *īl,)* which is the name of the god in the meaning of *al-nāṣiʿ al-bayāḍ* الناصع البياض (the shining white) or *al-nūr* (the light.) *Ibn Manẓūr* also listed the following Islamic *Ḥadīth* المقة من الله والصيت من السماء in which the word *al-Maqh* means "love". It is very likely, that the word *al-Miqh* is referring literally to the shining "moon god," as it is believed and agreed upon by most scholars, this what the Yemen's god al-Maqah was. However, based on the rest of the inscription, it can be a name of a golden statue, too. The meaning of *al-Maqh,* which conveys the image of bright light, fits the description of a shining golden statue, as well as a bright white moon, which is the exact given meaning of the word *miqh* by *Lisān al-ʿArab.*

The following word is likely *thuhūn* ثُهون or *thuhuna* ثُهُن, but it can also be *thahwān* ثهوان , or *thāhūn* ثاهون , all of which are related to the verb *thahata* ثَهَتَ or *thahana* ثَهَنَ (to pray, or call upon someone for help while crying with tears). The word is therefore a verb or verb-like title for the god *al-Miqh* in the meaning of *ikhshaʿū lahu* له اخشعو, *al-khushūʿ lahu* له الخشوع, *idʿū lahu* له ادعو, *al-duʿāʾ lah* له الدعاء (the one to pray to, or who is prayed to.) The practice of adding a verb after the name of a god is universal among the Arabs. Even after Islam, they used the verb *taʿālá* تعالى after *Allāh* (God.) Some believe *thuhūn* is a separate name, although based on the usage described in this inscription, such possibility is highly unlikely. It is possible though that this word was used alone (without *al-Miqh*) to refer to him, just as we say today *qala taʿālá* قال تعالى instead of *qāla Allāh taʿālá* قال الله تعالى both in the meaning of "God said".

In the next phrase *baʿl ʾwm*, the word *baʿl* could either mean *ṣanam* (statue of an idol) or *rab* or *ʾlāh* meaning "god of". In the Quran (37:125), we read the following verse أَتَدْعُونَ بَعْلًا وَتَذَرُونَ أَحْسَنَ

الْخَالِقِينَ which is translated "why do you pray to *a statue* and forget about the perfect God," clearly using the word *ba'l* to mean either "a statue" or as a name of a specific statue. *Lisān al-'Arab* explains that the word *ba'l* could mean "god" or "owner"; but it may have also been the name of a golden idol statue worshiped by the Arabs before Islam.

The word after *ba'l* is traced as *'wm*, as it did not include the *al* article. This word is most likely the name of the temple where the golden statue of the god *al-Miqh* is placed. The Arabic word *aww* أوّ (sheltering or shelter) can be a noun of the verbs *awā* أوا or *awá* أوى (sheltered) according to *Lisān al-'Arab*. Likely, the final letter *Mīm* is added to make it sound as a "grand shelter." Alternatively, the word can be a name, *Awwām* (the one –place- giving shelter,) but this is less likely because in standard Arabic the name should then be *aw-wā'*, as in *rawá* and *rawwā'*. To conclude, the phrase *Ba'l Awm* can therefore be "statue or idol of *Awm*", "*Ba'l* of *Awm*", or "god of *Awm*" where *Awm* is the temple name.

The first word, *ṣlmnh* صلمنه of the next two-word phrase is derived from *ṣalam* صلم, which was used throughout Arabia for a special type of *ṣanam* (statue of an idol). *Lisān al-'Arab* indicates that the word *ṣalam* was used to decribe someone (including an idol statue), whose ears were either cut off or it was simply earless — which is the case with most alabaster heads and votive figures found in *Ma'rib* and elsewhere. See Figure (12). *Lisān al-'Arab* also indicates that this word could be used as the verb *iqtaṭa'a* (cut from,) or the noun *qaṭ'* (piece of.) Adding the letters *Nūn* and *Hā'* at the end would make it *ṣalmanah* in the meaning of *qiṭ'ah* قطعة, or "piece" a feminine noun—that is how I read the word. Interestingly, the Hebrew Bible uses this word as the name of the geographical location, where according to the Jewish religion, Moses led his followers after speaking with God in Mount Sinai.

Line 4

The word *dhahabun* is *dhahab* ذهبٌ with Arabic *tanwīn*. Together with the previous word, the phrase becomes *ṣalamanah dhahbun* for either "an earless female statue made of gold," or "a piece of gold." The word *lwfī* is *li-wafyī* لوفيِ which means *li-ḥifẓ* لحفظ that is "to keep" or "to protect". This word is related to the noun *wafā'* وفاء. The word *mr'yhm* is *mar'ayhumu* مرئيهم derived from *mar'* مرء or *'umru'* (person). This word is used here in the meaning of "master." You may recall the name of the most important pre-Islamic king *Ūmru' al-Qays.* Based on classic Arabic grammar, adding the letter *Yā'* after a noun as in *mar'ayhumu* indicates that they were two masters. The name of the first king was *al-Shirḥ* ألشرح followed by the "wish verb" *Yaḥdhib* يحضب possibly in the meaning of "wish he will ignite more fire." Some referred to him as *'il Sharah*, possibly hinting at the Hebrew use of *'il* for god, similar to *'il Maqah*. Again, this is very unlikely since the word *al-Shirh* appears as one word, clearly indicating that *al* is the Arabic article "the"—added for extra respect.

Line 5

The second king's name is *Y'zil* يأزل followed by the word *bayyin* بيّن which is possibly a verb related in its meaning to *yubayyin,* "to differentiate between" or "to clarify." It may also be the adjective *bayyin* (clear.) The word that follows, *malikay* ملكي, is from *malik* (king.) It means "the two kings of;" this is another clear classical Arabic usage. The name *Saba'* is for the city or the tribes of *Saba'*. Originally, *Saba'* was likely the name of a tribe father, but afterwards became a name of the whole group, and eventually the name of the city/state kingdom of *Saba'* in southeastern Yemen.

The ensuing name *Dhrīdn* ذريدن is actually *Dhī Rīdin* ذي ريدن. As mentioned earlier, the letter *Dhāl* in the beginning of a noun is for *dhū*, *dhī*, or *alladhī*. This word means the people of *Rīdan*, a city (or the location or estate of tribe) near *Ma'rib*, which was conquered by the Kingdom of *Saba'* and became the capital around a century later. The phrase, therefore, could be read as "the two kings of *Saba'* and *Dhī Rīdan.*"

In examining the traced word *Saba'* in this line, one could also trace another word placed over it. It seems that, at one point in time, someone tried to erase the word *Saba'* to replace it with the word *ẓfr* ظفر. Convincingly, this could be the ancient city *Ẓafar* ظفار that was later replaced by the nearby city of *Ṣan'ā'* as the new capital of the Himyarite Kingdom of northern Yemen. In turn, this suggests that the Himyarite Kingdom was close to capturing the *Saba'* Kingdom in that period thus required scribes to change the kingdom name from "*Saba'* and *Dhī Rīdan,*" southeastern of Yemen today, to "*Ẓafar* and *Dhī Rīdan,*" which, not incidentally, are all situated in modern Yemen.

Alternatively, but more likely, the word *ẓfr* could be *Ẓifār* (*Ḥaḍramawt*), in modern Oman. This may suggest that the kingdom of *Saba'* was taken over by *Ẓifār* under the rule of the two brother kings and renamed their kingdom, *Ẓifar* and *Dhī Rīdan.* Since most historians consider the Himyarite king, *Shimr Yar'ish,* as the first king to unify all of Yemen, including *Ẓifār* (c. 300 CE,) and that the two southern Yemenite kings cited in this inscription had ruled directly before (or directly after) him. Consequently, it is my conviction that this inscription should be dated c. 250-300 CE. Regrettably, the final line that most likely listed the exact date was partially damaged.

As for the name of the father of the two kings, it was either *Fir'* فرع or *Fārī'* فارع and was followed by the letter *Mīm* for greatness. The "wish verb" after it, *Yanhib* ينهب possibly means, "Wish he get more war loots." Because this was a present tense verm, I think the name *Fārī'* is likely a tribe name which would make him a great grandfather. Surprisingly, on the next line, the first word was not *malk*, but clearly *'Ak* عك a known Arabic first name, which could be the kings' father's name and in such case *Saba'* could possibly be the name of their grandfather. As we have seen earlier, the inscription has already listed, in two other lines, a name of a grandfather: *Mūdhi'*, without using the usual Arabic *bin* (son of.) Alternatively, *'Ak* could be a title of some sort, and *Saba'*, is either their the name of the city/state or people. This fact would confirm Muslim historians' classification of the word *Saba'*. In the Quran, for example, the word *Saba'* appeares twice. The first in *Sūrat al-Naml* (27:21) وجئْتُكَ مِن سَبَإٍ بِنَبَإٍ يَقِينٍ. إِنِّي وَجَدتُّ امْرَأَةً تَمْلِكُهُمْ. The second in *Sūrat Saba'* (34:15) لَقَدْ كَانَ لِسَبَإٍ فِي مَسْكَنِهِمْ آيَةٌ. Both references use the word in the meaning of *Banī Saba'* (tribe of *Saba'*) similar to *Banī Asad*, or *Banī Nazār* for example.

Line 6

The word *wlwfī* ولوفي is actually *wa-li-wafyī*, or *wa-li-ḥifẓi* ولحفظ meaning "and to protect". The following word *'bdhmy* عبدهمي is likely *'abdahumá* عبداهمي in the meaning of *'abdahumā* عبدهما referring to *Sa'dTa'lib* alone, as being the slave of the two kings; but it also possible the word was *'abdāhumā* عبداهما, referring to both, *Sa'dTa'lib* and his cousin *al-Wahhāb as both being the slaves of the two kings.*

Line 8

The word *bdht* بذت in the phrase *wlwrthdm bdht* ولورثدم بذت means *bi-dhāta* بذاتَ or *bi-dhātih* بذاته (himself) referring to his uncle *Wirthdam*. Therefore, the entire phrase *wa-li-Wirthdam bi-dhāta* ولورثدم بذات, extending from the previous line, would mean *wa-li-hifẓi Wirthdam bi-dhātih* ولحفظ ورث الدم بذاته. Notice I have assumed the existance of the existence of the letter *Lām* in the damaged area. The word *hwfī* هوفى is *awfá*, replacing the letter *Alif* with *Hā'* according to local pronounciation, which means *ḥafaẓa*. This is similar to the word haqnayū for aqnayū in the third line. The letter *Yā'* of *hwfī* was *Alif Maqṣūrah* like we indicated in the word *ʿabdahumá* of the sixth line. Starting a sentence with a past tense verb is a standard Arabic practice in religious statements. Even today we say *ḥafaẓa Allāh Fulān* starting with past tense verb.

Line 9

The word *'mlṣ* أملص is most definitely *imlāṣ* إملاص which, according to *Lisān al-ʿArab*, means *inzilāq* انزلاق (slipping,) or *infilāt*, which probably means in this context: "falling to temptations", or "wrong doing". This could also indicates that *SaʿadTa'lib* was a young man. The last part at the end of the previous line above, shows the letter *Bā'* on its own. I tend to think though that this letter must have been followed by a partially damaged letter *Nūn* to make up the word *bin* used in the meaning of "from", as I explained in my reading of this word in the first line.

The word *sayamla'* سيملئ literally means "Will be filled up or completed." Again, my opinion is that it means "will be raised appropriately" since the following word was *bi-ʿammahū* بعمه as in *bi-fazl ʿammahu* بفضل عمه (by his uncle's kindness.) This, necessarily, confirms that *Saʾd Taʾlib*'s father was dead.

The word *ḥmdml* حمدمل is an interesting word as it appears in many other Sabaean inscriptions. It seems like a commonly used abbreviated vernacular phrase, in the meaning of present-day Arabic phrase "*hamdan lah,*" "*ḥamdan lillāh,*"or "*al-ḥamdu lillāh.*" I believe the letter *mīm* of *ḥamdam* (thanks to) is not Arabic *tanwīn* but Arabic *tamwīm* in the meaning of "*ḥamdan kabīr*" or "*ḥamdan ʿadhīm*" (many thanks to.) The following phrase *dht khyr* is *dhāt khayr* as in "generous one with good deed" or possibly "one who is well to do."

Line 10

The word *ḥlī* حلي or *ḥalī* takes the meaning of "dryness" among others. Possibly, it is used here in the meaning of "poverty" or "need" making the whole phrase read *min marḍ wa-ḥalī* من مرض وحلي in the meaning of "from sickness and poverty". The use of the word bin in the meaning of from in this phrase confirms my tracing in the previous line of a missing letter *Bāʾ*.

Line 11

This line was, evidently, the final line of the inscription since it restated the name of the person adding it, the gold, or both to the temple. Sadly, it was badly damaged; hence, I was only able to read it partially. The first word, extending from the previous line, is *ʿanhum* عنهم as in *bil-niyābati ʿanhum* بالنيابة عنهم (for them.) A clear Classical Arabic usage. It was followed by the word *dhẓfhw* ذظفهو for *dhū ẓāfahū* ذو ظافهو or *alladhi aẓāfahū* الذي اظافه (he who added it,) possibly referring to *Sa'dTa'lib*, or his offerings. The final partially legible word of the inscription was *thlthm'h* ثلثمئه for *thulthumā'ah*, or three hundreds, which was likely part of a precise date. Its final *Hā'* is an equivalent of *Tā' Marbūṭah.*

4

Summary of Part Two

Reading this inscription, one can see without any doubt, the extent of classical (or standard) Arabic language used throughout the words of the inscription! According to my detailed reading above, I can summarize the detailed English translation with appropriate explanation as follows:

> *Sa'adTa'lib* (name of the presenter), *Yaqliṭ* (meaning "to advance") son of *'Athkalān* (his father's name) *'Aṣayta* (meaning "did not succumb") and his cousin, (possibly and) his brother, *al-Wahhāb* (his name) *al-Suḥāḥ* (nickname meaning "the correct") *Wirthdam* (his father's name who is *Sa'adTa'lib* uncle and possibly stepfather) *Mūḍi'im* (*Mūḍi'*, their grandfather's name) *Yaghnim* (meaning "to prosper") offered *al-Maqh* (name of the god meaning "the shining light") *thuhūn* (meaning "pray to him" or "the one prayed to"), golden statue of *'Awwm* temple, a piece (or earless statue) of gold, to protect their two masters, *al-Shirḥ* (his name) *Yaḥḍib* (meaning "to ignite") and his brother *Yi'zil* (his name) *Bayyin* (meaning "to clarify or differentiate"), the two kings of *Saba'* (city or tribe) and *Dhī* (people of) *Raydin* (city or tribe), sons of *Fāri'im* (*Fāri'*, their father's name) *Yanhib* (meaning "to take over") *'Ak* (their grandfather's name, or a title) *Saba'* (name of a person or city/state name), and to protect their two slaves *Sa'adTa'lib* son of *'Athkalān*

> *Mūḍiʿim* and his brother *al-Wahhāb Wirthdam*, sons and grandsons of *Mūḍiʿi*, and to protect *Wirthdam* himself. May *al-Maqh* protect his slave *SaʿadTaʾlib* from wrongdoing, he will be raised by the kindness of his uncle who is, thanks to *al-Maqh* (the god), virtuous and prosperous, and may *al-Maqh* (the god), protect his slave *SaʿadTaʾlib* from sickness and poverty. For them, he who added it (the gold or inscription) in the day three hundreds ......

The above English reading can be translated in Arabic, with explanation, as follows:

سعدتألب (اسم المتقدم)، يقلط (بمعنى ليتقدم)، بن عثكلن (عثكلان، اسم ابيه)، عَصَيْتَ (بمعنى عصى عليهم) وبن عم واخيهو (وبن عمو اخيه، او وبن عم واخيه، ربما هو اخيه من أمه ايضا) ألوهب (وهاب، اسمه) أصحح (بمعنى صحّحْ او الصحاح، لقبه) ورِثدم (اسمِ ابيه وهو عم سعدتألب) يغنم (بمعنى ليغنم)، مُوضِعِم (موضعٍ، اسم جَدَيْهما او عشيرتهما)، هقنيو (أقْنَيَو أو وهبو) ألمقه (المقه: اسم الاله بمعنى الناصع البياض)، ثُهون (بمعنى الخشوع له)، بَعل (صنم او إله) أوْم (معبد أوم او أوام)، صلمنه ذَهَبَن (قطعة او صنم من ذهبٍ)، لوَفْيِ (لحفظ) مَرأيهمو (سيديهما) ألشرح (شرح، اسمه) يَحْضِب (بمعنى ليؤجج النار) واخيه يأزل (اسمه) بَيِّنْ (بمعنى وَضّح او ميّز)، ملكيّ سبأ (اسم مدينة او عشيرة) وذِي (اهل، قوم) ريدن (اسم مدينة او عشيرة)، بني (ابناء واحفاد) فرعم (فارعٍ، اسم اب او قوم) ينهب (بمعنى ليسلب) عَك (اسم او ربما اسم وظيفي) سبأ (اسم او ربما اسم مدينة او قوم)، ولوَفْي (ولحِفظ) عبدهمي (عبديهما) سعدتألب بن عثكلان مُوضِعِم واخيهُ إلوهاب ورثدم، بني (بنو أو أبناء) موضعم، ولورثدم (ولحفظ ورثدم) بذت (بذاته). هوفي (أوفى أو حَفَظَ) ألمقه (الإله المقه) عبده سعدتألب بن (من) إملص (إملاص اي انزلاق او عمل فاحش)، سيملئ (سيعيش برَغَد ويكتمل او يتربّى) بعمّه (بفَضْلِ عمه وربما زوج امه ايضا، ورثدم)، حمدمل (حمداً عظيماً له اي للإله المقه)، ذت خير (انه، اي ورثدم، ذات خير أي فاعل خير)، وهوفي (وحَفَظَ) ألمقه (الإله المقه) عَبده سعدتألب بن (من) مرض (مَرَضٍ) وحلي (فاقة، عوز، أو فقر). عنهم (نيابةً عنهم) ذظفهو (الذي أضافه، ربما يقصد الذهب او النقش) بيوم ثلثمئه (ثلاثِ مئة) ....

PART 3

Akkadian Inscriptional Sample: The Epic of Gilgamesh

1

Introduction to Part Three

The Epic of Gilgamesh is the oldest human literary work discovered. Gilgamesh was possibly a real Mesopotamian king, because a similar name was mentioned as the sixth king of Uruk in the list of the Sumerian kings, which was found in the royal tomb of Ur. Accordingly, he had possibly ruled around 2750 BCE.

Originally, it is believed that the earliest epic consisted of 12 tablets. However, some scholars do not consider the 12th tablet as being part of it, because it only included poems. Each tablet included around six columns, three on each side. A column contained around 50 lines of text. Accordingly, the full epic contained around 3000-3600 lines in total. In total, and after taking into account all editions of the epic, about one sixth of these lines are still missing. There are several editions of the epic in Cuneiform writing, dated approximately between 2000 BCE and 136 BCE. The so-called "Standard Edition" of the epic consists mainly of the tablets discovered by Layard in 1854 in the library of King Ashurbanipal's (668–626 BCE) palace in Nineveh (Mosul). These tablets are dated to about 1000 BCE. They are also referred to as the Assyrian tablets even though they were brought north, from Babylon. The additional tablets of the Standard Edition were discovered in Babylon and several surrounding areas.

Parts of what is believed to be an older edition of the Epic were also discovered. In total, we have two clearly older tablets, relatively in good shape, sharing similar writing style and physical characteristics. They belong to around 2000-2100 BCE. One is referred to as the "Yale Tablet" and the other as the "Pennsylvania Tablet". Both are Babylonian tablets believed to be dated to the first Babylonian dynasty and are part of one edition. The Pennsylvania Tablet was acquired by purchase in the spring of 1914 by the Museum of the University of Pennsylvania. The Yale Tablet was acquired around the same time by the Yale University. The Pennsylvania Tablet is considered the second of the older edition's 10-12 tablets.

In this section, I will read first only one column of the Pennsylvania Tablet. The text of this column was read initially by Stephen Langdon and then by Morris Jastraw, in the beginning of the twentieth century. This column includes the two so-called dreams of Gilgamesh as told to Enkido's female seducer, Samhat, who brought him out of the wild. Then, I will read the same two dreams as told by the Standard Edition, which consisted mainly of the Assyrian tablet and was compared meticulously and read by the British scholar, Andrew George, against fragments of several other tablets believed to belong to its same period. George also read the Pennsylvania Tablet. In my reading, I will refer to the first as the Babylonian tablet and to the second as the Assyrian tablet. I will allocate separate chapter for each tablet, numbering each text line as marked by George in his book *The Epic of Gilgamesh*, Penguin's edition. In my reading of each line, I will comment about words and usages as needed.

The main purpose for my reading of the two corresponding sections is to point out their clear and undisputed usage of pre-Islamic Classical Arabic words and grammar. Reading the two text samples utilizing Arabic did not only validate current readings, but also explained and corrected the mistakes currently circulated in the many modern translations of the epic. As my evidence, I will utilize five major historical etymological Arabic dictionaries by simply quoting from them in their original language, Arabic. These widely known Arabic references belong to 900-1300 CE making them ideal impartial material evidence. The five Arabic references are:

Lisān al-ʿArab: لسان العرب
Magāyīs al-Lughah: مقاييس اللغة
al-Ṣaḥḥāh fī al-Lughah: الصحاح في اللغة
al-Qāmūs al-Muḥīd: القاموس المحيط
al-ʿUbāb al-Zākhir: العباب الزاخر

Readers of this section should have a good understanding of the Arabic language. Translating what these references wrote can compromise their validity. I indicate each reference by name and place it between parentheses when quoting it.

As for modern Akkadian language dictionaries, I used several important ones. Among these references are:

The Chicago Assyrian Dictionary (CAD)
The Pennsylvania Sumerian Dictionary - Online (ePSD)
The Concise Dictionary of Akkacian (CDA)
Qamūs al-Lughah al-Akadiyyah قاموس اللغة الاكدية (QAL)

I will indicate each of these references by its abbreviation when quoting from it.

The Babylonian "Yale Tablet" of the Epic of Gilgamesh, ~2100 BCE. © Yale University.

2

About the Akkadian Arabic Language and Gilgamesh

Despite its reading challenges, we are fortunate that the Cuneiform writing system used in the Akkadian tablets has pointed out plenty of built-in soft vowel sounds. Soft vowels are crucial to recognizing words' derivations and meanings in Akkadian, a substantially Arabic language as I will demonstrate through undisputable evidence. In a way, the Nabataean, Musnad, and early Arabic writing systems took a huge step backward in comparison to the Akkadian Cuneiform writing system. However, the inherited Sumerian Cuneiform symbols, which were arguably adequate for the Sumerian, were not sufficient to cover the many additional sounds of the Akkadian Arabic language. Utilizing identical Cuneiform symbols for multiple sounds had clearly misrepresented the language of the Akkadians in writing, presenting major difficulties for scholars studying it several thousand years later. Very likely, this practice had also played a key role in distorting the original language and creating new derived languages in the area. Clearly, writing is a key factor in preserving the integrity of any language.

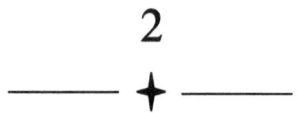

After studying the so-called Akkadian language for the first time, utilizing modern Western Akkadian references, my initial thought was: what a scandal! It was not, and still not, clear to me why did the European scholars decide to literally *construct* a new language complete with new independent dictionaries and new grammar rules, when the Akkadian language is undisputedly Arabic, a language well studied and equipped with many comprehensive historical etymological dictionaries and thesaurus, that were prepared by well-accomplished linguists and scholars many centuries ago. I can understand why Western scholars decided to transliterate the language as it was sketched on tablets. This is good intermediate classification methodology. However, I do not understand why one would recognize a word that is clearly Arabic, but call it otherwise. Such research approach cannot be justified by any scholarly reasons. This practice of reconstructing an Akkadian language separately from Arabic reminds me with modern attempts by some Western Scholars to reconstruct a new Quran from the early Kufic manuscript fragments found in Sana, Yemen!

Again and again, one reads unjustified and arbitrary claims by some Western scholars that we do not have neutral and unbiased etymological dictionaries for Arabic, a language as old as our earliest linguistic record, which contains plenty of archaic ancient marks. Some well-intentioned researchers have even created inferior manuals to fill this claimed etymological gap! One should wonder, if the etymological research of past Islamic Arab scholars was tainted by biased motives, as some Western accusers claim, why would one need to exclude similar motives from the work of modern day Western scholars! Historical Arabic etymological references, like *Lisān al-ʿArab*, are not only scientific, comprehensive, and unbiased, but because they were written centuries ago and include many older extinct usages, they are the best impartial and neutral references to consult with when studying a language like the Akkadian. The meanings of many Akkadian words in the modern Western dictionaries can easily be verified in these historical Arabic references. This by itself is undisputed evidence validating these old Arabic references.

Some may argue that the Akkadian language is much older than Classical Arabic as we know it. This is true. But Classical Arabic, as we know it, did not fall from the sky. At least one should call the Akkadian language, as evident in its inscriptions, old Arabic or proto-Arabic. It does not matter which language was recorded in writing earlier. The important fact is that all clear material evidence point out that the two languages are substantially the same. Hebrew, which some believe was *recoded* earlier than Classical Arabic, is equally important to the study of Akkadian. The Hebrew language was around during the late Akkadian period. However, as a distant geographically-limited transformed language of ancient Arabic, Hebrew's references are not the ideal ones to use to finalize Akkadian readings. Besides, as we will see after reading portions of the Epic of Gilgamesh, the remarkable Classical Arabic usages recorded in this great literary work leave us with no choice but to conclude that Classical Arabic was actually recorded long before Hebrew.

As for Sumerian, this language is still a highly speculative anthropological exercise, and will be "under construction" for a long time to come. The claim of some that Sumerian was "an isolate language" is highly debatable. Anyway, even if Sumerian was really a separate language, the fact is, we were only to decipher its sounds and words because we know Akkadian Arabic. In a way it is a "product" of modern Akkadian studies. In my opinion, it makes no sense to separate the two or to look primarily in Sumerian for Akkadian words' roots.

Simply put, to understand the language of the Akkadians, one must master Classical Arabic and be familiar with the Iraqi dialects. Building a new speculative language solely based on inscriptions is like building a “sand castle”. Professor *ʿAlī al-Jibūrī*, head of the Archeology department of the University of Mosul, and a well-known scholar of the Akkadian Language, has recently published a comprehensive Akkadian-Arabic dictionary, in 2009, based fully on the prominent Chicago Assyrian Dictionary (CAD), which is sponsored by the University of Chicago. He pointed out in his introduction that Akkadian is the closest historical language to Arabic. He also put an asterisk next to every word still being used in today’s day-to-day Arabic language, counting more than 1700 of such words! That is much more than the 200-300 words presented by some modern day Syriac scholars to prove that the old Syriac language was the actual language of the Akkadians, while ignoring Arabic entirely. What Professor *al-Jibūrī* did not point out thought —possibly he did not know— is that most of the rest of the words in CAD and his dictionary are also from Arabic and can easily be verified when consulting the historical etymological Arabic references, which did not only record the Arabic word usages of their time, but those abandoned thousands of years before their time!

Reading in CAD or the Concise Akkadian Dictionary (CAD), it is astonishing how many words are marked by “meaning unknown”. Many words in CAD have a large number of multiple meanings, which is also true in the etymological Arabic references. However, unlike CAD and other modern Akkadian dictionaries, the historical Arabic references give logically-derivable multiple meanings. Surely, I am not attempting to under estimate the value and importance of modern Western Akkadian dictionaries. The incredible work by many scholars over the past 100 years in these references is crucial to conduct any fruitful reading of the Akkadian texts. One dictionary, the Pennsylvania Sumerian Dictionary (PSD), with its electronic version (ePSD) hosted and sponsored by the University of Pennsylvania, is an incredibly useful and promising tool to unlock the language mysteries of not only the Sumerians, but also the Akkadians.

Still, one must be truthful and scientific. The Akkadian language claimed by today's Western references is not only far from being complete or well-defined language, but is also highly misleading. These references have confused and mixed plenty of sounds and word roots. It seems that words were introduced when certain meanings were needed! Surely, one can claim that the American English words "gonna" for "going to", and "wana" for "want to" are legitimate verbs in a non-British, independent language. However, it is deceiving to omit mentioning that English is the root of such words, let alone deriving new words and grammar rules for them. As for the so-called Akkadian grammar rules, assuming one manages to understand them, they are not only misleading, but lack connection even to other Semitic languages. To read an Akkadian inscription successfully one should consult old Arabic references, while keeping Arabic grammar rules in mind.

Based on the research of past Islamic Arab scholarship, it is my believe that the Akkadian people are indeed the earliest Nabataean Arabs who had migrated primarily from the Eastern and South Eastern Arabian regions of the Peninsula, carrying with them an earlier proto-Arabic language, which has evolved overtime, side-by-side the Arabic language of their ancestors. It is clear that the Cuneiforms symbolic writing system was not invented by the Akkadians, but the Akkadian Arabs should be credited as the earliest inventors of a semi-alphabetical Cuneiform writing system from the earlier primarily-pictorial one. The Akkadians are surely the first Arabs to create and maintain a civilization, which was not an isolated trend. More than 25 centuries later, newer Arab migrations triggered an equally important civilization in Baghdad, not far from where the Akkadians started theirs, Babylon.

After reading a number of important Nabataean inscriptions, I concluded that both linguistic and tracing mistakes are not only possible but unavoidable, no matter who the reader is. A final reading of an ancient inscription is difficult due to many factors. I have no doubt that there are many mistakes in the current tracings of Akkadian tablets. However, after accounting for a reasonable error percentage, the language of these tablets seems to me not only Arabic, but more Arabic than the late Nabataean Arabic.

To help the reader follow my examination of the Babylonian and Assyrian tablets, I have provided below a letter mapping table, linking the Roman letters used in the transliteration process of modern Akkadian dictionaries to the Arabic letters.

A (àáāâ)	ا أ آ ع	S	(س) ص ظ
B	(ب)	Š	(ش) س ض ذ ث ظ
D	(د) ذ ض ص ط ز ئ	Ṣ	(ص) ض ظ
E (èē)	أ إ ي ح ع غ هـ	T	(ت) ط ث ذ
G	(ج) ق غ	Ṭ	(ط)
H (ẖ)	(خ) ح هـ	Ū (úū)	ؤ و ع
I (íī)	إ ي ع ح	W	(و)
K	(ك) ق خ	Y	(ي)
L	(ل)	Z	(ز) ذ ص ظ
M	(م)	’ Hamzah	أ ع غ ح هـ ض ظ ث ذ
N	(ن)	a	◌َ
P	(ف) ب	e	◌َ ◌ِ
Q (ḵ)	(ق) ك	i	◌ِ
R	(ر)	u	◌ُ

This table should only be used as a general guide to de-root the Arabic origins of the Akkadian words. Although it is not complete, it is useful to start an investigation. To prepare it, I utilized the excellent tutorial provided in *Qamūs al-Lughah al-Akkadiyyah al-ʿArabiyyah* by *al-Jibūrī* and my personal observations. Please note, according to *al-Jibūrī*, a symbol for *Hamzah* (') was initially used by the Akkadians to represent all sounds/letters not available in the Sumerian Cuneiform writing system, which are أ ع غ ح ه ض ظ ث ذ. Later on, these sounds/letters were represented either by the vowels ā â ē ī ū, particularly ē, or by other consonant symbols. Also, please note, I have bolded the primary sound corresponding to each Roman letter and placed it between parentheses, followed by additional sound usages.

Explaining how many of the Akkadian words were transformed from Arabic words over more than two millenniums, *al-Jiburī* provided several observations like the one listed below. Although these observations are very useful, a reader of the Akkadian tablets should always, and additionally, sound out words with Arabic in mind, to arrive their correct, or most appropriate, roots.

Nūn with stop + Arabic lip letter -> Arabic lip letter repeated

kanpum -> kappum

anpum -> appum

Mīm + Arabic teeth letter -> Nūn + Arabic teeth letter

imtu -> intu

amiš -> aniš

Rā' + Nūn -> Nūn+Nūn

arnu -> annu

ibqurnisu -> ibqunnisu

Some assimilated repeated letter -> Nūn + single letter

inazziq -> inanziq

inaddi -> inandi

I would also like to offer here my own observation to help first-time readers of Akkadian inscriptions, with Arabic background, understand these inscriptions' excessive use of the syllable parts ša ذا, ši ذي, šu ذو, combined with verbs, nouns, and other words. Any confusion can easily be resolved—most of the time—, after replacing "š" with "t" or "h" in such words. This does not only make texts sound like Arabic, but can help tremendously with arriving to the right verb tense derivation and with identifying the correct subjects and objects. As for the –ma at the end of such words, it will be helpful to disregard the claim by some Western Akkadian dictionaries that this –ma was equivalent to "and", and to read it with its usual Arabic meaning, instead. Even if –ma was really used in the meaning of "and", such usage should be extremely isolated.

What does the name "Gilgamesh" really mean?

Before proceeding, I would like to discuss first the meaning of the word/name Gilgamesh, a highly debatable topic. According to the Epic of Gilgamesh, Gilgamesh was a large, powerful man. Some even thought he was half god half human. Enkindo, who came from the wild, was almost identical to him but smaller in size. Now, anyone with a minimum knowledge of Iraq, the Iraqis, and the strong Iraqi Arabic dialect, would not imagine for a moment his name would be as soft as "Gilgamesh". Gilgamesh sounds more like a European French name than an Iraqi Arabic name! It certainly does not fit the description of the epic's hero.

Furthermore, we do know that the earlier Babylonian tablets (~2000 BCE) used only Giš for the name Gilgamesh while the later Assyrian tablets (~1000 BCE) used Giš-gím-maš . This would certainly indicate that Giš was his actual name, while gím-maš is sort of a nick name, an adjective. According to my mapping table this Giš is clearly from Arabic root word *jiḥsh* جِحْش, in the meaning of "the defender" or "the mighty fighter", or "the mighty", avery common male name in Ancient Arabia. Old Arabic references listed many examples for its usage (see below). Even today, Iraqis call a strong mighty person *jaḥash* جحش:

جحش (لسان العرب)
الجَحْشُ: ولدُ الحمار الوحشيّ
وجَحَشَ عن القوم: تَنَحّى،
وجاحَشَ عن نفسه وغيرها جِحاشاً: دَافَعَ.
كُنْتُ أُجاحِشُ أَي أُحامِي وأُدافعُ.
والجِحاش أَيضاً: القتال. ابن الأَعرابي: الجَحْشُ الجهاد، قال: وتُحَوّلُ الشينُ سيناً:
وأَنشد: يَوْماً تَرانا في عِراكِ الجَحْشِ، نَنْبُو بأَجْلالِ الأُمُورِ الرُّبْشِ أَي الدَّواهِي العِظام.
وقد سمَّوا جَحْشاً ومُجاحِشاً وجُحَيشاً.
وبنو جِحاش: بطنٌ، منهم الشمّاخ بن ضِرار. الجوهري: جِحاشٌ أَبو حَيٍّ من غَطَفان، وهو جحاش بن ثَعْلَبَة بن ذُبْيان بن بَغِيض بن رَيْث بن غَطَفان. قال:
وهُم قوم الشماخ بن ضِرار؛ قال الشاعر: وجاءت جِحاشٌ قَضُّها بقَضِيضِها،
وجَمعُ عُوالٍ، ما أَدَقَّ وأَلأَما
جحش (الصّحاح في اللغة)
وجاحَشَهُ: أي دافعه.
والجَحيشُ: المتنحّي عن القوم.
جحش (مقاييس اللغة)
وكلمةٌ أخرى: جاحَشْتُ عنه إذا دافَعْتَ عنه.

قال الأعشَى:وأماّ الجَحْوَشُ، وهو الصبيُّ قبل أن يشتدّ، فهذا من باب الجَحْش،
وإنّما زيد في بنائه لئلا يسمَّى بالجَحْش،
الجَحْشُ (القاموس المحيط)
وهو جُحَيْشُ وحْدِه، كزُبيرٍ: مُستَبِدٌّ برأيِه، لا يُشاوِرُ الناسَ، ولا يُخالِطُهُمْ.
وجاَحَشَهُ: دافَعَهُ.
وزينبُ أُمُّ المؤمنينَ وأخَواها عبدُ اللهِ وعبدٌ بنو جَحْشِ بنِ رِئابٍ،
جحمش (لسان العرب)
الجَحْمَش: الصلُّب الشديد.

As for the word gím-maš, added in the newer Assyrian tablets, this word is most definitely an adjective, not part of his name. As we will see, the Assyrian tablets were far more elaborative and repetitive in comparison to the early Babylonian ones. The word Giš-gím-maš must be from Arabic words *jaḥmash* جحمش, *Jamash* جمش, or *jamas* جمس, all of which have the exact meaning: "stubborn", "rough", "rigid", "very old". Notice the use of "í" rather than "i" after the letter "g" in gím-maš. As I have indicated in my mapping table, the Akkadian words used the equivalent sounds of "ī", "ē" or "í" for the Arabic letter *Ḥā'* because the Cuneiform writing system had no symbol for it. We have numerous word examples attesting that.

جحمش (لسان العرب)
الجَحْمَش: الصلُّب الشديد.
وامرأة جَحْمَش وجُحْموش: عَجُوز كبيرة.
جمش (لسان العرب)
الجَمْش: الصَّوتُ.
يقال لِلَّذي لا يَقْبَل نُصْحاً ولا رُشْداً،
جمس (لسان العرب)
وجَمَس وجَمَدَ بمعنى واحد. ودَمٌ جَميسٌ: يابس.
وصخرة جامسة: يابسة لازمة لمكانها مقشعرّة.

والجُمْسَةُ القطعة اليابسة من التمر.
والجُمْسَةُ الرُّطَبَةُ التي رَطُبَتْ كلها وفيها يُبْسٌ. الأَصمعي: يقال للرُّطَبة والبُسْرَة إِذا دخلها كلها الإِرْطابُ وهي صلْبَةٌ لم تنهضم بَعْدُ فهي جُمْسَةٌ، وجمعها جُمْسٌ.
قال ابن الأَثير: قاله الخطابي، قال: وقال الزمخشري الجَمْسُ، بالفتح، الجامد، والجامُوسُ: نوع من البَقَر، دَخيلٌ، وجمعه جَوامِيسُ، فارسي معرّب، وهو بالعجمية كَوامِيشُ.

Despite its misleading similarity in sound, the word gím-maš is not the same as *Jamūs* جاموس, from the Persian word *kamūsh* for bull. Gilgamesh could have been depicted as a bull with human head, but he was a human; neither parts of his name meant bull. Equating his strength and stubbornness to that of a bull is only a metaphor.

Therefore, I believe the combined name Giš-gímmaš means "the stubborn fighter", "the steadfast fighter", or "the stubborn defender" or the "mighty fighter", and was pronounced initially as a compound name *Jiḥshi-jiḥmish* جِحْشِجِّحْمَش similar to modern Arabic *Jiḥsh al-Jiḥmash* جِحْش الجِحْمَش. Although the Arabs used the article *al* أل, for "the", long centuries before Islam, inscriptional evidence from Yemen and the rest of the Peninsula show they only wrote it when is fully pronounced. Many times they just used *hamzah* or the letter *Lām* alone in Musnad and Nabataean. This is not surprising since the writing systems for the Arabic language only matured after Islam, when it was finally capable of representing spoken Arabic accurately in texts, following the introduction of soft vowels and grammar rules. Here is how Accordingly, the name was originally:

Giš: Jish: جحْش
gím-maš: Jihmash جحْمَش or jimash جمَش
Giš-gímmaš: Jiḥši-jiḥmash: جِحْشِجِّحْمَش or Jiḥši-jimash جِحْشِجِّمَش
Jišši-jiḥmash: جِشِّجِّحْمَش or Jišši-jimash جِشِّجِّمَش

According to al-Jibūrī, though, in the later Babylonian (i.e. Assyrian) time period, the letter *Shīn* was assimilated into the letter *Lām* in many Akkadian words when one stops on it (i.e. pronounce it with *sukūn* vowel). Here is his observation:

Shīn with stop + Arabic teeth letter -> Lām + Arabic teeth letter

ištakana -> iššakana -> iltakana
išdu -> ildu
išṭur -> ilṭur
iššì -> ilšì

Note that according to *Lisan al-ʿArab*, the Arabic letter *Jīm*, *Shīn*, and *Ḍād* are in one sound category, coming from the front of the mouth: والجيم والشين والضاد ثلاثة في حيز واحد، وهي من الحروف الشجرية ، والشجر مفرج الفم، This would make the rule above applicable to it.

Applying the excellent observation by *al-Jibūrī* with little help from the Classical Arabic etymological references, one can easily explain how *Jiḥsh-ijiḥmash* was eventually pronounced *jilijiḥmash* جلّجحْمَش. Or, how *Jiḥsh-ijimash* was eventually pronounced *jilijimash* جلّجِمَش. It is also possible, *jilijiḥmash* itself was eventually pronounced *Jilijimash* جلجِمَش after further assimilation of the letter *Ḥā'* of *Jiḥmash* جِحْمَش. Accordingly, in the later Babylonian (i.e. Assyrian) time period, the combined name with nickname was transformed along one of two ways, depending on whether the second word was originally *Jihmash* جِحْمَش or *jimash* جِمَش. It is also likely, both of the letters *Ḥā'* and *Shīn* of the word *Jiḥsh* were assimilated. The two derivation scenarios shown below are based on the inscriptional facts of the Akkadian Arabic language and the impartial historical Arabic etymological references, not on linguistic speculations:

Jiḥshi-jimash -> Jishshi-jimash -> Jilli-jimash -> Jil-jimash
Jiḥshi-jiḥmash -> Jishshi-jiḥmash -> Jilli-jiḥmash -> Jil-jiḥmash

جحشِ جِّمَش -> جِشِّ جِمَش -> جِشِّجِمَش -> جِلِّجِمَش -> جلجِمَش
جحشِ جِّحْمَش -> جِشِّ جِحْمَش -> جِشِّجِحْمَش -> جِلِّجِحْمَش -> جلجِحْمَش

To validate my above readings, I would like to point out two facts supporting my explanation of the name Gilgamesh. According to prominent Iraqi scholar of Akkadian and Sumerian, *Ṭāhā Bāqir*, some Akkadian texts indicated his name meant 'the front fighter' (*Malḥamat Jiljamish: Ūdīsat al-ʿIrāq al-Khālidah*, pg. 19). I think the Akkadian texts quoted by *Bāqir* are accurate, since *Lisān al-ʿArab* had clearly listed the word *Jiḥsh* in the meaning of "the defender", or in other words "the fighter".

The second fact I would like to point out here is that some Akkadian tablets listed Gilgamesh's name as ^{d}Gish-bil-ga-mesh or ^{d}Gish-bíl-gi-mesh, both of which can literally be transliterated as "*Jiḥshi-bil-Jiḥmish*", or "*Jiḥsh abi al-Jiḥmish*" جحش ابي الجِّحْمَش, meaning "*Jiḥsh*, the father of stubbornness", which is a very common Arab and particularly Iraqi use of nicknames. It certainly indicates the word gím-maš was not part of his name.

To conclude, the evidence that the Arabic language was the language of the Akkadians is overwhelmingly clear. Classical Arabic tools are the key tools to use to understand Akkadian literature. Ignoring them would only lead to lost scholarly opportunities and inaccuracies. As I will demonstrate again and again, historical Arabic etymological references are the most valuable tools to map the Akkadian language, because they included tremendous information preserving the linguistic experience of Arabia for thousands of years.

3

A Comparative Detailed Reading in the Babylonian Tablets

In this chapter, I will read the first column of the so-called Pennsylvania Tablet where the two dreams of Gilgamesh were told. This tablet was the second of twelve tablets included in an earlier edition (~ 2100 BCE). According to Jastraw, the tablet measures 200.7 cm (79 inches) high, 40.6 cm (16 inches) wide, and 16.5 cm (6.5 inches) thick. It is about 17.8 cm (7 inches) taller than the Yale Tablet which belongs to the same Babylonian edition.

Below, I will first present the Roman transliteration of the text of the first column as traced by Jastraw and Langdon from Cuneiform. Next, I will transliterate the same text with Arabic letters, filling the sounds omitted due to both, the Roman transliteration process and the lack of equivalent Sumerian Cuneiform symbols for Akkadian sounds. Then, I will provide the translation by each of the three readers, Jastraw ("J"), George (“G”), and the author (“A”), in paragraph format, including punctuations. Finally, I will present a detailed comparative analysis and discussion of the three readings and translations:

1. it-bi-e-ma ^{d}Giš šú-na-tam i-pa-áš-šar
2. iz-za-kàr-am a-na um-mi-šú
3. um-mi i-na šá-at mu-ši-ti-ia

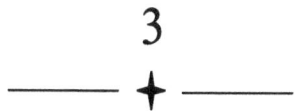

4. šá-am-ḫa-ku-ma at-ta-na-al-la-ak
5. i-na bi-ri-it it-lu-tim
6. ib-ba-šú-nim-ma ka-ka-bu šá-ma-i
7. [ki]-iṣ-rù šá A-nim im-ḳu-ut a-na ṣi-ri-ia
8. áš-ši-šú-ma ik-ta-bi-it e-li-ia
9. ú-ni-iš-šú-ma nu-uš-šá-šú ú-ul il-ti-ʾi
10. Uruk^{ki} ma-tum pa-ḫi-ir e-li-šú
11. it-lu-tum ú-na-šá-ku ši-pi-šú
12. ú-um-mi-id-ma pu-ti
13. i-mi-du ia-ti
14. áš-ši-a-šú-ma ab-ba-la-áš-šú a-na ṣi-ri-ki
15. um-mi ^{d}Giš mu-di-a-at ka-la-ma
16. iz-za-kàr-am a-na ^{d}Giš
17. mi-in-di ^{d}Giš šá ki-ma ka-ti
18. i-na ṣi-ri i-wa-li-id-ma
19. ú-ra-ab-bi-šú šá-du-ú
20. ta-mar-šú-ma [kima Sal] ta-ḫa-du at-ta
21. it-lu-tum ú-na-šá-ku ši-pi-šú
22. tí-iṭ-ṭi-ra-áš-[šú] [tu-ut]-tu-ú-ma
23. ta-tar-ra-[as-su] a-na ṣi-[ri]-ia
24. [uš]-ti-nim-ma i-ta-mar šá-ni-tam
25. [šú-na]-ta i-ta-wa-a-am a-na um-mi-šú
26. [um-mi] a-ta-mar šá-ni-tam
27. [šú-na-tu] [a-ta]-mar e-mi-a i-na su-ḳi-im
28. [šá Uruk]^{ki} ri-bi-tim
29. ḫa-aṣ-ṣi-nu na-di-i-ma
30. e-li-šú pa-aḫ-ru
31. ḫa-aṣ-ṣi-nu-um-ma šá-ni bu-nu-šú
32. a-mur-šú-ma aḫ-ta-du a-na-ku
33. a-ra-am-šú-ma ki-ma áš-šá-tim
34. a-ḫa-ab-bu-ub el-šú
35. el-ki-šú-ma áš-ta-ka-an-šú

36. a-na a-ḫi-ia
37. um-mi ^{d}Giš mu-da-at [ka]-la-ma
38. [iz-za-kàr-am a-na ^{d}Giš]
39. [^{d}Giš šá ta-mu-ru amêlu]
40. [ta-ḫa-ab-bu-ub ki-ma áš-šá-tim el-šú]
41. áš-šum uš-[ta]-ma-ḫa-ru it-ti-ka
42. ^{d}Giš šú-na-tam i-pa-šar

The following is a possible equivalent transliteration of the above text using Arabic letter and soft vowel diacritics:

1. اتبِغّم جِحش شأنتم يفسرّ
2. إذكرم عنى امي ذو
3. امي حين ساعة مسيتيّ
4. شَمَخْكُمَ اتَنَلَك
5. حين بريت عتلوتِم
6. ابذونم ككبو سماءِ
7. قِصرْ ُ ذا أنيم إمقعُت عنَ ظهريّ
8. عسُّذوم اكتبت حليّ
9. ونسذوم نساّ ذو ول التعي
10. اروك مَثُم فَخِر حل ذو
11. عتلوتم أُنَشَقو ظيفي ذو
12. وأُمِدمَ فوتي
13. يمِدو اياتي
14. عسّيا ذوم أبعلى ذو عنَ ظهركِ
15. امّ جِحش مُهديت كلأم
16. اذكرم عن جِحش
17. مِنذِ جِحش ذا كيما كاتِ
18. حين ظهري اولدم
19. وربي ذو سعدو

20. تأمرذوم [كيما سل] تخذو اتّ
21. عتلوتم انشقو ظيفي ذو
22. تطّرأ ذو تتؤمَ
23. تتذرا ذو عنَ ظهريّ
24. اتِنئِم اتأمر ثانِتم
25. شأنت اتوأم عن امي ذو
26. أُمي اتأمر ثانِتم
27. شأنت. اتأمر حميّ حين سوقم
28. ذا اوروك ربيتم
29. خصينو نَدَْيِمَ
30. حلي ذو فخرو
31. خصينُمَ شعنِ (سعنِ؟) بون ذو
32. أمُرذوم اختذو أنَكو
33. ارأم ذوم كيما أساتِم
34. احبب إلذو
35. إلكي (حلقي؟) ذوم استكن ذو
36. عنَ أخيّ
37. أمِّ جِحش مُهديت كلأم
38. [اذكرم عنَ جِحش]
39. [.........................]
40. [.........................]
41. آذم استمخارو إتيك
42. جِحش شأنَتم إفّسر

Jastraw's Translation

Gish sought to interpret the dream; Spoke to his mother:

"My mother, during my night I became strong and moved about among the heroes;

And from the starry heaven a meteor(?) of Anu fell upon me:
I bore it and it grew heavy upon me, I became weak and its weight I could not endure.
The land of Erech gathered about it.
The heroes kissed its feet
It was raised up before me.
They stood me up.
I bore it and carried it to thee."

The mother of Gish, who knows all things, Spoke to Gish:
"Someone, O Gish, who like thee in the field was born and whom the mountain has reared, thou wilt see (him) and [like a woman] thou wilt rejoice.
Heroes will kiss his feet.
Thou wilt spare [him and wilt endeavor] to lead him to me."

He slept, he saw another dream, which he reported to his mother:
["My mother,] I have seen another [Dream.] My likeness I have seen in the streets [Of Erech] of the plazas.
An axe was brandished, and they gathered about him;
And the axe made him angry.
I saw him and I rejoiced, I loved him as a woman, I embraced him.
I took him and regarded him as my brother."

The mother of Gish, who knows all things, [Spoke to Gish]:
["O Gish, the man whom thou sawest, whom thou didst embrace like a woman].
(means) that he is to be associated with thee."

Gish understood the dream.

George's Translation

Gilgamesh rose to relate the dream, saying to his mother:

> "oh mother during the course of my night I walked hale and hearty among the young men.
> Then the stars of sky *hid* from me, a *piece* of the sky fell down to me.
> I picked it up, but it was too heavy for me, I pushed at it but I could not dislodge it.
> The land of Uruk was gathered about it, the young men were kissing its feet.
> I braced my forehead and they helped me push, I picked it up and carried if off to you."

The mother of Gilgamesh, well versed in everything, said to Gish:

> "For sure, Gilgamesh, someone like yourself was born in the wild and the upland has reared him.
> You will see him and you will rejoice, the young men will kiss his feet.
> You will embrace him and bring him to me."

He lay down, and had another dream. He rose and spoke to his mother:

> "O mother, I have had another dream.
> ..... in the street of Uruk-the-Town-Square, an axe was lying with a crowd gathered around.
> The axe itself, it was strange of shape; I saw it and I grew glad.
> [Like a wife I loved it, caressed it and embraced it,] I took it up and set it at my side."

The mother of Gilgamesh, well versed in everything, [said to Gilgamesh]:

" ..... so that I shall make him your equal."

As Gilgamesh related the dream,

Author's Translation

Jiḫsh demanded his vision be explained. He recounted it to his mother:

"Mother, during my early night hours, your mighty (loud voice?) came to you.
While among the warriors, from between the stars of heaven, [like] a horse of Anim fell upon me.
I roamed with him (flew?) in the dark, he held tight around me.
And I rushed him, his speed did not scare me.
Uruk-of-the-Fertile-Land gathered proudly around him.
The warriors sniffed his legs, and laid down before me, helping me.
We roamed him in the dark, carried him upon you."

The mother of *Jiḫsh*, the guider of his vision, said to *Jiḫsh*:

"Since this *Jiḫsh* existed, his look-alike existed.
When my back delivered him and his high star reared him, seeing after him like a son you adopt, the warriors sniffed his feet.
You will face him suddenly; you will take him like a twin.
You will bring him upon me."

He wailed; he saw for a second time, a vision. He conveyed it to his mother:

"Mother, I am seeing, for a second time, a vision.
I am seeing a heated gathering (fight?) in the market of Uruk-of-the-Hill.

An axe fell (thrown?) around (over?) a proud one (a miniature goat?).
The axe of (falling on) the shabby one (goat?) missed him.
I saw him, I took him myself.
I caressed him like a mother, kissing all over him.
I shaved (fed?) him, tamed (calmed?) him to (me) his brother."

The mother of *Jiḥsh*, guider of his vision, [explained to *Jiḥsh*:]
[..................................]
[..................................]
this (means): his real-life transformed equal is selected to you."

Jiḥsh, his vision became clear.

Discussion and Analysis

1. it-bi-e-ma ^{d}Giš šú-na-tam i-pa-áš-šar
اتبِغّم جِحش شُأنتم يفسّر

(J) Gish sought to interpret the dream;
(G) Gish rose to relate a dream,
(A) *Jiḥsh* demanded his vision be explained.

it-bi-e-ma:
Jastraw derived this word from Akkadian tibû meaning "to want", which is clearly from the Arabic root verb *baghā* بغا. This derivation is possible, but I think the word here means "to demand":

بغا (لسان العرب)
وابتغاه وتَبَغَّاه واسْتَبْغاه؛ بَغَيتُ الشيءَ طلبته

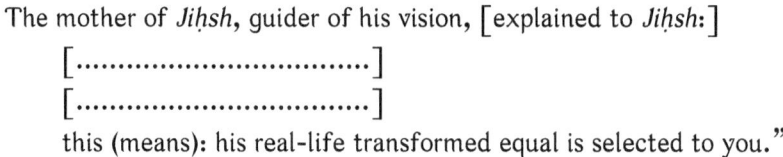

وأَبغاه الشيءَ: طلبه له أَو أَعانه على طلبه، وقيل: بَغاه الشيءَ طلبه له، وأَبغاه إياه أَعانه عليه.
وقال اللحياني: اسْتَبْغَى القومَ فَبَغَوْه وبغَوْا له أي طلبوا له.

George derived the same word from Akkadian tebû, in the meaning of "rose up". However, this word in CAD is not only a bad match, but is clearly mixing up two Arabic words. The first is *ṭabā* طبا from root verb *ṭabiya* طبي, in the meaning of "called upon him", which would involve raising one's hand. The second is the verb root word *tabā* تبا , meaning "to attack", "to plunder", or "to loot":

ePSD: tebû: to raise the hand; to rise; to plunder; to loot; to levy; to muster; to swell

تبا (لسان العرب)
ابن الأَعرابي: تَبَاَ إذا غَزَا وغنم وسَبَى.
طبي (لسان العرب)
يقال: طَبَاهُ يَطْبُوه ويَطْبِيه إذا دَعاهُ وصَرَفَه إليه واختارَه لنَفْسِه، واطَّباه يَطَّبِيه افْتَعَلَ منه، فقُلِبَت التاءُ طاءً وأُدْغِمَت.

Although less likely, I believe this word could also been derived from *baghama* بغم, meaning "spoke with deep voice". We will see a possible similar word usage in line#28.

بغم (لسان العرب)
والمُباغَمَةُ: المُحادثةُ بصَوْتٍ رَخِيمٍ؛

^{d}Giš:

I am not sure why George used the word "Gilgamesh" for the name when it was clearly "giš". The use of "giš" as the name in the early Babylonian tablet is a significant piece of information. It is the key to decipher the meaning and eventual usage of the name Gilgamesh as the epic hero. I have already discussed the word Giš in the previous chapter and indicated it stands for Jiḥsh جحش, a well-known old Arabic name. The middle letter *Ḥā'*, like the letter *Ghayn* in the word above, it-bi-e-ma, was assimilated to heavy *Yāʾ*, a standard practice by the Gulf area Arabs —both letters had no symbols in Sumerian Cuneiform writing.

šú-na-tam:

Both Jastraw and George thought this word means "dream". Jastraw derived it from Hebrew *išênu*, the verb underlying *šittu*, "sleep," and *šuttu*, "dream" according to him. It is possible that *šittu* is from *išênu*. The letter *Nūn* assimilation into *Tāʾ* was common as we mentioned earlier. The word *išênu*, which means "asleep" or "old" in Hebrew is clearly related to the Arabic root verb *shanana* شنن in a similar meaning. Therefore, I believe *šú-na-tam* is derived from Arabic *shaʾn* شأن rather than Hebrew *šuttu*. This would open the possibility that this word actually means "vision", "insight", "foretelling", "prophecy", "hallucination", not necessarily "night dream". Notice the relation between the following Arabic root words:

شنن (لسان العرب)
والشَّنُّ: الضعف، وأصله من ذلك.
وتَشَنَّنَ جلد الإنسان: تَفَضَّنَ عند الهَرَم.
وشَنَّتِ العينُ دَمْعَها كذلك.
شأن (لسان العرب)
الشَّأْنُ: الخَطْبُ والأَمْرُ والحال، وجمعه شُؤونٌ وشِئانٌ؛
وما شَأَنَ شأْنَه؛ عن ابن الأَعرابي، أَي ما شَعَرَ به،
وحكى اللحياني: أَتاني ذلك وما شَأَنْتُ شَأْنَه أَي ما عَلِمتُ به
والشَّأْنُ مَجْرى الدَّمْعِ إِلى العين، والجمع أَشْؤُنٌ وشُؤُون.
شون (لسان العرب)
التهذيب: والتَّشَوُّنُ خفة العقل

2. iz-za-kàr-am a-na um-mi-šú
إذكرم عنَ امي ذو

(J) Spoke to his mother:

(G) saying to his mother:

(A) he recounted it to his mother:

a-na:

This very 2-3 letter combining word is used in many meanings in old Classical Arabic, depending on the vowel sounds and other connected words. It could mean "from", "in", "about", "over", "within", "how", "where", and a lot more. It is also possible that the word in the tablet was actually ʿana عَنَ as in *ʿala* على.

أنّ (القاموس المحيط)

وأنّى: تكونُ بمعنَى حيثُ، وكيفَ، وأيْنَ، وتكونُ حَرْفَ شَرْطٍ.

وصِلَةً للاسْمِ المَوْصولِ: ﴿وآتَيْنَاهُ من الكُنُوزِ ما إنَّ مفاتِحَهُ﴾

أنن (لسان العرب)

﴿فلَا تَعْضُلُوهُنَّ أَنْ يَنْكِحْنَ أَزْوَاجَهُنَّ﴾

واحتمَل الكلام تقدير من أو عن، وذكَر آيات أخرى يقدَّر فيها حرف الجر من أو إلى

عنن (لسان العرب)

وقال الأَزهري في ترجمة عنا، قال: قال المبرد من وإلى ورب وفي والكاف الزائدة والباء الزائدة واللام الزائدة هي حروف الإِضافة التي يضاف بها الأَسماء والأَفعال إلى ما بعدها،

وربما وضعت موضع على

وهو الذي يَقْبَلَ التوبةَ عن عباده؛ أي من عباده

وعَنِّي: بمعنى علَيَّ

قال: وقد جاء عن بمعنى بعد؛

3. um-mi i-na šá-at mu-ši-ti-ia

امي حين ساعة مسيتيّ

(J) "My mother, during my night

(G) "oh mother during the course of my night
(A) "Mother, during my early night hours,

mu-ši-ti-ia:

مسا (لسان العرب)
والمَساء بعذ الظهر إلى صلاة المغرب، وقال بعضهم إلى نصف الليل.

4. šá-am-ḫa-ku-ma at-ta-na-al-la-ak
شَمَخْكُمَ اتَنَلَكَ

(J) I became strong and moved about
(G) I walked hale and hearty
(A) Your mighty (loud voice?) came to you.

شمخ (لسان العرب)
الشامخ: العالي.
صمخ (لسان العرب)
ويقال: صمخ الصوتُ صِماخَ فلان.
سمخ (لسان العرب)
ويقال: سَمَخَني بِجدّةِ صوته وكثرة كلامه، ولغة تميم الصَّمْخُ.

5. i-na bi-ri-it it-lu-tim
حين بريت عتلوتم

(J) among the heroes;
(G) among the young men
(A) While among the warriors,

i-na:
This word is likely *ḥīna* حين which means "while", "during", "in". It is still being used in southern Iraq in these meanings and more.

bi-ri-it:

This word is bi-ni-it بينت, "among", from Arabic *bayn* بين. Exchanging the letter *Nūn* with *Rā'* is consistent with Nabataean inscriptions. Iraqis today say *bināt* بينات for "among".

it-lu-tim:

عتل (لسان العرب)

والعُتُلُّ الشديد، وقيل: الأَكُول المَنُوع، وقيل: هو الجافي الغليظ، وقيل: هو الجافي الخُلُق اللئيم الضرِّيبة، وقيل: هو الشديد من الرجال والدواب.

6. ib-ba-šú-nim-ma ka-ka-bu šá-ma-i

ابذونم ككبو سماء

(J) And from the starry heaven

(G) Then the stars of sky *hid* from me,

(A) from between the stars of heaven,

ib-ba-šú-nim-ma:

It seems that George read this word as *ibdunima* ابدونم, meaning "without". However, even if it was correct, this usage does not fit with the meaning "to hide". Besides, in the Assyrian Tablet, when Gilgamesh's mother addressed him, repeating the events of his vision in his own words, she used the word ib-šu-nik-ka, instead. Specifically, she exchanged the word šú-nim-ma with šú-nik-ka. This indicates that this word is a demonstrative pronoun, from Arabic *dū*, but used to point to plural. The initial part ib-ba is not part of the word, but the equivalent of the letter *Bā'*. Iraqis pronounce it "ib" rather than "bi.

با (لسان العرب)

الباء حرف هجاء من حروف المعجم، وأَكثر ما تَرِد بمعنى الإِلْصاق لما ذُكِر قَبْلَها من اسم أَو فعل بما انضمت إليه، وقد تَرِدُ بمعنى المُلابسة والمُخالَطة، وبمعنى من أَجل ، وبمعنى في ومن وعن ومع،

7. [ki]-iṣ-rù šá A-nim im-ḳu-ut a-na ṣi-ri-ia
قِصْرُ ذا أنيم إمقعُت عنَ ظهريّ

(J) a meteor(?) of Anu fell upon me:
(G) a *piece* of the sky fell down to me,
(A) [like] a horse of Anim fell upon me

[ki]-iṣ-rù:
I think this word means "horse". Clearly, the meaning of "troop", below, is consistant with horse.

ePSD: kiṣru: "troop"

قصر (لسان العرب)
ويقال للمَحْبُوسة من الخيل: قَصِير؛

im-ḳu-ut:

مقع (لسان العرب)
ومُقِعَ فلان بسَوْءَةٍ مَقْعاً: رُمِيَ بها.
ويقال: مَقَعْتُه بشرٍّ ولقَعْتُه معناه إذا رميْته به.

8. áš-ši-šú-ma ik-ta-bi-it e-li-ia
عسُّذوم اكتبت حليّ

(J) I bore it and it grew heavy upon me,
(G) I picked it up, but it was too heavy for me,
(A) I roamed with him (flew?) in the dark, he held around me,

áš-ši-šú-ma:
Both Jastraw and George derived the verb *áš-ši* from *našû* which means "to lift". However, the letter *Nūn* in this word is part of the root verb and cannot be omitted in any derivation:

ePSD: našû: to lift; to raise; to carry

نصص (لسان العرب)
النَّصُّ: رفْعُكَ الشيء. نَصَّ الحديث يَنُصُّه نصاً: رفَعَه.
ونصَّ المتاعَ نصاً: جعلَ بعضه على بعض.
ونَصَّ الدابةَ يَنُصُّها نصاً: رَفَعَها في السير، وكذلك الناقة.

I think the verb áš-ši is likely derived from the Arabic root verb *ʿasasa*, which means "to roam at night":

عسس (لسان العرب)
عسَّ يَعُسُّ عَسَساً وعَساً أي طاف بالليل؛

ik-ta-bi-it:

كتب (لسان العرب)
والكَتْبُ الجمع، تقول منه: كَتَبْتُ البَغْلَة إذا جمَعْتَ بين شُفْرَيْها بحَلْقَةٍ أو سَيْرٍ.
وكَتَّبَها تَكْتِيباً، وكَتَّبَ عليها: صَرَّرها.
كتب (الصّحاح في اللغة)
وأكْتَبْتُ القِربَةَ أيضاً: شددتها بالوكاء؛

e-li-ia:

The first letter can be the letter *ʿayn* to make the word *ʿalayya* عليّ or "on me". However, the writer used a-na عني earlier in that meaning. Therefore, this word must be *ḥiliyyah* حلي from *ḥawliya* حولي which means "around me" or "near me". Even today, southern Iraqis say *ḥilli* in the meaning of "near me".

ṣi-ri-ia:

The word ṣi-ri sould be pronounced ظهر or "back".

9. ú-ni-iš-šú-ma nu-uš-šá-šú ú-ul il-ti-'i

ونسذوم نسّا ذو ول التعي

(J) I became weak and its weight I could not endure.

(G) I pushed at it but I could not dislodge it.

(A) and I rushed him, his speed did not scare me.

ú-ni-iš-šú-ma:

Both Jastraw and George derived the verb *ni-iš-šú* from *enšu*, from Arabic *ḥinṣ* حنص, which means "weak", possibly believing that the root was *nšu*. However, the letters *Ḥā'* (or *Nūn* too) in this word is part of the root and cannot be omitted in any derivation:

ePSD: enšu: (to be) weak; (to be) thin; (to be) low; weak person

حنص (لسان العرب)

الحِنْصأْوةُ من الرجال الضعيفُ. يقال: رأيت رجُلاً حِنْصأْوةً أي ضعيفاً

نيص (لسان العرب)

النَّيْصُ الحركة الضعيفة.

The verb *ni-iš-šú* is likely derived from Arabic root verb *nasasa*, which means "to rush"or "to drive fast", including "to fly fast", which fits well with the previous line:

نسس (لسان العرب)

النَّس السوق الشديد، والتَّنْساس السير الشديد

ونَسْنَس الطائر إِذا أَسرع في طَيَرانِه

nu-uš-šá-šú:

The noun word *nu-uš-šá* does not mean "weight". It seems that Jastraw and George desperately linked it to *enšu* which they already got wrong earlier. The Akkadian word for "weight" is *šuqultu*, from Arabic thuql ثقل:

ePSD: šuqultu: weight.

il-ti-'i:

This word is derived from Arabic *la'a'a* لعع meaning "to be scared".

لعع (لسان العرب)

وتَلَعْلَعَ الرجلُ: ضَعُفَ.

واللَّعْلاعُ: الجبانُ.

لعا (لسان العرب)

واللاعي: الذي يُفزِعه أَدنى شيء؛

10. Uruk[ki] ma-tum pa-ḫi-ir e-li-šú

أروك مَثُم فَخِر حل ذو

(J) The land of Erech gathered about it.
(G) The land of Uruk was gathered about it,
(A) Uruk-of-the-Fertile-Land gathered proudly around him.

ma-tum:

This word is from the Arabic root *mayth* ميث for "soft land". Recall, Cuneiform had no symbol for the letter *Thā'*. The word clearly points to the fertile marshland of southern Iraq, Sumer, and should be pronounced *maythum* مَيثُم, the way it was pronounced in later editions.

ePSD: mātu: the Land (of Sumer)

ميث (لسان العرب)
ماثَ الشيءَ مَيْثاً: مَرَسَه.
وماثَ المِلحَ في الماءِ: أذابه؛ وكذلك الطين، وقد انماثَ.
والمَيْثاءُ: الأَرضُ اللينةُ من غير رمل وكذلك الدَّمِثَة؛ وفي الصحاح: المَيْثاء الأَرض السَّهلة، والجمع مِيثٌ،

11. it-lu-tum ú-na-šá-ku ši-pi-šú

عتلوتم أُنَشَقو ظيفي ذو

(J) The heroes kissed its feet.
(G) the young men were kissing its feet.
(A) The warriors sniffed his legs,

ši-pi-šú:

The word ši-pi is from Arabic *ẓifī* ظيفي. Recall, Cuneiform writing did not include a symbol for the letters *Ẓā'*. Also, Western scholars used the letter "p" to represent the letter *Fā'*.

وظف (لسان العرب)
والوَظِيفُ لكل ذي أَربع: ما فوق الرُّسْغ إلى مَفْصِل الساق.
ووَظِيفا يدي الفرس: ما تحت رُكْبَتَيْه إلى جنبيه، ووظيفا رجليه: ما بين كعبيه إلى جنبيه.

12. ú-um-mi-id-ma pu-ti
وأُمِدمَ فوتي،

(J) It was raised up before me.
(G) I braced my forehead
(A) and laid down before me,

مدد (لسان العرب)
وشيء مَدِيد: ممدود
فوت (لسان العرب)
الفَوْتُ: الفَواتُ. فاتَني كذا أَي سَبَقَني،

13. i-mi-du ia-ti
يمِدو اياتي

(J) They stood me up.
(G) and they helped me push,
(A) helping me.

مدد (لسان العرب)
ومَدَدْنا القومَ: صِرْنا لهم أَنصاراً ومدَداً وأَمْدَدْناهم بغيرنا.

14. áš-ši-a-šú-ma ab-ba-la-áš-šú a-na ṣi-ri-ki
عسّيا ذوم أبعلى ذو عنَ ظهركِ

(J) I bore it and carried it to thee."
(G) I picked it up and carried it off to you."
(A) We roamed him in the dark, carried him upon you."

áš-ši-a-šú-ma:
Notice, the writer used áš-ši-a, here, but used áš-ši earlier (line #8). This word should be pronounced *ʿassaya* عسّيا for plural vs. *ʿassa* عسّ for single, exactly as Classical Arabic does.

ab-ba-la-áš-šú:

بعل (لسان العرب)
وهو بَعْلٌ على أهله أي ثِقْلٌ عليهم.

15. um-mi ^{d}Giš mu-di-a-at ka-la-ma
امّ جِحش مُهديت كلأم

(J) The mother of Gish, who knows all things,
(G) The mother of Gish, well versed in everything,
(A) The mother of *Jiḥsh*, guider of his vision,

It seems that there are several contradictions in George's reading of this line, which was repeated several times in both editions.

mu-di-a-at:
Both Jastraw and George derived this root word from *idû* or *edû* which according to CAD means "to clarify" or "to guide". I agree with this meaning, as this word is derived from Arabic *hadiya* هدي, since the Cuneiform writing system did not include a symbol for the letter *Hāʾ* and Western scholars unjustifiably used several sound symbols to represent it.

هدي (لسان العرب)
وقوله تعالى: أَوَلَم يَهْدِ لهم؛ قال أَبو عمرو بن العلاء: أَوَلَم يُبَيِّنْ لهم.

ka-la-ma:
This word was read by both scholars as the equivalent of Arabic *kul* كل for "all". That is possible. However, the addition of *–ma* indicates that the word here is likely a noun, particularly since this same

word was given by CAD the meanings "to clarify" or "to guide", too. I think this word was from Arabic *kala'ma* كلأم, in the meaning "his vision".

كلأ (لسان العرب)
ويقال: كَلأْتُ في أَمْرِك تكْلِيئاً أَي تأَمَّلْتُ ونَظَرتُ فيه، وكَلأْتُ في فلان: نَظَرْتُ إِليه مُتأَمِّلاً،

16. iz-za-kàr-am a-na ^{d}Giš

اذكرم عن جحش

(J) Spoke to Gish:
(G) said to Gish:
(A) said to *Jiḥsh*:

17. mi-in-di ^{d}Giš šá ki-ma ka-ti

منذ جحش ذا كيما كات

(J) "Someone, O Gish, who like thee
(G) "For sure, Gish, someone like yourself
(A) "Since this *Jiḥsh* existed, his look-alike existed.

mi-in-di:

Jastraw thought this word meant "someone" while George thought it meant "for sure" or "truly". However, neither claim can be supported by solid linguistic evidence. Here are the definitions of this word according to standard Western Akkadian references.

CAD: mindê: perhaps; since
ePSD: mindê: as if

I agree with the above two meanings. I believe this word is actually from Arabic *mindhu*منذ, but it was used in its original historical Classical Arabic equivalent *min idh kāna* من إذ كان meaning "since *such* was".

منذ (لسان العرب)

قال الليث: مُنْذُ النون والذال فيها أَصليان،

وسئل بعض العرب: لم خفضوا بمنذ ورفعوا بمذ فقال: لأَن منذ كانت في الأَصل من إذ كان كذا وكذا، وكثر استعمالها في الكلام فحذفت الهمزة وضمت الميم، وخفضوا بها على علة الأَصل، قال: وأَما مذ فإِنهم لما حذفوا منها النون ذهبت الآلة الخافضة وضموا الميم منها ليكون أَمتن لها، ورفعوا بها ما مضى مع سكون الذال ليفرقوا بها بين ما مضى وبين ما لم يمض؛

وحكي عن بني سليم: ما رأَيته مِنذ سِتٍّ، بكسر الميم ورفع ما بعده.

šá:

George desperately claimed this word meant "someone" because he needed the word "someone" to bring Enkidu in the scene. However, I think this word is the usual Arabic *dhā* for "this".

ki-ma:

Both scholars read this word as كيما for "like". I agree. However, I think here it meant "like him" or "his look-alike", a remarkable old Classical Arabic usage.

ka-ti:

Western Akkadian references claim *ka-ta* meant "you", just as the word at-ta did. The last one is clearly from Arabic an-ta meaning "you", with the letter *Nūn* assimilated. I believe ka-ta is actually *kana-ta* for "s/he was" or "he existed". The letter *Nūn* was assimilated here, too. The word *ka-ti* is therefore *kānati* referring to the look-alike existence. CDA listed kânu in the meaning of Arabic *kāna* كان from *yakūn* يكون. Accordingly, the statement was "*min idh kāna Gish dhā, kima kānat*" من اذ كان جيش ذا، كيما كانت. This would mean the next few lines are referring to the look-alike. In other words, this look-like (Enkidu) was possibly her son, too! Alternatively, it is possible the statement was "*min idh kāna Gish, dhā kima kānat*" من اذ

كان جيش، ذا كيما كنت. In such case *dhā kima* would mean together "his look-alike".

كون (لسان العرب)

الكَوْنُ: الحدَثُ، وقد كان كَوْناً وكَيْنُونة؛

وقال الجوهري: لم يك أَصله يكون، فلما دخلت عليها لم جزمتها فالتقى ساكنان فحذفت الواو فبقي لم يكن، فلما كثر استعماله حذفوا النون تخفيفاً، فإِذا تحركت أَثبتوها، قالوا لم يَكُنِ الرجلُ، وأَجاز يونس حذفها مع الحركة؛

غيره: وكان تدل على خبر ماضٍ في وسط الكلام وآخره، ولا تكون صلَةً في أَوَّله لأَن الصلة تابعة لا متبوعة؛

روي عن ابن الأَعرابي في قوله عز وجل: كُنتُم خَيْرَ أُمَّة أُخرجت للناس؛ أَي أَنتم خير أُمة، قال: ويقال معناه كنتم خير أُمة في علم الله

18. i-na ṣi-ri i-wa-li-id-ma

حين ظهري اولدم

(J) in the field was born and

(G) was born in the wild

(A) When my back delivered him

ṣi-ri:

Jastraw and CAD claim this word, which means "back", also means "field". I think do not think this word was used in that meaning. According to CAD, the Akkadians used eqlu for "field", clearly from Arabic *ḥiql* حقل. George modified its meaning arbitrarily to "wild", possibly because he was not convinced with CAD's meaning. Additionally, both scholars misread the line grammatically. I think the word ṣi-ri meant "back", which agrees with the way Iraqis refer to the process of giving birth to a child, even today.

19. ú-ra-ab-bi-šú šá-du-ú

وربي ذو سعدو

(J) whom the mountain has reared,
(G) and the upland has reared him.
(A) and his high star reared him,

šá-du-ú:
Although šá-du from Arabic *sadd* سد can possibly mean "mountain", but the writer's use of *á* rather than *a* indicates that the word was actually *sa'du* from Arabic *sa'd* سعد, which means star. The addition of –ú makes it "his star".

ePSD: šadû: mountain

سدد (لسان العرب)
والسَّدُّ، بالفتح والضم: الردم والجبل؛
سدا (لسان العرب)
وتَسدَّاه أَي علَاه
سعد (لسان العرب)
وسعد مرتفع به وجمعه سُعود.
والسُّعُدُ والسُّعود، الأَخيرة أَشهر وأَقيس: كلاهما سعود النجوم، وهي الكواكب التي يقال لها لكل واحد منها سَعْدِ

20. ta-mar-šú-ma [kima sal(?)] ta-ẖa-du at-ta
تأمرذوم [كيما سل] تخذو اتّ

(J) Thou wilt see (him) and [like a woman] thou wilt rejoice.
(G) You will see him and you will rejoice,
(A) seeing after him like a son you adopt,

ta-mar-šú-ma:
This unusual word is derived from amáru or amāru أمار, meaning "to see" according to Western Akkadian dictionaries. Even though this word is a bit peculiar, but it still seems to be related from the Arabic word *'ará* أرى meaning "to see", an already complicated word, or from *'amar* أمر, meaning "to see something happen" or "to order".

رأرأ (لسان العرب)
رأرأ : الرأرأة : تحريك الحدقة وتحديد النظر
مَنْ رأَ مِثْلَ مَعْمدانَ بنِ يَحْيَى، إذا ما النِّسْعُ طال على المَطِيَّهْ؟ ومَنْ رأَمثلَ
مَعْدانَ بن يَحْيَى، إذا هَبَّتْ شآمِيَةٌ عَرِيَّهْ؟ أَصل هذا: من رأَى
وجاء في الحديث: لا يتَمَرَّأَى أَحدُكم في الماء لا يَنْظُر وَجْهَه فيه،
تقول: جعلتُ الشَّيْءَ رَأْيَ عَيْنِك وبمَرْأًى مِنْكَ أَي حِذاءَكَ ومُقابِلَك بحيث تراه،
مرا (لسان العرب)
المرو : حجارة بيض براقة تكون فيها النار وتقدح منها النار
أمر (لسان العرب)
رجل إذا نزل به أمر ائتمر رأيه أي شاور نفسه وارتأى فيه قبل مواقعة الأمر ،

sal(?):

سلل (لسان العرب)
والسَّلِيلُ: الولد حين يخرج من بطن أُمه

21. it-lu-tum ú-na-šá-ku ši-pi-šú
عتلوتم انشقو ظيفي ذو

(J) Heroes will kiss his feet.
(G) The young men will kiss his feet.
(A) the warriors sniffed his legs.

22. tí-iṭ-ṭi-ra-áš-[šú] [tu-ut]-tu-ú-ma
تطّرأ ذو تتؤمَ

(J) Thou wilt spare [him and wilt endeavor]
(G) You will embrace him
(A) You will face him suddenly; you will take him like a twin.

tí-iṭ-ṭi-ra-áš-[šú]:
I an not sure how Jastraw came up with the meaning of "spare" for this word. Western Akkadian sources listed either šūzubu, clearly

from the Arabic root verb *shadhaba* شذب, in the meaning of "to protect" or "to save from harm", or padû, clearly from Arabic root verb *fadá* فدى, in the same meaning. George thought this word meant "embrace", but I found no trace to such usage. The word for "embrace" according to ePSD is edēru.

فدي (لسان العرب)
فَدَيْتُه فِدًى وفِداء وافْتَدَيْتُه؛
شذب (لسان العرب)
وشَذَبَ عنه شَذْباً أَي ذَبَّ.
كذلك كلُّ شيءٍ نُحِّي عن شيءٍ، فقد شُذِبَ عنه؛ كقوله: نَشْذِبُ عن خِنْذِفَ، حتى تَرْضَى أي ندفع عنها العِدا؛

I think this word is derived from Arabic *ṭar'a* طرأ, "to meet suddenly" particularly since the writer used –áš rather than –aš at the end of the word:

طرأ (لسان العرب)
طَرَأَ على القوم يَطْرَأُ طَرْءاً وطُرُوءاً: أَتاهم مِن مَكانٍ، أَو طَلَعَ عليهم من بَلَدٍ آخَرَ، أَو خرج عليهم مِن مكانٍ بَعيدٍ فُجاءة، أَو أَتاهم من غير أَن يَعْلَمُوا، أَو خَرَج عليهم من فَجْوةٍ.

[tu-ut]-tu-ú-ma:

It is very likely that the damaged symbols were ti-it, not tu-ut. Regardless, there are several possibilities for the meaning of this word, but none of them relates to Jastraw's "endeavor". I think this word is Arabic *titaw'ima* تتؤم. It is either in the meaning of "take him like a twin", or "to get along with":

تأم (لسان العرب)
وتاءَمَ أَخاه: وُلِدَ معه،
قال: والتَّوْأَمُ في أكثر ما ذكرتُ الأَصل فيه وَوْأَمٌ.
فالتَّوْأَمُ وَوْأَمٌ في الأَصل

وأم (لسان العرب)
واءَمَه وِئاماً ومُواءَمةً: وافقه.
وواءَمْتُه مُواءَمةً ووِئاماً: وهي المُوافَقة أَن تفعل كما يفعل.
إِنه لَيُوائمُ أَي يُوافِق؛ وقال أَبو زيد: هو إِذا اتَّبَع أَثَره وفعل فِعْلَه،

23. **ta-tar-ra-[as-su] a-na ṣi-[ri]-ia**
تتذرا ذو عنَ ظهريّ

(J) To lead him to me."
(G) and bring him to me."
(A) You will bring him upon me."

ta-tar-ra-[as-su]:
Jastraw and George probably derived this word from tarû, likely from the Arabic root word *dharā* ذرا. This is a good possibility. Recall, the letter *dhāl* did not have a Cuneiform symbol representation and was many times written with the sound of the letter *Tāʾ*. However, this word could also be from the Arabic root verb *tarar* ترر, in the meaning "to throw" or "push on":

ePSD: tarû: to lay down, cast, place; to set in place, imbue; to throw down; to release, let go; to pour out; to lead away

ذرا (لسان العرب)
وأَذْرَيْتُ الشيءَ إِذا أَلْقَيْتَه
وذَرى الشيءُ أَي سَقَط،
قال: وإِنما قيل أَذْرَيْت الشيءَ عن الشيء إِذا أَلقَيْتَه؛
ترر (لسان العرب)
وتَرَّ بِسَلْحِه يَتِرُّ: قذف به.
وتَرَّ النَّعامُ: أَلقى ما في بطنه.
وتُرَّ في يده: دفع.

24. [uš]-ti-nim-ma i-ta-mar šá-ni-tam

اتنِئم اتأمر ثانِتم

(J) He slept, he saw another

(G) He lay down, and had another

(A) He wailed, he saw, for a second time,

[uš]-ti-nim-ma:

This word is very likely it-ti-nim-ma from Arabic *n'ama* نأم meaning "to sigh" or "to wail", possibly in a dream or in a day vision. This would agree with the Assyrian tablet which did not explicitly mention sleeping, as we will see. However, "slept" or "dowsed" are possible meanings here.

نأم (لسان العرب)
النأْمةُ، بالتسكين: الصوتُ. نأَم الرجلُ يَنْئِمُ ويَنأَمُ نَئِيماً، وهو كالأَنِينِ،
والتَّناوُم: من النَّوْم،
نوم (لسان العرب)
النَّوْم: معروف. ابن سيده: النَّوْمُ النُّعاسُ. نامَ يَنامُ نَوْماً ونِياماً؛ عن سيبويه،
والاسمُ النِّيمةُ، وهو نائمٌ إذا رَقَدَ.

25. [šú-na]-ta i-ta-wa-a-am a-na um-mi-šú

شأنت اتوأم عن امي ذو

(J) dream, which he reported to his mother:

(G) dream. He rose and spoke to his mother:

(A) a vision. He conveyed it to his mother:

i-ta-wa-a-am:

This is the same word we saw in line #22, but it is used in a different meaning here:

تأم (لسان العرب)
قال: والتَّوأَمُ في أَكثر ما ذكرتُ الأَصل فيه وَوأَمٌ.

فالتَّوأمُ ووَأمٌ في الأَصل
وأتأَمَها أي أفْضاها؛
فضا (لسان العرب)
وأفْضى فلان إلى فلان أي وَصلَ إليه

26. [um-mi] a-ta-mar šá-ni-tam
أمي اتأمر ثانِتم

(J) ["My mother,] I have seen another
(G) "O mother, I have had another dream.
(A) "Mother, I am seeing, for a second time,

27. [šú-na-tu] [a-ta]-mar e-mi-a i-na su-ḵi-im
شأنت. اتأمر حميّ حين سوقم

(J) [Dream.] My likeness I have seen in the streets
(G) ..... in the street
(A) a vision. I am seeing a heated gathering (fight?) in the market

e-mi-a:
It is strange how Jastraw derived the meaning "my likeness" from this word. He read it as *ḥimiyya* حميّ and thought it was related to *ḥimu* حمو, which in Akkadian and Arabic stands for "in-law". George conveniently ignored the word! This word is yet, another example of the fruitless approach of inventing sounds for a separate, *made-up* Akkadian language, rather than using existing historical Arabic etymological references. Let's examine the following confused word entries in CAD:

CAD: emmu: hot	[related to Arabic ḥāmi حمِو]
CAD: emmūtu: hotness	[related to Arabic ḥumūtu حُموتو]
CAD: emu: in-law	[related to Arabic ḥamū حَمو]
CAD: emētu: aunt	[related to Arabic ʿammitu عمِتو]

With a little help from the Iraqi dialect, *e-mi-a* is clearly *ḥamiyyah* حَمِيّة meaning "heated argument", "heated fight", "heated gathering", or "heated contest". This word is a solid classical Arabic word.

حما (لسان العرب)
حَمْوُ المرأة وحَمُوها وحَماها
وحَمِيَت الشمسُ والنارُ تَحْمَى حَمْياً وحُمِياً وحُمُواً، الأَخيرة عن اللحياني: اشتدَّ حَرُّها، وأَحْماها اللهُ، عنه أَيضاً. الصحاح: اشْتَدَّ حَمْيُ الشمسِ وحَمْوُها بِمعْنىً.
والحِمْيَةَ والحِمَى: ما حُمِيَ من شيءٍ،
وفلان ذُو حَمِيَّةٍ مُنْكَرَةَ إذا كان ذا غضب وأَنَفَةٍ.
والحُمَيّاً شِدَّةُ الغضب وأَوَّلُه.

28. **[šá Uruk]^{ki} ri-bi-tim**
ذا اوروك ربيتم

(J) [Of Erech] of the plazas.
(G) of Uruk-the-Town-Square,
(A) of Uruk-of-the-Hill.

ri-bi-tim:

ربا (لسان العرب)
والرَّبْوُ والرَّبْوَةُ والرُّبْوَةُ والرِّبْوَة والرَّباوة والرُّباوة والرِّباوَة والرَّابِيَة والرَّباةُ: كلُّ ما ارْتَفَعَ من الأَرض وربَا؛

29. **ḫa-aṣ-ṣi-nu na-di-i-ma**
خصينو نَدْيِمَ

(J) An axe was brandished, and
(G) An axe was lying
(A) An axe fell (thrown?)

ḫa-aṣ-ṣi-nu:

خصن (لسان العرب)
ابن الأَعرابي: من أَسماء الفأْس الخَصِينُ والحَدَثانُ والمِكْشاح.

na-di-i-ma:

ندي (لسان العرب)
والنَّدَى: ما يَسْقُط بالليل،
ويقال : ما نَدِيَني من فلان شيء أَكْرَهُه أي ما بلَّني ولا أَصابني
ونَوادي النَّوى: ما تَطايرَ منها تحت المِرْضَخة.
ندأ (لسان العرب)
نَدَأَ اللحمَ يَنْدَؤُه نَدْءاً: أَلقاهُ في النار، أَو دَفَنَه فيها.

30. e-li-šú pa-aḫ-ru
حلي ذو فخرو

(J) They gathered about him;
(G) with a crowd gathered around.
(A) around (over?) a proud one (a miniature goat?)

pa-aḫ-ru:
A similar word pa-ḫi-ir (gathered proudly, or prided itself), clearly a verb, was used in line #10 *before* e-li-šú (meaning "around him") and *after* a subject, "Uruk". This prompted both scholars to rush in explaining it identically! However, here it is *after* e-li-šú and *after* a verb, "thrown". Most importantly, here, the word is pa-aḫ-ru, not pa-ḫi-ir, clearly a noun, following šú in the meaning "belong to", to make the term *dhū fakhr* ذو فخر, either a nickname "the one with pride", or "son of pride", a classical Arabic usage. I think "e-li-šú pa-aḫ-ru" together means "around the one with horns"—a goat or gazelle—, or "around a proud one"—a person.

31. ḫa-aṣ-ṣi-nu-um-ma šá-ni bu-nu-šú
خصينُمَ شعنِ (سعنِ؟) بون ذو

(J) And the axe made him angry.
(G) The axe itself, it was strange of shape;

(A) The axe of (falling around) the shabby one (goat?) missed him.

ḫa-aṣ-ṣi-nu-um-ma:

The previous word was ḫa-aṣ-ṣi-nu, axe, while this was ḫa-aṣ-ṣi-nu-um-ma, "axe of".

šá-ni:

I think this word is either *sha'ni* شعن, meaning "someone with long, not groomed, hair", or *sa'ni* سعن, meaning "a miniature goat". If it is miniature goat, which was historically equated by the Arabs with bad luck, according to *Lisān al-'Arab*, this may indicate that the axe was intentionally targeting him. Both meanings fit well with the character of Enkidu in the epic.

شعن (لسان العرب)

اشْعَنَّ الشعر: انْتَفَشَ.

والعرب تقول: رأَيت فلاناً مُشْعانَّ الرأْس إذا رأَيته شَعِثاً مُنْتَفِشَ الرأس مُغْبَرّاً أَشْعَثَ.

وفي الحديث: فجاء رجل مُشْعانٌّ بغنم يسوقها؛ هو المُنْتَفِش الشعر الثائر الرأْس. يقال: شَعَرٌ مُشْعانّ ورجل مُشْعانٌّ ومُشْعانُّ الرأْس، والميم زائدة.

سعن (لسان العرب)

وقيل: السَّعْنة من المِعْزى صغار الأَجسام في خَلْقها،

وقيل: السَّعْنة المشؤُومة

bu-nu-šú:

This word is the key word to understand the reason for the gathering. Jastraw correctly believed it was a verb, but his meaning, "made him angry" referring to "my likeness", is wrong. Certainly, it does not explain or justify the astonished gathering mentioned in the Assyrian tablet as we will see in the next chapter. George thought the word was a noun, meaning "its shape", referring to the axe, an even less astonishing event. Historical Classical Arabic teaches us that the verb/noun root, *bawn* بون, relates to distance. In this case, it was used as a verb to indicate that the axe had *miraculously* missed him (or was visually diverted), falling next to him. This event can certainly justify a gathering and/or an astonishment!

بون (مقاييس اللغة)

الباء والواو والنون أصلٌ واحدٌ، وهو البُعْد. قال الخليل: يقال بينهما بَوْنٌ بعيد وبُونٌ -على وزن حَوْر وحُور- وبَيْنٌ بعيدٌ أيضاً، أي فَرْقٌ.قال ابنُ الأعرابيّ: بانَني فلان يَبُونُني، إذا تَباعَدَ مِنك أو قَطَعَك. قال وبانَني يَبينُني مثله.

32. a-mur-šú-ma aḫ-ta-du a-na-ku

أمُرذوم اختذو أنَكو

(J) I saw him and I rejoiced,

(G) I saw it and I grew glad.

(A) I saw him, I took him myself.

aḫ-ta-du:

The meanings "became glad" or "rejoiced" for this word can both be correct. This word is from *'akhadha* أخذ, meaning "took". Taking anything can bring joy. However, I think here it does mean "took".

أخذ (لسان العرب)

الأَخْذ: خلاف العطاء

وقولهم: أَخَذْتُ كذا يُبدلون الذال تاء فيُدْغمونها في التاء، وبعضهم يُظهرُ الذال، وهو قليل.

a-na-ku:

This is an interesting word. Professor *al-Jibūrī* thought it was *anā* or "I" from *anā*+akū أكو + أنا, using the well-known Iraqi word akū from *'akun* أكُن. He is right. However, I think it means "I, myself" not just "I" because the Akkadians also used *anā* alone in many cases.

33. a-ra-am-šú-ma ki-ma áš-šá-tim

ارأم ذوم كيما أساتِم

(J) I loved him as a woman,

(G) Like a wife I loved it,

(A) I caressed him like a mother,

a-ra-am-šú-ma:

رأم (لسان العرب)

رَئِمتِ الناقةُ ولدها تَرْأَمُهُ رأْماً ورَأَماناً: عطفتْ عليه ولزمته،

وكل من لزم شيئاً وأَلِفَهُ وأَحبَّه فقد رَئِمَهُ؛

وكلُّ من أَحبَّ شيئاً وأَلِفَهُ فقد رَئِمَهُ.

والرُّئِمُ: الاست؛ عن كراع، حكاها بالألف واللام

áš-šá-tim:

While it is possible that the Akkadians had used this word to mean "woman", I think it was likely for an "adult woman" or "mother". This word literally means "the one with the big bottom" in Arabic. Because this is not likely to refer to young women, and because the word was used with *r'ama* رأم for "motherly caressing", it was very likely in the meaning of "mother".

سته (لسان العرب)

السَّتْهُ والسَّتَهُ والاسْتُ: معروفة،

والاسْتُ العَجُزُ

والسَّتِهُ: الطالبُ للاسْتِ،

34. a-ḫa-ab-bu-ub el-šú

احبب إلذو

(J) I embraced him.

(G) caressed it and embraced it,

(A) kissing all over him.

a-ẖa-ab-bu-ub:

Eventhough this word is related to *ḥub* حب, or love, Iraqis, even today, use it in the meaning of "kiss". It is typical in southern Iraq to say "*ḥib īdah*" meaning "kiss his hand"!

35. el-ki-šú-ma áš-ta-ka-an-šú

حلقي (إلكي؟) ذوم استكن ذو

(J) I took him and regarded him

(G) I took it up and set it

(A) I shaved (fed?) him, tamed (calmed?) him

el-ki-šú-ma:

I am not sure how both, Jastraw and George, concluded that this word means "took" since there is no trace for it anywhere I looked. Possibly they thought it meant "to me" followed by šú (dhū), a far-fetched desperate reading. They possibly assumed -ki, Sumerian for "with (in math)" was used here to indicate "addition of something".

I believe this word was either from Arabic *'alaka* ألك (or 'alaka علك) meaning "to make one chew" or "to feed", or from the Arabic root verb *h'alaqa* حلق, meaning "to cut hair" or "to shave" for people and goats! Both meanings would fit with the events of the epic. The second word seems extremely old, because it has pages and pages of usages in the historical Classical Arabic references. The Akkadian words kasāsu and kuš, from Arabic root *qaṣaṣa* قصص, meaning "to cut", are also used in Akkadian, but for lamb shearing.

ألك (لسان العرب)

في ترجمة علج: يقال هذا أَلوكُ صِدْقٍ وعَلوك صِدْقٍ وعَلُوج صِدْقٍ لما يؤكل، وما تَلَوَّكْتُ بأَلوكٍ وما تَعَلَّجْتُ بعَلوج. الليث: الأَلوك الرسالة وهي المأْلُكة، على مَفْعُلة، سميت أَلوكاً لأَنه يُؤْلَكُ في الفم مشتق من قول العرب: الفرس يأْلُك

اللُّجُمَ، والمعروف يلوك أو يَعْلُك أي يمضغ. ابن سيده: أَلَكَ الفرسُ اللجام في فيه يأْلُكه علَكه.

علك (مقاييس اللغة)

العين واللام والكاف أصلٌ صحيح يدلٌّ على شيء شبه المضغ والقبض على الشّيء. من ذلك قول الخليل: العَلْك: المضغ.

ويقال: علَكت الدّابّةُ اللّجامَ، وهي تعلُكُه علْكاً.

ePSD: kasāsu: gnaw; to shear, pluck wool

ePSD: kuš7: horse (groom)

حلق (لسان العرب)

والاحْتِلاقُ: الحلْق. يقال: حلَق مَعَزه، ولا يقال: جَزّه إلا في الضأْن، وعنز مَحلْوقة، وحُلاقة المِعزى، بالضم: ما حُلِق من شعره.

ويقال: إن رأْسه لَجيدٌ الحِلاق. قال ابن سيده: الحلْق في الشعر من الناس والمعز كالجزّ في الصوف، حلَقه يَحلِقه حلْقاً فهو حالقٌ وحلاقٌ وحلَقه واحْتلَقه؛

36. a-na a-ḫi-ia

عنَ أخيّ

(J) As my brother."

(G) at my side."

(A) to (me), his brother.

a-ḫi-ia:

George read the word a-ḫi-ia, which means "my brother", as "my side", a desperate attempt to justify his believe that this dream involved the axe being transformed to a person! For this word, I agree with Jastraw's reading, which was in the meaning of "as a brother".

37. um-mi ^{d}Giš mu-da-at [ka]-la-ma

أمّ جِحش مُهديت كلأم

(J) The mother of Gish, who knows all things,

(G) The mother of Gish, well versed in everything,

(A) The mother of *Jiḥsh*, guider of his vision,

38. [iz-za-kàr-am a-na ^{d}Giš]

[اذكرم عنَ جِحش]

(J) [Spoke to Gish]:

(G) [said to Gish]:

(A) [said to Gish]:

39. [^{d}Giš šá ta-mu-ru amêlu]

[..........................]

(J) ["O Gish, the man whom thou sawest,]

(G) [...............................]

(A) [...............................]

40. [ta-ẖa-ab-bu-ub ki-ma áš-šá-tim el-šú]

[..........................]

(J) [Whom thou didst embrace like a woman].

(G) [...............................]

(A) [...............................]

41. áš-šum uš-[ta]-ma-ẖa-ru it-ti-ka

آذم استمخارو إتيك

(J) (means) that he is to be associated with thee."

(G) .... so that I shall make him your equal."

(A) this (means): his real-life transformed equal is selected to you."

uš-[ta]-ma-ẖa-ru:

Although the previous three lines were damaged, this line is more or less clear. The root verb of this word is clearly *makhara* مخر. This word was used several times in the Assyrian Tablet, too. However, the writer there used ul rather than uš, the usual Arabic language approach to either derive a noun or a certain verb tense. Compare the following usages of the word in both tablets. Notice that the "š" was assimilated to "l" in the later edition, as we saw when deriving the name for Gilgamesh:

uš-[ta]-ma-ḫa-ru
ul-ta-maḫ-ḫar-šú
tul-tam-ḫi-ri-šú
ul-tam-ḫi-ra-šú

The two primary meanings of the root verb behind this word in all historical Arabic references were "to sail or cut through" or "to choose a person". In their explanations, they compared the process of choosing a person to sailing through in a "sea" of human waves to select that special someone. All this indicates that this word was possibly used by the Akkadians to mean some sort of a transformation/creation/selection process, likely done by a god or someone with special powers, to deliver an "equal", "clone", or a "chosen person". This would agree with the readings by both Jastraw and George. Even though, the main meaning of the word maḫāru according to CAD and ePSD fully agrees with all historical Arabic etymological references, neither one listed the meaning "to choose", indicated by the Arabic references:

ePSD: maḫāru: to confront; to oppose; to withstand; to face; to block

مخر (لسان العرب)
والمَخْرُ في الأَصل: الشَّقُّ. مَخَرَتِ السفينةُ الماءَ: شقَّتْه بِصَدْرِها وجَرَتْ.
ومَخَرَ الأَرضَ إِذا شقها للزراعة.
وامْتَخَرَ الشيءَ: اخْتارَه.
ومَخَرَ البيتَ يَمْخَرُه مَخْراً: أخَذَ خِيارَ متاعِه فذهب به.

مخر (الصّحّاح في اللغة)
وامْتَخَرْتُ القومَ: انتقيت خيارهم ونُخْبَتَهُم.
والمِخْرَةُ والمُخْرَةُ: الشيء الذي تختاره.
مخر (مقاييس اللغة)
وقولهم: امتخَرْتُ القومَ، إذا انتقيْتَ خِيارَهم، كأنّه شقّ النّاس إليه حتّى انتخبَه.
مَخَرَتِ (القاموس المحيط)
وفي لَفْظٍ: "استَمْخِروا الريحَ"
خرت (لسان العرب)
الخَرْتُ والخُرْتُ: الثّقْبُ في الأُذن،
والمَخْروتُ المَشقوقُ الشّفَة.

42. ᵈGiš šú-na-tam i-pa-šar
جِحش شأنتم إفَسر

Gish understood the dream.
As Gish related the dream,
Jiḥsh, his vision became clear.

i-pa-šar:

Notice the writer used the word i-pa-áš-šar in the first line, adding the part -áš- in the middle. This was not arbitrary. In the first line the word was equivalent to Arabic *yufassar* يُفسّر . In this line it is likely *itfassar* إتفسّر or *yitfssar* يِتفسر, in the meaning "was explained" or "became clear".

فسر (لسان العرب)
الفَسْرُ: البيان. فَسَرَ الشيءَ يفسِرُه، بالكَسر، وتَفْسُرُه، بالضم، فَسْراً وفَسَّرَه: أبانه، والتّفْسيرُ مثله. ابن الأَعرابي: التّفْسيرُ والتأْويل والمعنى واحد.
وقوله عز وجل: وأَحْسَنَ تَفْسيراً؛ الفَسْرُ: كشف المُغَطّى، والتّفْسير كَشف المُراد عن اللفظ المُشْكل، والتأْويل: ردّ أَحد المحتملين إلى ما يطابق الظاهر.
واسْتَفْسَرْتُه كذا أي سأَلته أن يُفَسِّره لي.

4

A Comparative Detailed Reading in the Assyrian Tablets

I will read in this chapter the section of the Standard Edition (~1000 BCE) —mainly from the Assyrian tablets—, where the two dreams of Gilgamesh were told. We are fortunate to have several copies of this edition. Many damaged areas were cross checked between them to fill in and confirm the actual Cuneiform text on lines.

Below, I will first present George's Roman transliteration of the text of that section, which is part of the first tablet in the Assyrian edition. I will not list every line from other alternative tablets. Instead, I will only list one line incorporating the completed text. When an alternative word or line is listed, I will place them between curly brackets.

Next, I will transliterate the same text in Arabic letters filling the sounds omitted as a result of both, the Roman transliteration and the lack of equivalent Sumerian Cuneiform symbols. Then, I will provide two translations in paragraph format including punctuations, the first by George ("G"), and other one by the author ("A"). Finally, I will present a detailed comparative analysis and discussion of the two readings and translations. Note that many lines of these tablets included some assumed Sumerian Cuniform words. I will only translate and analyze the Akkadian words and substitute most Sumerian words with an ellipsis "..." symbol:

244. ^{d}GIŠ-gím-maš ina ŠÀ UNUG^{ki} i-na-aṭ-ṭa-la šu-na-te-ka
245. it-bé-ma ^{d}GIŠ-gím-maš šu-na-ta BÚR-ár MU-ra a-na AMA-šú
246. um-mi MÁŠ.GI_6 aṭ-ṭu-la mu-ši-ti-ia
247. ib-šu-nim-ma MUL.MEŠ AN-e
248. GIM ki-iṣ-ru ša da-«nim» {im-ta-naq-qu-tú}{im-taq-qu»-ta} e-lu EDIN-ia
249. áš-ši-šu-ma «da»-an e-li-ia
250. ul-tab-lak-ki-is-su-«ma» ul e-le-'-i-a nu-us-«su»
251. UNUGki ma-a-tum iz-za-az UGU-[šu]
252. [ma-a-tu pu-uḫ-ḫu-rat] in[a muḫ-ḫi-šú]
253. [i-tep-pi-ir um-m]a-nu U[GU E]DIN-[šú] {with line 254}
254. [GURUŠ.MEŠ uk]-tam-ma-ru UGU-[šú]
255. [ki-i šèr-ri la]-«'»-i ú-na-šá-qu GÌR.[MEŠ-šú]
256. [a-ram-šú-ma GI]M áš-šá-te UGU-šú aḫ-bu-[ub]
257. [áš-šá-áš-šu-ma a]t-ta-di-šú ina šap-li-[ki] { with 258}
258. [u at-ti tul_5-t]a-maḫ-ri-šu it-ti-[i]a
259. [um-mi dGIŠ-gím-maš {em-qet}{en-qet} mu-d]a-at ka-la-ma i-de MU-ár ana EN-[š]á
260. [^{f}ri-mat-^{d}n]in-sún {em-qet}{en-qet} mu-da-a-tú ka-la-ma i-de MU-ár ana ^{d}GIŠ-gímmaš
261. [ib-š]u-nik-ka {MUL AN-e}{ MUL.MEŠ [ ]}
262. [ki]-<ma ki>-ṣir šá da-nim {im-ta-qu-ut e-lu [ ]} {[šá] ŠUB.MEŠ UGU EDIN-ka}
263. taš-ši-šu-ma {«da»-nu}{[ ]-an} {e-l[i-k]a} {UGU-ka}
264. tul-tab-lak-kit-su-ma ul te-le-'-i-a nu-us-su
265. taš-šá-áš-šum-ma «ta»-ad-di-šú ina šap-li-ia
266. u a-na-ku {ul-[ta]m-ḫi-raš-šú}{[-ma]ḫ-ḫar-šu}{it-ti-ka} {KI$^{!}$(DI)-[ ]}
267. ta-ram-šu-ma «GIM» DAM {e-li-šú taḫ-[bu-ub]}
268. il-la-«kak»-kúm-«ma dan»-nu tap-pu-ú mu-še-zib ib-ri
269. ina KUR da-an {e-mu-qí-šú}{e-mu-qí i-[šu/i]}
270. «ki-ma ki»-ṣir šá da-nim du-un-nu-nu e-mu-qa-a-šú

271. «ta-ram-šu»-ma GIM DAM {ta-ḫab-bu-bu UGU-šú} { e-li-šú taḫ-b[u-ub]}
272. [«šu-ú dan»-nu uš-te-n]é-zeb-ka ka-[a]-«šá» {«šu-ú dan»-nu ú-še-zeb ka-a-šú}
273. šá-ni-tum i-ta-mar šu-na-at-tú
274. [i]t-bé-e-ma i-te-ru-ub ana IGI ^{d}15 AMA-šú
275. «d»GIŠ-gím-maš ana šá-ši-ma MU-«ár» ana AMA-šú
276. [i]p-pu-un-na-a AMA-a a-ta-mar šá-ni-ta šu-ut-ta
277. [ina SILA] šá UNUGki re-bi-tum :
278. ḫa-ṣi-nu na-di-ma UGU-šú {paḫ-ru}{paḫ-ri}
279. [UNUGk]i ma-a-tú iz-za-zu UGU-šú
280. [ma-a-tú puḫ]-ḫu-rat ina muḫ-ḫi-šú
281. i-te-ep-pir [<ummānu> UG]U EDIN-šú
282. [GURUŠ.MEŠ u]k-«tam»-mar UGU-šú :
283. áš-šá-áš-šum$^{!}$-ma {at-ta-di-iš} { at-ta-di-šu} ina šap-li-ku
284. [a-ram-š]u-ma ki-i áš-šá-te UGU-šú aḫ-bu-ub
285. [u at-ti t]ul^{5}-ta-maḫ-ḫa-ri-šu it-ti-ia
286. «AMA ^{d}giš-gím-maš» em-qet mu-da-at ka-lá-ma i-de MU-ra ana DUMU-šá
287. «fri-mat-dnin-sún en-qet mu-da-at ka-lá-ma i-de MU-ra ana dGIŠ-gím-maš
288. [DUM]U! ḫa-ṣi-in-nu šá ta-mu-ru ib-ri
289. ta-ram-šu-ma GIM DAM ta-ḫab-bu-bu UGU-šú
290. u a-na-ku ul-ta-maḫ-ḫar-šú it-ti-ka
291. il-la-ka-ak-kúm-ma dan-nu tap-pu-ú mu-še-zib ib-ri
292. ina KUR da-an e-mu-qa «i»-[šu]
293. ki-ma ki-ṣir šá da-nim dun-nu-nu / e-mu-qa-a-šú
294. «d»GIŠ-gím-maš ana šá-ši-ma MU-ár a-na AMA-šú
295. [u]m-ma ina KA ^{d}en-líl ma-lik lim-qut-a[m-ma]
296. ib-ri ma-li-ku a-na-ku lu-ur- ur-ši
297. [lu-u]r-ši-ma ib-ri {ma-li-ku} {ma-lik} a-na-ku
298. [i-t]a-mar šu-na-t[i-šu :]

244. جِحْشجِّحْمَش إنّ ذا أروك انّطلَ شأْناتكَ
245. اتبغم جِحْشجِّحْمَش شأنتَ ... عنَ امي ذو
246. أمي ... أطل مسيتيّ
247. ابذونم ...
248. كيما قصر ذا انيم امتنقتو {امتقت} حلي
249. عسٌّ ذوم ذعن حليّ
250. التبلك ذوم ول العيّ نسّ ذو
251. اروك مَيثُم عِزّز [حلي] ذو
252. مَيثو فُخُرت إن مخي ذو
253. اتفر أُمّعنو حولي ... ذو
254. ... أُقتمرو حلي ذو
255. كي سِهري لَعي أُنشقو [أرجله]
256. ارأم ذوم كيما أساتَ حلي ذو أحببُ
257. عسس ذوم أعتّدِ ذو إنَ سَفلِك
258. وانت تُلتَمخري ذو إتيّ
259. أمي جِحْشجِّحْمَش عِمقَت مُهديت كلأم يذ ... عنَ ذا
260. رِيمَت نِنْسون عِمقَت مُهديت كلأم يذ .. عنَ جِحْشجِّحْمَش
261. ابذونك ...
262. كيما قصر ذا انيم إمتَقُت حلي ...
263. تعسّي ذوم دَعَن حلِّك
264. تُلتَبلَكت ذوم ول تلّعيّ نسّ ذو
265. تعساّ ذوم تعدّ ذو إن سفليّ
266. وانَكو أُلتمخِرا ذو إتيكَ
267. ترأم ذوم كيما أسات، تحبُبُ حلي ذو
268. اليكَ كوم ذأن تفو مشذب إبر
269. ان [ارض] ذعنْ حمُقي يذو
270. كيما قِصر ذا انيم ذُعُنٌّ حمقى أ ذو
271. ترأم ذوم كيما أسات، تَحبُبَ حلي ذو

272. ذوو ذأن أُشتنَذَبْكَ كا ذا {ذوو ذأن أُشذَب كا ذو}

273. ثانِيتُم إتأمر شأّنتو

274. اتبغم يتَرعُب عنَ ... امي ذو

275. ... جِحْشجّحْمَش عنَ ساسِمَ ... عنى امي ذو

276. أفنّا أمّاه أتأمر ثانِتَ شأّنتَ

277. إنَ ... اروك ربيتم

278. خصين نَديمَ حلي ذو فَخرْ

279. أروك ميَثو عِزّزحلي ذو

280. مَيثو فُخُرت أنَ مُخي ذو

281. إتّفِر أُمّعنو حلي ... ذو

282. ... أُقتمرو حولي ذو

283. عساّذوم أعتدّ ذو إنَ سفَلِك

284. أرأم ذوم كي أساتَ حلي ذو أحبُب

285. وأتّ تلُتَمَخري ذو إتيّ

286. امي جِحْشجّحْمَش عِمقَت مُهديت كلأم يذ ... عنَ ذا

287. رِيمَت نِنْسون عِمقَت مُهديت كلأم يذ ... عنَ جِحْشجّحْمَش

288. ... خَصينو ذا تمعُرو ابر

289. ترأم ذوم كيما أسات، تَحبُبَ حلي ذو

290. وانَكو أُلتمخَرَ ذو إتيكَ

291. اليكَ كومَ ذأن تَفو مُشَذّب إبرِ

292. إنَ أرض ذعنْ حمقي يذو

293. كيما قصر ذا انيم ذُعُنُّ حمُقى أ ذو

294. .. جِحْشجّحْمَش عنَ ساسِمَ ... عنى امي ذو

295. أُماّه إنَ كا إنليل ملَك لإمقُعتَمَ

296. إبرِ ملِكو أنَكو لأُرسي

297. لأُرسِيمَ إبرِ ملِكو أنَكو

298. ... اتأمر شأّنتي ذو

George's Translation

Gilgamesh in Uruk was seeing you in dreams. Gilgamesh rose to relate a dream, saying to his mother:
"O mother, this is the dream I had in the night –
"The stars of the heavens appeared above me,
like a rock from the sky one fell down before me.
I lifted it up, but it weighted too much for me,
I tried to roll it, but I could not dislodge it.
The land of Uruk was standing around it,
[the land was gathered] about it.
A crowd [was milling about] before it,
[the menfolk were] thronging around it.
[Like a babe-in]-arms they were kissing its feet,
like a wife [I loved it,] caressed and embraced it.
[I lifted it up,] set it down at your feet,
[and you, O mother, you] made it my equal."

The mother of Gilgamesh was clever and wise, well versed in everything, she said to her son. Wild-Cow Ninsun was clever and wise, well versed in everything, she said to Gilgamesh:
"The stars of heaven [appeared] above you,
[like a] rock from the sky one fell down before you.
You lifted it up, but it weighed too much for you,
you tried to roll it, but you could not dislodge it.
You lifted up, set it down at my feet,
and, I, Ninsun, I made it your equal.
Like a wife you loved it, caressed and embraced it:
a mighty comrade will come to you, and be his friend's saviour.
Mightiest in the land, strength he possesses,
his strength is as mighty as a rock from the sky.
Like a wife you will love him, caress and embrace him,

he will be mighty, and often will save you"

Having had a second dream, he rose and entered before the goddess,
his mother. Said Gilgamesh to her, to his mother:
"Once more, O mother, have I had a dream -
"[In the street] of Uruk-the-Town-Square,
an axe was lying with a crowd gathered around.
The land [of Uruk] was standing around it,
[the country was] gathered about it.
A crowd *was milling about* before it,
[the menfolk were] thronging around it.
"I lifted it up and set it down on your feet,
like a wife [I loved] it, caressed and embraced it,
[and you O mother,] you made it my equal"

The mother of Gilgamesh was clever and wise, well versed in everything, she said to her son. Wild-Cow Ninsun was clever and wise, well versed in everything, she said to Gilgamesh:
"My son the ax you saw is a friend,
like a wife you will love him, caress and embrace him,
and I, Ninsun, I shall make him your equal."
A mighty comrade will come to you, and be his friend's saviour,
mightiest in the land, strength he possesses,
his strength is as mighty as a rock from the sky."
Said Gilgamesh to her, to his mother,
"May it befall me, O mother, by Counselor Enlil's command!
Let me acquire a friend to counsel me,
a friend to counsel me I will acquire"

[So did Gilgamesh] saw his dreams!

Author's Translation

Jiḫshi-Jiḫmash in this Uruk saw ahead your (coming) visions.
Jiḫshi-Jiḫmash demanded his vision be explained, he recounted to his mother:
"Mother, during my early evening, from between those stars of heaven, [like] a horse of Anim fell around me.
I roamed with him (flew?) in the dark, he obeyed (wrapped around?) me.
I rushed him around, not afraid of his speed.
Uruk-of-the-Fertile-Land gathered with honor around him.
The land became proud by his purity (pure bones?).
He astonished and puzzled a large crowd before him.
[Their men] gathered under moon light around him.
[Like freighted babies] they smelled his legs.
I caressed him, like his mother, kissing all over him.
I roamed him in the dark, prepared him down at your feet.
And you transformed/selected his real equal to me.

Mother of *Jiḫši-jiḫmash* thought deeply, the guider of his vision, said to him. The-Favorite-of-Ninsūn thought deeply, the guider of his vision, said to *Jiḫši-jiḫmash*:
From between those stars of heaven, like a horse of Anim fell upon you.
You roamed with him in the dark, he obeyed (wrapped around?) you.
You rushed him around, not afraid of his speed.
You roamed with him in the dark, prepared him down at my feet.
And I, myself, had transformed/selected his real equal to you.
You will caress him, like his mother, kissing all over him.
To you, he is a look-alike, a loyal mighty one, a saver of a comrade.
On earth, he is obedient; (his) devotion is entirely to you.

Like the horse of Anim had obeyed, (with his) devotion to you.
You will caress him, like his mother, kissing all over him.
The mighty one will ask you to save (him), as he will (save) you"
{The mighty one will save (you), as you will (save) him"}

For a second time he had his vision. He demanded, trembling, from the goddess, his mother; *Jiḫshi-Jiḫmash* screamed to her, said to his mother:
"Help me, O mother, I am seeing for the second time his vision.
[In the Market] of Uruk-of-the-Hill,
an axe fell (thrown?) around (over?) a proud one (a goat?).
Uruk-of-the-Fertile-Land gathered with honor around him.
The land became proud by his purity (pure bones?).
He astonished and puzzled a large crowd before him.
[Their men] gathered under moon light around him.
I roamed him in the dark, prepared him down at your feet.
I caressed him, like his mother, kissing all over him.
and you, transformed/selected his real equal to me."

Mother of *Jiḫši-jiḫmash* thought deeply, the guider of his vision, said to him. The-Favorite-of-Ninsūn thought deeply, the guider of his vision, said to Jiḫši-jiḫmash:
"My son, this axe saves (sees after? recognizes?) a comrade.
You will caress him, like his mother, kissing all over him.
and I, myself, had transformed/selected his real equal to you.
To you, he will be a look-like, a mighty loyal one, a saver of a comrade.
On earth, he is obedient; his devotion is entirely to you.
Like the horse of Anim had obeyed, (with) his devotion to you."

Jiḫši-jiḫmash, screamed to her, to his mother:

"O mother, by Counselor Enlil, let me have one to fall upon him.
A comrade, I have for myself, to safeguard me.
Let me safeguard a comrade, I have for myself."

[So, *Jiḥshi-Jiḥmash*] saw your (coming) visions!

Analysis and Discussion

244. ^{d}GIŠ-gím-maš ina ŠÀ UNUG^{ki} i-na-aṭ-ṭa-la šu-na-te-ka

جِحْشِجِّحْمَش إنّ ذا أروك إنّطلَ شُأناتَكَ

(G) Gilgamish in Uruk was seeing you in dreams:
(A) *Jiḥshi-Jiḥmash* in this Uruk saw ahead your (coming) visions:

i-na-aṭ-ṭa-la:
This line illustrates remarkable usages of Classical Arabic words in a astonishing flawless Classical Arabic sentence! The meaning of the underlining word naṭālu in the Western Akkadian dictionaries is also given in the Classical Arabic etymological references. This word is from Arabic naṭala نطل or na'ṭala نأطل also indicating the meanings of "seeing ahead", or "geniusely seeing ahead".

CAD: naṭālu: to see ahead; to see, to watch; to examine;

نطل (لسان العرب)
والنِّئْطِلُ والنَّيْطلُ: الداهية.
ورجل نَيْطَل: داهٍ.
الأَصمعي: يقال جاء فلان بالنِّئْطِل والضِّئْبِل، وهي الداهية؛ قال ابن بري: جمع النِّئْطِل نآطِل؛ وأَنشد: قد علم النآطِلُ الأَصْلالُ، وعلماءُ الناسِ والجهّالُ، وَقْعي إِذا تَهافَتَ الرُّؤالُ قال: وقال المتلمس في مفرده: وعَلِمْتُ أَنّي قد رُمِيتُ بِنِئْطِلٍ، إِذْ قيلَ: صارَ مِنَ آلِ دَوْفَنَ قَوْمَسُ دَوْفَنَ: قبيلة، وقَوْمَس: أَمير.

245. it-bé-ma ^{d}GIŠ-gím-maš šu-na-ta BÚR-ár MU-ra a-na AMA-šú

اتبغم جِحْشِجِّحْمَش شأنتَ ... عنَ امي ذو

(G) Gilgamish rose to relate a dream, saying to his mother:
(A) *Jiḥshi-Jiḥmash* demanded his vision be explained, he recounted it to his mother:

246. um-mi MÁŠ.GI$_{6}$ aṭ-ṭu-la mu-ši-ti-ia

أمي ... أطل مسيتيّ

(G) "O mother, this is the dream I had in the night –
(A) Mother, during my early evening,

aṭ-ṭu-la:

طلل (لسان العرب)
والإطْلال: الإشْرافُ على الشيء.
وأطَلّ عليه أي أشْرَفَ؛

247. ib-šu-nim-ma MUL.MEŠ AN-e

ابذونم ...

(G) "The stars of the heavens appeared above me,
(A) from between those stars of heaven,

248. GIM ki-iṣ-ru ša da-«nim» {im-ta-naq-qu-tú}{im-taq-qu-ta} e-lu EDIN-ia

كيما قصر ذا انيم امتنقتو {امتقت} حلي

(G) like a rock from the sky one fell down before me.
(A) [like] a horse of Anim fell around me.

249. áš-ši-šu-ma «da»-an e-li-ia

عسُّ ذوم ذعن حليّ

(G) I lifted it up, but it weighted too much for me,

(A) I roamed with him (flew?) in the dark, he obeyed (wrapped around?) me.

da-an:

This word can be from Arabic *daʿan* دعن which means "wrapped around like in a net", matching the meaning of the corresponding word used in line #8 of the older Babylonian tablet, ik-ta-bi-it. This word also means "to ride an animal until he is exhausted". However, it is more likely that this word was from Arabic *dhaʿana* ذعن, meaning "obeyed quickly and blindly".

دعن (لسان العرب)

الدَّعْن: سَعَف يضم بعضه إلى بعض ويُرَمَّلُ بالشَّريط ويبسط عليه التمر، أَزْدِيّة.

وقال أَبو عمرو في تفسير شعر ابن مُقبل: أُدْعِنَت الناقةُ وأُدعن الجمل إذا أُطيل ركوبه حتى يَهْلِك، رواه بالدال والنون

ذعن (لسان العرب)

قال ابن الأَعرابي: مُذْعِنين مقرّين خاضعين، وقال أَبو إسحق: جاء في التفسير مسرعين، قال: والإذعان في اللغة الإسراع مع الطاعة، تقول: أَذعَن لي بحقي، معناه طاوَعَني لما كنت أَلتمسه منه وصار يُسْرِع إليه؛ وقال الفراء: مُذْعِنين مطيعين غير مستكرهين، وقيل: مذعنين منقادين.

والإذعان: الانقياد.

وأَذعَنَ الرجلُ: انقاد وسلَس، وبناؤه ذَعِن يَذْعَن ذَعَناً.

وناقة مِذْعان: سلِسةُ الرأْس منقادة لقائدها.

250. ul-tab-lak-ki-is-su-«ma» ul e-le-'-i-a nu-us-«su»

التبلك ذوم ول العيّ نسّ ذو

(G) I tried to roll it, but I could not dislodge it.
(A) I rushed him around, not afraid of his speed

ul-tab-lak-ki-is-su-ma:
Compare this word with the word ú-ni-iš-šú-ma used in line #9 of the older Babylonian tablet, which has a similar meaning: rushed him around. The word *labaka* لبك means "to rush or pressure", or "to confuse" someone, a word still commonly used by Iraqis.

لبك (لسان العرب)
اللَّبْكُ: الخَلْطُ، لَبَكْتُ الأَمْرَ أَلْبُكُه لَبْكاً.

251. UNUGki ma-a-tum iz-za-az UGU-[šu]
اروك مَيثُم عِزّز [حلي] ذو

(G) The land of Uruk was standing around it,
(A) Uruk-of-the-Fertile-Land gathered with honor around him

ma-a-tum
Compare this word with ma-tum in the Babylonian edition. As I explained earlier, it is from Arabic *mayth* ميث and should be pronounced *māthum* مَيثُم. Notice the usage of additional –a- in the middle of the word, which proves our point. The additional letter *Mīm* at the end is consistent with the Arabic usages in all Musnad inscriptions from Yemen. It is used to add importance.

252. [ma-a-tu pu-uḫ-ḫu-rat] in[a muḫ-ḫi-šú]
مَيثو فُخُرت إن مخي ذو

(G) [the land was gathered] about it.
(A) The fertile land became proud by his purity (pure bones?)

muẖ-ẖi-šú:
While historical Arabic refrences gave a clear meaning to this word, Western Akkadian dictionaries offered confused unconnected basic meanings. This word is derived from Arabic root *makhakha* مخخ meaning "to purify" or "to extrude":

ePSD: muẖẖu: skull, pate; first section of a balanced account, capital; on, over, above; against; more than; top

مخخ (لسان العرب)
المُخُّ: نِقْيُ العظم؛
مخ (مقاييس اللغة)
الميم والخاء كلمةٌ تدلُّ على خالصِ كلِّ شيء.

253. [i-tep-pi-ir um-m]a-nu Ú[GÚ E]DIN-[šú] {with line 254}
اتفر أُمّعنو حولي ... ذو

(G) A crowd [was milling about] before it,
(A) He astonished and puzzled a large crowd before him.

i-tep-pi-ir:
The usage of this word was confirmed in line #281. It is from the Arabic root verb *farā* فرا meaning "to astonish".

فرا (لسان العرب)
والفَرِيُّ: الأمر العظيم.
وفَرِيتُ: دَهِشْتُ وحِرْتُ؛ قال الأَعلم الهذلي: وفَرِيتُ مِنْ جَزَعٍ فلا أَرْمِي ، ولا وَدّعْتُ صاحِبْ أَبو عبيد: فَرِيَ الرجل، بالكسر، يَفْرَى فَرًى، مقصور، إذا بُهِتَ ودَهِشَ وتَحَيَّر . قال الأصمعي: فَرِيَ يَفْرَى إذا نظر فلم يدر ما يَصْنَع.
والفَرْيَة: الجلَبة .

um-ma-nu:

This word is possibly from Arabic *ummah* أمة, meaning "the mass". It was possibly pronounced, earlier, *umma'nu*, from Arabic *umma'a* أُمَّعة, meaning "followers". The writer used ā for the letter *'Ayn.*

CAD: ummānu: a crowd; common people, soldiers, masses

أمم (لسان العرب)
وأُمَّةُ الرجل: قومُه.
أمع (لسان العرب)
الإمَّعةُ والإمَّعُ، بكسر الهمزة وتشديد الميم: الذي لا رأْي له ولا عَزْم فهو يتابع كل أَحد على رأْيه ولا يثبت على شيء، والهاء فيه للمبالغة.

254. [GURUŠ.MEŠ uk]-tam-ma-ru UGU-[šú]
... أُقتمرو حلي ذو

(G) [the menfolk were] thronging around it.
(A) [Their men] gathered under moon light around him.

uk-tam-ma-ru:

This confirms that Gilgamesh's vision and gathering took place in a clear starry sky, contrary to George's Babylonian tablet reading.

قمر (لسان العرب)
وأَقْمَرَ الرجلُ: ارْتَقَبَ طلُوعَ القَمَرِ؛

255. [ki-i šèr-ri la]-«'»-i ú-na-šá-qu GÌR.[MEŠ-šú]
كي سِهري لَعي أُنشقو [أرجله]

(G) [Like a babe-in]-arms they were kissing its feet,
(A) [Like freighted babies] they smelled his legs,

šèr-ri:

This is an interesting usage of the Arabic root word *sihr* سهر. Recall, the sound of the letter *Hā'* was not present in Cuneiform symbols.

Notice the misleading current Romanization system of the Akkadian words. Compare the words: ṣehru, šerru, and šèr-ri!

ePSD: ṣehru; šerru: child; small child; baby; (to be) babyish; weak; a low social class; (to be) small;

سهر (لسان العرب)
السَّهَرُ: الأَرَقُ.
وقد سَهِرَ، بالكسر، يَسْهَرُ سَهَراً، فهو ساهِرٌ: لم ينم ليلاً؛
قال: وإِنما الرواية أَسهرته أَي لم تدعه ينام،

la-'-i:
We saw this exact word in line# 9 of the Babylonian tablet with the same meaning, "scared".

256. [a-ram-šú-ma GI]M áš-šá-te UGU-šú aḫ-bu-[ub]
ارأم ذوم كيما أساتَ حلي ذو أحبُب

(G) like a wife [I loved it,] caressed and embraced it.
(A) I caressed him, like his mother, kissing all over him.

257. [áš-šá-áš-šu-ma a]t-ta-di-šú ina šap-li-[ki] {with line# 258}
عسس ذوم أعتّدِ ذو إنَ سَفلِكِ

(G) [I lifted it up,] set it down at your feet,
(A) I roamed with him in the dark, prepared him down at your feet.

Notice, in this edition of the epic, no one laid down before him or gave him help, and no carrying was involved. He just roamed with the horse alone, then brought him to his mother. Hence, the writer used áš-ši-šú-ma عسّ ذوم or áš-šá-áš-šu-ma عسس ذوم, instead of áš-ši-a-šú-ma عسّيا ذوم, which the writer of the Babylonian edition used to indicate a plural action.

at-ta-di-šú:

عتد (لسان العرب)
وأَعْتَدَ الشيءَ: أَعَدَّه؛ قال الله عز وجل: وأَعتدَت لهن مُتَّكَأً أَي هَيَّأَتْ وأَعَدَّت.

258. [u at-ti tul$_5$-t]a-maḫ-ri-šu it-ti-[i]a
وانت تُلتَمخري ذو إتيّ

(G) [and you, O mother, you] made it my equal."
(A) And you, transformed/selected his real-life equal to me.

259. [um-mi dGIŠ-gím-maš {em-qet}{en-qet} mu-d]a-at ka-la-ma i-de MU-ár ana EN-[š]á
أمي جِحْشجِّحْمَش عِمقَت مُهديت كلأم يذ ... عنَ ذا

(G) "The mother of Gilgamish was clever and wise, well versed in everything, she said to her son-
(A) Mother of *Jiḥši-jiḥmash* thought deeply, the guider of his vision said to him.

em-qet:
This word (sometimes was en-qet) was not used in the Babylonian tablet. George thought it meant "was clever and wise", based on the CAD definition of the word. The meaning of this word fits well with the Arabic root word *'imq* عمق, for "deep". However, em-qet should be a past tense verb, here, indicating a feminine subject.

ePSD: emqu: wise, clever

عمق (لسان العرب)
ورجل عُمْقِيُّ الكلام: لكلامه غَوْرٌ.
وعَمِّق النظر في الأُمور تَعْمِيقاً وتَعَمَّق في كلامه أَي تَنَطَّع.
وتَعَمَّق في الأَمر: تَنَوَّقَ فيه، فهو مُتَعَمِّق.

260. [^{f}ri-mat-^{d}n]in-sún {em-qet}{en-qet} mu-da-a-tú ka-la-ma i-de MU-ár ana ^{d}GIŠ-gímmaš

ريِمَت نِنْسون عِمقَت مُهديت كلأم يذ .. عنَ جِحْشجّحْمَش

(G) Wild-Cow Ninsun was clever and wise, well versed in everything, she said to Gilgamesh:

(A) The-Favorite-of-Ninsūn thought deeply, the guider of his vision said to *Jiḥši-jiḥmash*:

^{f}ri-mat-^{d}nin-sún:

The known name of the Mesopotamian goddess was "Ninsun" or "Ninsuna". I am going to use this name "as is" without analyzing it. Evidently, the compound term ^{f}ri-mat-^{d}nin-sún is transliterated into Akkadian as *rīmat-nin-sūn*. This clearly sounds Arabic for "the gazelle of Ninsūn". However, since we know that Gilgamesh's mother was a human, and since we also know that the Arabs used the gazelle as a symbol of beauty and preference for women, I think this compound term means "the favorite of Ninsūn".

ريم (لسان العرب)

والرِّيمُ الظَّبْيُ الأَبيض الخالص البياض؛

261. [ib-š]u-nik-ka {MUL AN-e}{ MUL.MEŠ [ ]}

ابذونك ...

(G)"The stars of heaven [appeared] above you,

(A) From between those stars of heaven,

262. [ki]-<ma ki>-ṣir šá da-nim {im-ta-qu-ut e-lu [ ]} {[šá] ŠUB.MEŠ UGU EDIN-ka}

كيما قِصر ذا انيم إمتَقُت حلي ...

(G) [like a] rock from the sky one fell down before you.

(A) like a horse of Anim fell upon you.

263. taš-ši-šu-ma {«da»-nu}{[ ]-an} {e-l[i-k]a} {UGU-ka}
تعسّي ذوم دَعَن حلّك

(G) You lifted it up, but it weighed too much for you,
(A) You roamed with him in the dark, he obeyed (wrapped around?) you

264. tul-tab-lak-kit-su-ma ul te-le-'-i-a nu-us-su
تُلتَبلَكت ذوم ول تلّعيّ نسّ ذو

(G) you tried to roll it, but you could not dislodge it.
(A) You rushed him around, not afraid of his speed.

265. taš-šá-áš-šum-ma «ta»-ad-di-šú ina šap-li-ia
تعسّا ذوم تعدّ ذو إن سفليّ

(G) You lifted up, set it down at my feet,
(A) You roamed with him in the dark, prepared him down at my feet.

266. u a-na-ku {ul-[ta]m-ḫi-raš-šú}{[-ma]ḫ-ḫar-šu}{it-ti-ka} {KI!(DI)-[ ]}
وانكو ألتمخرا ذو إتيكَ

(G) and, I, Ninsun, I made it your equal.
(A) and I, myself, transformed/selected his real-life equal to you.

267. ta-ram-šu-ma «GIM» DAM {ta-ḫab-bu-bu UGU-šú}{e-li-šú taḫ-[bu-ub]}
ترأم ذوم كيما أسات، تحبُبُ حلي ذو

(G) Like a wife you loved it, caressed and embraced it:
(A) You will caress him, like his mother, kissing all over him.

Eventhough, according to George's transliteration this line was identical to lines #271 & #289, he translated it with a past tense verb, while translating the other two with a future tense verb using "will". I think it should be read the same as way the other two.

268. il-la-«kak»-kúm-«ma dan»-nu tap-pu-ú mu-še-zib ib-ri
اليكَ كوم ذأن تفو مشذب إبر

(G) a mighty comrade will come to you, and be his friend's saviour.
(A) to you he is a look-alike, a loyal mighty one, a saver of a comrade.

This is another very remarkable and clear Classical Arabic sentence with solid old Classical Arabic usages.

il-la-kak-kúm-ma:
It is very likely this word is actually two words: il-la-ka kúm-ma. The word il-la-ka, is clearly from Arabic *ilayka* إليك for "to you". The use of the word kúm-ma here, from Arabic *kama* كما, is similar to the usage of the word ki-ma in line #17 of the Babylonian tablet. Regardless, in both cases it means "look-alike".

tap-pu-ú:
Clearly from Arabic root word *wafī* وفي, meaning "to be loyal".

وفي (لسان العرب)
الوفاءُ: ضد الغَدْر،

dan-nu:
George probably confused this word with another word used extensively in the tablet, da-an, which was either from *da'na* دعن or *dha'na* ذعن, as explained earlier. After comparing dan-nu with da-an, I believe the word dan-nu is from the Arabic root word *dha'n* ذأن,

meaning "mighty" or "strong", which matched Western Akkadian references.

eSPD: dannu: strength; force; (to be) strong, powerful, mighty, great; (to be) resistant, obstinate, combative, quarrelsome; a noble; (crook of the) arm; wrestler; to reinforce; to provide for.

ذأن (لسان العرب)
الذُّؤْنُونُ والعُرْجُون والطُّرْثُوث من جنس: وهو مما ينبت في الشتاء، فإِذا سَخُنَ النهار فسد وذهب. غيره: الذُّؤْنون نبت ينبت في أُصول الأَرْطى والرِّمْث والأَلاء، تنشقُّ عنه الأَرض فيخرج مثل سواعد الرجال لا ورق له، وهو أَسْحَمُ وأَغْبَرَ، وطرفه مُحَدَّد كهيئة الكَمَرَة، وله أَكمام كأَكمام الباقلى وثمرة صفراء في أَعلاه، وقيل: هو نبات ينبت أَمثال العراجين من نبات الفُطْرِ، والجمع الذَّآنِينُ.
قال آخر: غَداةَ توليتم كأَنَّ سيوفكم ذآنينُ في أَعناقِكم لم تُسَلَّلِ وفي حديث حذيفة: قال لجُنْدُب بن عبد الله: كيف تصنع إذا أَتاك من الناس مثلُ الوَتِدِ أَو مثل الذُّؤْنون يقول اتَّبِعْني ولا أَتبعك؟

mu-še-zib:

Compare how the ePSD pronounced the two related words, having similar meanings, then examine the Arabic word *shadhaba* شذب. This is one more misrepresentation of a word by the Western Akkadian dictionaries. The letter *Shīn* cannot be omitted in any derivation.

ePSD: šūzubu: to spare
ePSD: ezēbu to set aside, leave behind; to save, keep back, hold back

شذب (لسان العرب).
وشَذَبَ العُودَ، يَشْذُبُه شَذْباً: أَلقَى ما عليه من الأَغْصانِ حتى يَبْدُوَ؛ وكذلك كلُّ شيءٍ نُحِّي عن شيءٍ، فقد شُذِبَ عنه؛ كقوله: نَشْذِبُ عن خِنْدِفَ، حتى تَرْضَى أَي ندفع عنها العِدا؛
وقال شمر: شَذَبْتُه أَشْذِبُه شَذْباً، وشلَلْتُه شلاًّ، وشَذَّبْتُه تَشْذِيباً، بمعنى واحد؛ وقال بُرَيقُ الـهُذليُّ: يُشَذِّبُ بالسَّيْفِ أَقرانَه، * إِذْ فَرَّ ذُو اللـِّمَّةِ الفَيْلَمُ وأَنشد شمر قول ابن مقبل: تَذُبُّ عنه بلِيفٍ شَوْذَبٍ شَمِلٍ، * يَحْمِي أَسِرَّةَ، بَيَن الزَّوْرِ والثَّفَنِ بلِيفٍ أَي بذَنَبٍ.

وفي حديث علي، كرّم اللّه وجهه، شَذّبهم عَنا تَخَرَّمُ الآجال.
وشَذَبَ عنه شَذْباً أَي ذَبَّ.

ib-ri:

While it is possible that this word was used in the meaning of "friend", I think , based on Arabic references, it was more likely "comrade" or "associate".

CAD: ibru: associate; friend; co-worker
CAD: ibertu: forearm bone;

أبر (لسان العرب)

والآبر: العامل.

وإبرة الذراع: مُسْتَدَقُّها. ابن سيده: والإبْرة عُظَيْم مستوٍ مع طَرَف الزند من الذراع إلى طرف الإصبع؛ وقيل: الإبرة من الإنسان طرف الذراع الذي يَذْرَعُ منه الذراع؛ وفي التهذيب: إبرَةُ الذارع طرف العظم الذي منه يَذْرَع الذارع، وطرف عظم العضد الذي يلي المرفق يقال له القبيح، وزُجّ المِرْفق بين القَبِيح وبين إبرة الذراع، وأَنشد: حتى تُلاقي الإبرةُ القبيحا وإبرة الفرس: شظِيّة لاصقة بالذراع ليست منها

269. ina KUR da-an {e-mu-qí-šú}{e-mu-qí i-[šu/i]}

ان [ارض] ذعنْ حمُقي يذو

(G) Mightiest in the land, strength he possesses,
(A) On earth, he is obedient; (his) devotion is entirely to you.

e-mu-qí-šú:

This word is from Arabic *ḥimq* حمق. It can sometimes mean "enthusiasm" or " excessive devotion". Its main meaning in Arabic is "foolish" or "crazy", but it can be used indirectly for "fanatic", or "extreme".

<u>حمق</u> (لسان العرب)
الحُمْقُ: ضدّ العَقْل.
وفرس مُحْمِقٌ: نِتاجُها لا يُسْبَق؛

270. «ki-ma ki»-ṣir šá da-nim du-un-nu-nu e-mu-qa-a-šú
كيما قِصر ذا انيم ذُعُنٌ حمقى أ ذو

(G) his strength is as mighty as a rock from the sky.
(A) Like the horse of Anim had obeyed, (with his) devotion to you.

e-mu-qa-a-šú:
Notice the usage of -a-šú أذو rather than -šú ذو by the speaker to point to Gilgamesh, possibly an old Classical Arabic usage.

271. «ta-ram-šu»-ma GIM DAM {ta-ḫ̱ab-bu-bu UGU-šú} { e-li-šú taḫ̱-b[u-ub]}
ترأم ذوم كيما أسات، تَحبُبَ حلي ذو

(G) Like a wife you will love him, caress and embrace him,
(A) You will caress him, like his mother, kissing all over him.

272. [«šu-ú dan»-nu uš-te-n]é-zeb-ka ka-[a]-«šá»
{«šu-ú dan»-nu ú-še-zeb ka-a-šú}
ذوو ذأن أُشتنَذَبْكَ كا ذا
{ذوو ذأن أُشَذَب كا ذو}

(G) he will be mighty, and often will save you"
(A) The mighty one will ask you to save (him), as he will (save) you."
(A) The mighty one will save (you), as you will (save) him."

Although George was able to arrive to the appropriate meaning of this line, which was written with a completely different style on two separate tablets, he was unable to illustrate the remarkable Classical Arabic grammar usage in the line. I included my Arabic transliteration of both lines for the interested reader, to illustrate why I believe that the Akkadian language was substantially Arabic, and the Epic of Gilgamesh was written in the earlier Classical Arabic.

Notice the derivation and transformation of the verb *shadhaba* شذب. Also, notice the careful usage of dhū ذو, dhawū ذوو, and dhā ذا!

273. šá-ni-tum i-ta-mar šu-na-at-tú

ثانِيتُم إتأمر شُأنتو

(G) Having had a second dream,
(A) For a second time he had his vision.

274. [i]t-bé-e-ma i-te-ru-ub ana IGI ^{d}15 AMA-šú

اتبغم يتَرعُب عنَ ... امي ذو

(G) he rose and entered before the goddess, his mother.
(A) He demanded, trembling, from the goddess, his mother;

i-te-ru-ub:

This word is from the Arabic root word *ra'aba* رعب, meaning "to scare". George used erēbu, in the meaning of "to enter". Examining Western Akkadian dictionaries, it is possible that this word was actually used in the meaning of "to enter" or "to leave", but I think only with an additional "scare" element added to it.

ePSD: erēbu: to enter; take away; to remove, to bring out; to leave; a bird of prey or a vulture;
CAD: erēbu: enter on a goddess; attack; to enter; to leave

رعب (لسان العرب)
الرُّعْبُ والرُّعُبُ: الفَزَع والخَوْفُ.

Compare this line to line #24 of the Babylonian edition. Notice there is no mentioning of "sleep" here, which confirms that the word uš-ti-nim-ma meant "wailed" or "sighed" rather than "slept".

275. «d»GIŠ-gím-maš ana šá-ši-ma MU-«ár» ana AMA-šú
.. جِحْشِجِّحْمَش عنَ ساسِمَ ... عنى امي ذو

(G) Said Gilgamesh to her, to his mother,
(A) *Jiḥshi-Jiḥmash* screamed to her, said to his mother:

šá-ši-ma:
George simply ignored this word from the Arabic root *'asasa* أسس, which can also mean "to scream". It is confirmed by CAD, which listed ša-sù in the same meaning. However, it is a very important one as it confirms that Gilgamesh was angry after his second vision.

CAD: ša-sù: shout

أسس (لسان العرب)
وأَسَّ بها: زجرها
سوس (لسان العرب)
والسَّوْسُ: الرِّياسَةُ، يقال ساسوهم سَوْساً، وإِذا رأَّسُوه قيل: سَوَّسُوه وأَساسوه.
السُّوسُ (القاموس المحيط)
وسُسْتُ الرَّعِيَّةَ سِياسَةً: أمرْتُها ونَهَيْتُها.
شسأ (لسان العرب)
أَبو منصور في قوله: مكان شِئسٌ، وهو الخَشِنُ من الحجارة، قال: وقد يخفف،
فيقال للمكان الغليظ: شأْسٌ وشأْزٌ، ويقال مقلوباً: مكانٌ شاسِئٌ وجاسِئٌ غليظ.
شسا (لسان العرب)
التهذيب في المعتل: ابن الأَعرابي الشَّسا البُسْرُ اليابس.

276. [i]p-pu-un-na-a AMA-a a-ta-mar šá-ni-ta šu-ut-ta
أفّنا أمّاه أتأمر ثانِت شُأنتَ

(G) "Once more, O mother, have I had a dream -
(A) "Help me, O mother, I am seeing for the second time his vision.

ip-pu-un-na-a:
One more word confirming Gilgamesh was stressed and mad after his second vision. It is from Arabic *faniya* فني "to calm" or "to help". Therefore, *iffunā* إفّنا would mean "help us" in Classical Arabic. I am not sure how George arrived at the meaning "once more".

فني (لسان العرب)
والمُفاناة: المُداراة.
وفانَيْت الرجل: دارَيْته وسكّنْته؛

277. [ina SILA] šá UNUGki re-bi-tum :
إنَ ... اروك ربيتم

(G) "[In the street] of Uruk-the-Town-Square,
(A) "[In the market] of Uruk-of-the-Hill.

278. ḫa-ṣi-nu na-di-ma UGU-šú {paḫ-ru}{paḫ-ri}
خصين نَديمَ حلي ذو فَخْر

(G) an axe was lying with a crowd gathered around.
(A) An axe fell (thrown?) around (over?) a proud one (a miniature goat?).

Notice this sentence is identical to the corresponding one in the Babylonian tablet, lines #29 & #30. Also notice that the word used here was either paḫ-ru or paḫ-ri, both of which are nouns. In lines #252 & #280, the word pu-uḫ-ḫu-rat فُخُرَت was used, a verb.

279. [UNUGk]i ma-a-tú iz-za-zu UGU-šú

أروك مَيثو عِزّحلي ذو

(G) The land [of Uruk] was standing around it,

(A) Uruk-of-the-Fertile-Land gathered with honor around him.

280. [ma-a-tú puḫ]-ḫu-rat ina muḫ-ḫi-šú

مَيثو فُخُرت أنَ مُخي ذو

(G) [the country was] gathered about it.

(A) The land became proud by his purity (pure bones?)

281. i-te-ep-pir [<ummānu> UG]U EDIN-šú

إتّفِر أُمّعنو حلي ... ذو

(G) A crowd *was milling about* before it,

(A) He astonished and puzzled a large crowd before him.

282. [GURUŠ.MEŠ u]k-«tam»-mar UGU-šú :

... أُقتمرو حولي ذو

(G) [the menfolk were] thronging around it.

(A) [The crowd] gathered under moon light around him.

283. áš-šá-áš-šum$^{!}$-ma {at-ta-di-iš} { at-ta-di-šu} ina šap-li-ku

عسّاذوم أعتدّ ذو إنَ سَفلِك

(G) "I lifted it up and set it down on your feet,

(A) I roamed with him in the dark, prepared him down at your feet.

Notice that, here, we are not dealing with a horse. Therefore, there were no additional lines about rushing someone or sniffing his legs.

Gilgamesh simply roamed with, without riding, the person or goat before bringing him to his mother.

284. [a-ram-š]u-ma ki-i áš-šá-te UGU-šú aḫ-bu-ub
أرأم ذوم كي أساتَ حلي ذو أحبُب

(G) like a wife [I loved] it, caressed and embraced it,
(A) I caressed him, like his mother, kissing all over him.

285. [u at-ti t]ul^{5}-ta-maḫ-ḫa-ri-šu it-ti-ia
وأتّ تُلتَمَخري ذو إتيّ

(G) [and you O mother,] you made it my equal."
(A) and you, transformed/selected his real equal to me."

286. «AMA ^{d}giš-gím-maš» em-qet mu-da-at ka-lá-ma i-de MU-ra ana DUMU-šá
امي جِحْشجّحْمَش عِمقَت مُهديت كلأم يذ ... عنَ ذا

(G) "The mother of Gilgamesh was clever and wise, well versed in everything, she said to her son-
(A) Mother of *Jiḥši-jiḥmash* thought deeply; the guider of his vision, said to him;

287. «^{f}ri-mat-^{d}nin-sún en-qet mu-da-at ka-lá-ma i-de MU-ra ana ^{d}GIŠ-gím-maš
رِيمَت نِنْسون عِمقَت مُهديت كلأم يذ ... عنَ جِحْشجّحْمَش

(G) Wild-Cow Ninsun was clever and wise, well versed in everything, she said to Gilgamesh:
(A) The-Favorite-of-Ninsūn thought deeply; the guider of his vision said to Jiḥši-jiḥmash:

288. [DUM]U! ẖa-ṣi-in-nu šá ta-mu-ru ib-ri
... خَصينو ذا تمعُرو ابر

(G) "My son the ax you saw is a friend,
(A) My son, this axe saves (sees after? recognizes?) a comrade.

This line is the key to understand the second vision by Gilgamesh in this tablet. George thought the word "friend" or "associate" was linked to the axe because his mother was referring to the axe as the object. Not so. Analyzing the line carefully with Arabic grammar in mind, it is clear that the axe was the subject here and the friend/associate was the object.

ta-mu-ru:
The spelling of this word, assuming it means "saw", is a bit different than previously written. It was written everywhere as ta–mar or ta–mur, not ta-mu-ru. Let's examine this word from the previous texts in both tablet versions. The asterisks indicate what I believe was a wrong reading by both, Jastraw and George:

i-ta-mar šu-na-at-tú (having had seen)	إتمأر	(line # 273)
a-ta-mar šá-ni-tum (I have seen)*	أتمأْر	(line # 276)
i-ta-mar šu-na-ti-šu (he saw)	إتَمأْر	(line # 298)
a-mur-šú-ma (I saw him)	أمؤرذوم	(line # 32)
a-ta-mar šá-ni-tam (I have seen)*	أتمأْر	(line # 26)
i-ta-mar šá-ni-tam (he saw)	إتَمأْر	(line # 24)
a-ta-mar e-mi-a (I have seen)*	أتمَأْر	(line # 27)
ta-mar-šú-ma (will see (him))	تمأَْر	(line # 20)

It is possible that this word was actually "saw", as both scholars thought. However, I think it could also be derived from the Arabic root verb *m'ara* معر, meaning "to miraculously escape a hit". This would be a good match to what really happened: the axe miraculously made the person or goat miss a hit. Similarly, "saw" can also match the meaning, assuming his mother was telling him that this axe had missed a special person because it saw or distinguished him.

معر (لسان العرب)
مَعِرَ الظُّفُرُ يَمْعَرُ مَعَراً، فهو مَعِرٌ: نَصَلَ من شيء أَصابه؛

289. ta-ram-šu-ma GIM DAM ta-ḫab-bu-bu UGU-šú
ترأم ذوم كيما أسات، تَحبُبَ حلي ذو

(G) like a wife you will love him, caress and embrace him,
(A) You will caress him, like a mother, kissing all over him.

290. u a-na-ku ul-ta-maḫ-ḫar-šú it-ti-ka
وانَكو اُلتمخَر ذو إتيكَ

(G) and I, Ninsun, I shall make him your equal."
(A) and I, myself, had transformed/selected his real-life equal to you.

291. il-la-ka-ak-kúm-ma dan-nu tap-pu-ú mu-še-zib ib-ri
اللكَ كومَ ذأن تَفو مُشَذّب إبرِ

(G) A mighty comrade will come to you, and be his friend's saviour,
(A) To you he will be a look-like, a mighty loyal one, a saver of a comrade.

292. ina KUR da-an e-mu-qa «i»-[šu]
إنَ أرض ذعنْ حمقي يذو

(G) mightiest in the land, strength he possesses,
(A) On earth, he is obedient; his devotion is entirely to you.

293. ki-ma ki-ṣir šá da-nim dun-nu-nu / e-mu-qa-a-šú

كيما قصر ذا انيم ذُعُنّ حمقى أ ذو

(G) his strength is as mighty as a rock from the sky."

(A) Like the horse of Anim had obeyed, (with) his devotion to you."

294. «d»GIŠ-gím-maš ana šá-ši-ma MU-ár a-na AMA-šú

.. جِحْشِجِّحْمَش عنَ ساسِمَ ... عنى امي ذو

(G) Said Gilgamesh to her, to his mother,

(A) *Jiḥshi-Jiḥmash* screamed to her, said to his mother:

295. [u]m-ma ina KA [d]en-líl ma-lik lim-qut-a[m-ma]

أمّاه إنَ كا إنليل مَلك لإمقُعتَمَ

(G) "May it befall me, O mother, by Counselor Enlil's command!

(A) O mother, by Counselor Enlil, let me have one to fall upon him.

This line and the next two lines are truly eloquent. They sound like Classical Arabic poetry. Notice the use of the word lim-qut-am-ma, *li-amqutama* لأمقعتم. This is derived from the same word used in line #248 in the beginning of the text.

296. ib-ri ma-li-ku a-na-ku lu-ur- ur-ši

إبرِ مَلِكو أنَكو لأُرسي

(G) Let me acquire a friend to counsel me,

(A) A comrade, I have for myself, to safeguard me.

lu-ur- ur-ši:

This word is derived from the classical Arabic root verb *rasā* رسا, meaning "to settle down" or "to safegaurd".

رسا (لسان العرب)
سَا الشَّيءُ يَرْسُو رُسُوّاً وأَرْسَى: ثَبَتَ، وأَرْساه هو.
ورَسَا الجَبَلُ يَرْسُو إذا ثَبَتَ أَصلهُ في الأَرض، وجبالٌ راسِياتٌ.
ورَسَتْ قَدَمُه: ثَبَتَتْ في الحَرْب.
ورَسَتِ السَّفِينَةُ تَرْسُو رُسُوّاً: بَلَغَ أَسفلُها القَعْرَ وانتهى إلى قرارِ الماءِ فثَبَتَت
وبَقِيت لا تَسِير، وأَرْساها هو.

297. [lu-u]r-ši-ma ib-ri {ma-li-ku} {ma-lik} a-na-ku
لأُرسِيمَ إبرِ مَلِكو أنَكو

(G) a friend to counsel me I will acquire"
(A) Let me safeguard a comrade, I have for myself.

lu-ur-ši-ma:
Notice the classical Arabic use of −*ma* in this word and in many other lines, compared to previous line. Jastraw, and the most updated Concise Dictionary of Akkadain (CDA), which Andrew George helped editing, claim that a final -*ma* could mean "and". In other words, it could be like Arabic *Wāw* for "and". I disagree. From reviewing all its usages in both tablets so far, I see no indication it was used to mean "and".

298. [i-t]a-mar šu-na-t[i-šu :]
... اتأمر شُأنتي ذو

(G) [So did Gilgamesh] saw his dreams!
(A) [So, *Jiḫshi-Jiḫmash*] saw your (coming) visions!

5

Summary of Part Three

A comparative study of the section containing the two dreams/visions by Gilgamesh, as told by two editions of the Epic of Gilgamesh separated by about 1000 years, was performed. In the study, the author compared his reading, utilizing historical classical Arabic etymological references, with other readings, by Jastraw and George, utilizing modern Western Akkadian dictionaries.

Western Akkadian dictionaries, which are primarily derived from the Chicago Assyrian Dictionary (CAD), utilize new *speculated* grammar rules, and new "invented" root words rather than using Arabic. Because they use inscriptions alone as primary sources, a fruitless approach plagued with expected imperfections and incompleteness, these dictionaries contain plenty of inaccuracies and contradicting entries. It seems that, often, the authors of these references arrive to the meanings of words based on their *assumed* readings of inscriptional texts. As a result, many meanings are not logically connected. The current Akkadian dictionaries do not only deprive the Akkadian language from its overwhelmingly-clear Arabic etymological roots, but they lack any consistent and verifiable word root system, of their own. They are very poor etymological references, and certainly inferior to the available historically-established Arabic etymological references.

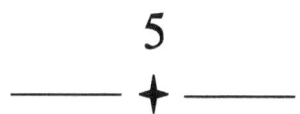

In comparison, the historical Arabic dictionaries, which were written many centuries before the discovery of the Akkadian and Sumerian tablets, are based on solid and consistent word roots and meanings. Checking Akkadian words against these references and observing Arabic grammar rules and sentence structures, I produced a much clearer and coherent translation of the two sample texts, arriving to identical, non-contradicting translation of the two dreams in both the Standard and Babylonian editions. Eventhough, I analyzed and translated only a small portion of the Epic of Gilgamesh as a sample, my conclusions should be valid for the rest of the epic.

Despite the clear inaccuracies of the Western Akkadian dictionaries, they are very valuable and even crucial linguistic tools to use in any translation process. The Chicago Assyrian Dictionary, for example, accumulated over many decades a large number of actual transliterated words taken directly from a wide range of inscriptional tablets. However, while these dictionaries are excellent initial references to consult, they should be treated only as secondary references to conclude words' meanings in Akkadian texts. Surely, one should consult the authoritative historical Arabic etymological references to both confirm and derive actual meanings.

The above point can clearly be illustrated by observing the contradictions in the translations of both Jastraw and George of the two dreams of Gilgamesh. For example, in Jastraw's reading regarding the meteor, Gilgamesh was able to carry it, initially, which is very unreasonable assumption. In fact, I am not even sure if the Akkadians knew what a meteor is! Besides, why would the people of Uruk kiss the feet of a meteor, or even better, why would a meteor have feet to start with. Furthermore, according to Jastraw's reading, Gilgamesh was soon unable to carry the meteor anymore and he was abandoned by the crowd, but then he picked it up and carried it to his mother. This contradicting story is not even possible in a dream.

Similarly, George wanted to convince us that the whole people of Uruk have gathered around an axe laying on the ground for some reason. Let's suppose that the axe had a strange shape, as he claimed, why would the writer of the epic neglect to inform his readers what kind of shape abnormality it possessed. George needed to translate the word "brother" as "my side" to fit his story. Even worse, after Gilgamesh carries the axe to his mother, she made it equal to him. Why should a small abandoned axe become equal to the mighty Gilgamesh?

It is important to realize that the process of tracings historical inscriptions cannot be 100% accurate due to many factors. Besides, the authors of these inscriptions can also make mistakes. However, the tracing of the Epic of Gilgamesh is fairly accurate. Regardless of whose translation was the correct one, the reader of Part Three should realize that all of the words of the sample text being studied were present, with matching meanings, in the historical Arabic etymological references. This, by itself, is a powerful undisputable evidence that the language of the Akkadians was substantially Arabic, and that Classical Arabic was at the heart of the Akkadian literature. Any translation of the Epic of Gilgamesh will undoubtedly include mistakes because of several factors, among them our lack of in-depth knowledge of historical Classical Arabic. However, the fact that the epic was written with an early proto Classical Arabic is unmistakably clear.

Selected Bibliography

1. Abulhab, Saad D. *DeArabizing Arabia: Tracing Western Scholarship on the History of the Arabs and Arabic Language and Script.* New York: Blautopf Publishing, 2011.
2. ʿAlī, Jawād. *Tarīkh al-ʿArab qabla al-Islam*. Baghdad: al-Mujammaʿ al-ʿIlmī al-ʿIrāqī, 1959.
   جواد علي. تأريخ العرب قبل الاسلام. بغداد: المجمع العلمي العراقي، 1959.
3. Assyrian Information Management. *Aramaic Lexicon and Concordance.* www.atour.com/dictionary/
4. Bazrāwī, Bāsil. "al-Tāʾ fī al-Lughah al-ʿArabiyyah: Khaṣaʾisuhā al-ṣawtiyyah wa-Istikhdāmātihā." pul-pit.alwatanvoice.com
   باسل بزراوي. التاء في اللغة العربية: خصائصها الصوتية واستخداماتها
5. Beeston, A. F. L. "Languages of Pre-Islamic Arabia." *Arabica,* June-September: 178-186.
6. Beeston, Alfred Felix L. "Pre-Islamic Arabia to the 7th Century AD." Encyclopedia Britannica, Academic Edition. www.britannica.com/EBchecked/topic/31568/history-of-Arabia/45972/Himyarites#ref484255
7. Bellamy, James A. "A new Reading of Namārah Inscription." *Journal of the American Oriental Society* 105 (1985): 31-48.
8. Bellamy, J. A. "Arabic Verses From The First/Second Century: The Inscription Of ʿEn ʿAvdat", *Journal Of Semitic Studies*, 35: (1990), 73-79.

9. Butts, Aaron Michael and Hardy, Humphrey Hill II. A Revised Reading of a Nabataean Inscription from Umm al-Jimāl. *Journal of Semitic Studies*. LV/2 Autumn.

10. al-Fawzān, ʿAbd Allāh bin Ṣāliḥ. *Dalīl al-Sālik ilá Alfiyyat bin Mālik*. al-Maktabah al-ʿIlmiyyah.
Alfuzan.islamlight.net
عبد الله بن صالح الفوزان. دليل السالك الى الفية بن مالك. المكتبة العلمية.

11. Ḥaṭṭāb, Muḥammad Jamīl. *Muʿjam Maʿānī Asmāʾ al-Mudun wa-al-Qurá fī Muḥāfaẓat Ṭarṭūs*. al-Lādhiqiyyah: Dār al-Mirsāh lil-Ṭibāʿah wa-al-Nashir wa-al-Tawzīʿ, 2008.
محمد جميل حطاب. معجم معاني اسماء المدن والقرى في محافظة طرطوس. اللاذقية: دار المرصاح للطباعة والنشر والتوزيع، 2008.

12. Healey, J. F and Dhuyayb, Sulaymān ibn ʿAbd al-Raḥmān. *The Nabataean Tomb Inscriptions of Madaʾin Salih*. London: Oxford University Press, 1993.

13. Healey, J. F. and Smith, G.R. "The Earliest Dated Arabic Document 267 AD." *Atlal: The Journal of Saudi Arabian Archaeology*. 12 (1989): 77-84.

14. Hoyland, Robert G. *Arabia and the Arabs: From the Bronze Age to the Coming of Islam*. London: Routledge. 2001.

15. Ibn Khaldūn. *Ta'rīkh Ibn Khaldūn*. Part 1, Chapter 47.
ابن خلدون. تأريخ ابن خلدون. الجزء الاول. الفصل 47
al-eman.com/IslamLib/viewchp.asp?BID=163&CID=42

16. Ibn Mālik, Jamāl al-Dīn bin Muḥammad bin ʿAbd Allāh. *Alfiyyat Ibn Mālik*. al-Maktabah al-Ḥurrah. **ar.wikisource.org/wiki/**
ابن مالك، جمال الدين بن محمد بن عبد الله. الفية ابن مالك. المكتبة الحرة

17. Ibn Manẓūr, Abū al-Faḍl Jamāl al-Dīn Muḥammad bin Mukarram. *Lisān al-ʿArab*.
http://www.baheth.net
ابن منظور، ابو الفضل جمال الدين محمد بن مكرم. لسان العرب.

18. al-Khawārizmī. *Muftāh al-ʿŪlūm*. al-Bāb al-Sādis, fī al-Akhbār. al-Maktabah al-Ḥurrah.

ar.wikisource.org/wiki/

الخوارزمي. مفتاح العلوم. الباب السادس: في الاخبار. المكتبة الحرة.

19. Lendering, Jona. "*Sasanians. Ancient Persia.*"

www.livius.org/sao-sd/sassanids/sassanids.htm

20. Littmann, Enno. *Semitic Inscriptions*. Div. IV, Section A: *Nabataean Inscriptions from the Southern Hauran*. Publications of the Princeton University Archaeological Expeditions to Syria in 1904-1905 and 1909 1914. Leyden: J. Brill Publishers and Printers. 1914

21. Littmann, Enno, Ph.D. *Semitic Inscriptions*. Part IV of the Publications of an American Archaeological Expedition to Syria in 1899-1900 under the Patronage of V. Evert Macy, Clarence M. Hyde, B. Talbot B. Hyde, and I. N. Phelps Stokes. New York: The Century Company. October 1904.

22. Mādūn, Muḥammad ʿAlī. *Khaṭṭ al-Jazm ibn al-Khaṭṭ al-Musnad*. al-Ṭabʿah al-ʾŪlá. Dimashq: Dār Ṭlās lil-Dirāsāt wa-al-Terjamah wa-al-Nashr, 1989.

محمد علي مادون. خط الجزم ابن الخط المسند. الطبعة الاولى. دمشق: دار طلاس للدراسات والترجمة والنشر. 1989.

23. al-Maghribī, ʿIyāḍ bin Mūsá al-Yaḥṣibī al-Sabtī. *al-Sīrah al-Nabawiyyah: Kitāb al-Shafāʾ bi-Taʿrīf Ḥuqūq al-Muṣṭafá*. Dār al-Fikr, 2002.

عياض بن موسى اليحصبي السبتي. السيرة النبوية: كتاب الشفاء بتعريف حقوق المصطفى. دار الفكر، 2002.

24. al-Maḥallī, Jalāl al-Dīn, and Jalal al-Dīn al-Sayyūṭī. *Tafsīr al-Jalālayn*. Bayrūt: al-Ṭabʿah al-Thālithah. Dār al-Maʿrifah, 1984.

جلال الدين المحلي وجلال الدين السيوطي. تفسير الجلالين. الطبعة الثالثة. بيروت: دار المعرفة، 1984

25. Makhlūf, Ḥusayn Muḥammad. *Ṣafwat al-Bayān li-Maʾānī al-Qurʾān.* al-Kūwayt: Wizārat al-Awqāf wa-al-Shuʾūn al-Islāmiyah, 1987. al-Ṭabʿah al-Thālithah.

حسين محمد مخلوف. صوت البيان لمعاني القرآن. الطبعة الثالثة. الكويت: وزارة الاوقاف والشؤون الاسلامية، 1978.

26. al-Maʿrifah: al-Mawsūʾah al-Ḥurrah li-Khalq wa-Jamʿ al-Muḥtawá al-ʿArabī. *Mamlakat Tannūkh.* **www.marefa.org**

مملكة تنوخ. المعرفة: الموسوعة الحرة لخلق وجمع المحتوى العربي.

27. al-Marīkhī, Mishliḥ bin Kamīkh, Ghubān, ʿAlī Ibrāhīm. "*Naqsh Wāʾil bin al-Jazzāz al-Tidhkārī al-Muʾarrakh ʿām 410 Mīlādī.*" Mudāwalāt al-Liqāʾ al-ʿIlmī al-Sanawī al-Thālith lil-Jamʿiyyah. Masqaṭ, Jāmiʿat al-Sulṭān Qābūs, 2001.

مشلح بن كميخ المريخي وعلي ابراهيم غبان. نقش وائل بن الجزاز التذكاري المؤرخ 410 ميلادي. مداولات اللقاء العلمي السنوي الثالث للجمعية. مسقط: جامعة السلطان قابوس، 2011.

28. MacDonald, M. C. A. "Reflections on the Linguistic map of Pre-Islamic Arabia." Arabian *Archeology and Epigraphy* 11 (2000): 28-79.

29. al-Munjid al-Abjadī. al-Ṭabʿah al-Ūlá. Bayrūt: Dār al- Mashriq, 1967.

المنجد العربي. الطبعة الاولى. بيروت: دار المشرق، 1967.

30. al-Nadīm, Ibn. *The Fihrest of al-Nadim.* Translated and Edited by Bayard Dodge. New York: Columbia University Press, 1970.

31. Negev, A. "Obodas The God", *Israel Exploration Journal*, 36, 1/2 (1986): 56-60.

32. O'Connor, M. "The Arabic Loanwords in Nabataean Aramaic." *Journal of Near Eastern Studies.* 45, no. 3 (July 1986): 213-229

33. Patrich, Joseph. *The Formation of Nabataean Art: Prohibition of a Graven Image among the Nabataeans.* Jerusalem: The Magnes press.

34. Rabin, Chaim. *Ancient West Arabian*. London: Taylor's Foreign Press, 1951.

35. al-Ṣan'ānī, Muḥammad bin Isma'īl al-Amīr. *Subul al-Salām: Sharh Bulūgh al-Marām min Adillat al-Iḥkām*. Bayrūt: Dār al-Kutub al-'Ilmiyyah, 2006.

محمد بن اسماعيل الامير الصنعاني. سبل السلام: شرح بلوغ المرام من ادلة الاحكام. بيروت: دار الكتب العلمية، 2006.

36. Shahid, I. Philological Observations on Namara Inscription. *Journal of Semitic Studies*. 24 (1979): 33-42.

37. al-Ṭabarī, Abū Ja'far Muḥammad bin Jarīr. *Ta'rīkh al-Ṭibarī: Ta'rīkh al-Rusul wa-al-Mūlūk*. al-Qāhirah: Dār al-Ma'ārif, 1977.

ابو جعفر محمد بن جرير الطبري. تأريخ الطبري: تأريخ الرسل والملوك. القاهرة: دار المعارف، 1977.

38. al-Theeb, Solaiman Abdal-Rahman (1989) A comparative study of Aramaic and Nabataean inscriptions from North-West Saudi Arabia. Doctoral thesis, Durham University. Available at Durham E-Theses Online:
etheses.dur.ac.uk/1421/

39. Wenning, Robert. "The Betyls of Petra." *Bulletin of the American Schools of Oriental Research* 324 (November 2001): 79-95.

40. Wikībīdyah: al-Mawsū'ah al-Ḥurrah. "al-Manādhirah."
ar.wikipedia.org

المناذرة. وكيبيديا: الموسوعة الحرة.

41. Winnett, F. V. "A Himyaritic Inscription from the Persian Gulf Region." *Bulletin of the American Schools of Oriental Research*. 102 (April 1946): 4-6.

42. Wright, W. *A Grammar of the Arabic Language*. London: Cambridge University Press, 1955. Third Edition.

ABOUT THE AUTHOR

Arabic type designer, librarian, systems engineer, and independent scholar. Born 1958 in Sacramento, California, and grew up in Karbala and Baghdad, Iraq. Moved in 1979 to New York, where he earned a Bachelor of Science in Electrical Engineering and a Master of Science in Library and Information Science. Served for 12 years as a Senior and Supervising Librarian in the New York Public Library, specializing in Arabic, Science, and Business subjects. Served for 15 years as a Systems Librarian and a library Director of Technology in the City University of New York (CUNY.) A known and active Arabic type designer especially noted for his non-traditional, innovative, Arabic typeface designs. Awarded a US design patent in 2000 and a utility patent in 2003 for his Mutamathil Type Style, an open template for simplified, technology-friendly, Arabetic font designs. Published a book and several articles in scholarly journals about Arabic language and script's history, typography, and computing. Contributes regularly to discussions of Arabic related topics on international typography and archeology forums.

www.ingramcontent.com/pod-product-compliance
Lightning Source LLC
Chambersburg PA
CBHW050441240426
43661CB00055B/2467
9780984984343

www.ingramcontent.com/pod-product-compliance
Lightning Source LLC
Chambersburg PA
CBHW050425240426
43661CB00055B/2278
* 9 7 8 0 7 8 8 4 2 2 5 0 8 *